# TRAFFICKING OF CHILDREN
# FOR SEXUAL EXPLOITATION

# TRAFFICKING OF CHILDREN FOR SEXUAL EXPLOITATION

PUBLIC INTERNATIONAL LAW 1864–1950

SUNIL SALANKEY RAO

OXFORD

UNIVERSITY PRESS

# OXFORD
### UNIVERSITY PRESS

Oxford University Press is a department of the University of Oxford.
It furthers the University's objective of excellence in research, scholarship,
and education by publishing worldwide. Oxford is a registered trademark of
Oxford University Press in the UK and in certain other countries

Published in India by
Oxford University Press
YMCA Library Building, 1 Jai Singh Road, New Delhi 110 001, India

ISBN-13: 978-0-19-808492-1
ISBN-10: 0-19-808492-7

Typeset in Minion Pro 10.5/12.5
at MAP Systems, Bengaluru 560 082, India
Printed in India by G.H. Prints Pvt Ltd, New Delhi 110 020

*In loving memory of M.R. Satwaji Jadav (Bapu)
and Nagubai Salankey (Aggi)*

and

*to my parents, Narayana and Pramila Rao
and to my sisters, Samitha and Sowmya*

# Contents

*Foreword by* Susan Kneebone     ix

*Introduction*     xi

1   Early History     1

2   The Grounding of Protection in International Law:
    The Convention of 1921     24

3   Expanding the Scope for Action: The Convention of 1933     52

4   Unification and Progressive Development in the
    Convention of 1949     88

*Conclusion*     142

*Endnotes*     147

*Index*     212

*About the Author*     216

# Foreword

⤜ ❧

This book is a valuable and welcome contribution to the literature on human trafficking. As the author points out, discussion on this issue often begins and ends with the the 2000 United Nations Convention against Transnational Organised Crime framework which includes the Protocol to Prevent, Suppress and Punish Trafficking in Persons, Especially Women and Children (2000)('the Trafficking Protocol'). This was the period in which a renewed interest in the problem of human trafficking led to it being cast as an issue of irregular migration and border security. As Sunil Salankey Rao sets out to establish, human trafficking is not a new problem, but rather one with strong historical antecedents. It is also an issue which disproportionately affects children in Asia. Rao's focus is upon trafficked children, whose plight is often subsumed in legal and policy responses in the larger global narrative on trafficking.

Much of the literature on human trafficking, particularly that which deals with trafficking of women and girls into prostitution, focuses upon the five 'White Slave' treaties made between 1904 and 1949, and provides a feminist analysis. Rao takes his research back to 1864, focuses upon children of both genders, and gives a broad analysis of the issues. He provides a detailed commentary on how international instruments in that period relate to the issue of trafficking of children for sexual exploitation. He weaves into this discussion, a focus on race and gender, and examines the development of approaches to criminalization of prostitution. This book thus provides a nuanced understanding of the development of responses to the problem of human trafficking, and in particular of trafficking in children. This is a particularly important discussion as the European treaties, which Rao analyses, provide the background for policy responses to the extensive problem of trafficking in children in non-European contexts. Thus this book advances the understanding of the competing discourses which underlie international law responses to human trafficking.

22 July 2013

Susan Kneebone
Faculty of Law
Monash University

# Introduction

⚘ ⚘

The trafficking of children for sexual exploitation of prostitution is an insidious crime perpetrated against the most vulnerable of all human beings. It is unequivocally a grave violation of the canons of human rights that are inalienable to us all. Sadly, it is not a new phenomenon, nor is its transcendental nature. It has existed in almost all civilizations and cultures throughout history, and continues to exist today, perhaps with an even greater presence, as a consequence of its inevitable merging with the advent of globalization. To this end, it is now, as it was then, a failure of human kind.

In the fight to eradicate this abhorrent trade in children, a number of treaties have been adopted that reflect the various perspectives the subject has been conceptualized within over its history. Common among these are: slavery, labour, migration, and human rights perspectives. In relation to the human trafficking perspective, the adopted treaties can be segmented into two distinct periods. That is, treaties adopted prior to 1950, and treaties adopted after 1950. In this regard, from 1864–1950, a total of five treaties were adopted. The first treaty, adopted in 1904, was the International Agreement for the Suppression of the White Slave Traffic. The second treaty, the International Convention for the Suppression of the White Slave Traffic, was adopted in 1910. Eleven years later, in 1921, the International Convention for the Suppression of the Traffic in Women and Children was adopted. A further twelve years on, in 1933, the International Convention for the Suppression of the Traffic in Women of Full Age was adopted. The final treaty relevant to this period, the Convention for the Suppression of the Traffic in Persons and of the

Exploitation of the Prostitution of Others was adopted in 1949. After 1950, only a singular treaty, in relation to the human trafficking perspective, has been adopted—the Protocol to Prevent, Suppress and Punish Trafficking in Persons, Especially Women and Children—supplementing the United Nations Convention against Transnational Organized Crime (Trafficking Protocol). This treaty was adopted in 2000.

In order to understand how international law in relation to the trafficking of children for sexual exploitation of prostitution developed to its present stage, the key areas in which that development occurred, and the pace of that development in those areas, both the period prior to 1950, and the period after 1950, needs to be examined. However, the majority of the discourse on the treaties is based on the period after 1950, and the subsequent adoption of the Trafficking Protocol. In particular, the discourse examines the origin and drafting history of this treaty comprehensively, whilst the five treaties adopted prior to 1950 are not afforded the same comprehensive consideration. The result is, first, a disjunct in the understanding of the development of international law on the subject to its present stage, and second, misconceptions are formed. In relation to the former, many questions arise, including how and why did the treaties adopted prior to 1950 originate? What were the major issues that gave rise to their adoption? What drafting process resulted in their adoption? What were the debates, the contentious issues, the compromises, and the omissions in relation to these treaties? Was there unanimous agreement or did States have reservations? And how did States react and respond to these treaties? These questions are considered in relation to the origin and drafting history of the Trafficking Protocol but not the treaties adopted prior to this treaty. In relation to the latter, without reference to the origin and drafting history of the treaties adopted prior to 1950, misconceptions arise. Most notably, the discourse suggests that the International Convention for the Suppression of the Traffic in Women of Full Age, 1933, was applicable to adult females only. This assumption appears to be based on the title of this treaty and the wording of its provisions. However, examination of the origin and drafting history of this treaty discloses that it was applicable to minor girls and developed out of the context where minor girls were being trafficked with the use of false birth certificates to show that they were of full age.

Apart from these aspects, the discourse also tends to conflate the examination of the trafficking of children along with all forms of sexual exploitation including prostitution (for example, dancing and pornography) or more broadly with all forms of exploitation, sexual and otherwise, such as labour exploitation. Additionally, it examines the subject from a number of perspectives—human rights, slavery and slavery-like practices, migration, labour, law enforcement, and gender, to name a few.

This book recognizes that the history of the treaties adopted in the period prior to 1950 is of fundamental importance to understanding not only how international law developed to its present stage, the key areas in which that development occurred, and the pace of that development in those areas, but also, the relevance to contrary assumptions often made. This book also recognizes the indirectness of conflating children with other forms of exploitation, and other perspectives and/or dimensions, and seeks to avoid them to ensure a comprehensive and direct examination.

Accordingly, this book examines from a human trafficking perspective, the treaties adopted during the period 1864–1950 in relation to the trafficking of children for sexual exploitation of prostitution. Each treaty is examined in light of its origin, drafting history, relevance to children trafficked for sexual exploitation of prostitution, and progressive developments in the areas of gender, race, administrative and legal measures, description of the act of trafficking, and connection between the act of trafficking and the exploitative end purpose of prostitution.

Chapter 1 traces the early history of international law from 1864 until the commencement of World War I, examining the origins of the International Agreement for the Suppression of the White Slave Traffic, 1904, and the International Convention for the Suppression of the White Slave Traffic, 1910. It also details the legislative and administrative measures of these instruments and the relevance to children trafficked for sexual exploitation of prostitution. Early conceptualizations of gender and race are presented as to the implicit connection between the act of trafficking and the exploitative end purpose of prostitution. Further, the developments during this period, most notably, the introduction of a trafficking offence and a more broad description of the act of trafficking in the International Convention for the Suppression of the White Slave Traffic, 1910, are also detailed.

Chapter 2 examines the origin and drafting history of the International Convention for the Suppression of the Traffic in Women and Children, 1921. It also details the new measures to supplement the International Agreement for the Suppression of the White Slave Traffic, 1904, and the International Convention for the Suppression of the White Slave Traffic, 1910, and the relevance of these new measures to children trafficked for sexual exploitation of prostitution. Developments are also presented, in particular, the removal of the gender and the race specific nature of the earlier treaties and the extension of the scope of the trafficking offence set down in the International Convention for the Suppression of the White Slave Traffic, 1910.

Chapter 3 traces the development of the International Convention for the Suppression of the Traffic in Women of Full Age, 1933. It examines the origin and drafting history of this treaty, emphasizing the contextual concern that gave rise to this treaty—the problem of the traffic in girls underage by traffickers who presented them as being overage by the use of false birth certificates and passports. It also examines the relevance of the treaty's measures to children trafficked for sexual exploitation of prostitution.

Chapter 4 examines the origin and drafting history of the International Convention for the Suppression of the Traffic in Persons and of the Exploitation of the Prostitution of Others, 1949. It also summarizes the provisions of this treaty, examines the relevance of the treaty to children trafficked for the sexual exploitation of prostitution, and details progressive developments including unification of the earlier treaties, the introduction of new offences, and the express connection between the act of trafficking and the exploitative end purpose of prostitution.

Chapter 5 draws together the developments in international law from 1864–1950, detailed in Chapters 1–4, in order to illustrate in a stand alone chapter the progressive international law response to the trafficking of children for the sexual exploitation of prostitution.

# 1

# Early History

Prostitution in England was unregulated until the anxiety of naval and military authorities about the incidence of venereal disease among sailors and soldiers provided the impetus for State regulation.[1] Compulsory treatment of infected women was considered necessary to prevent further spread of infection, and this led to the passage of the first of the Contagious Diseases Acts in 1864. 'Diseases' was a misleading title because the Act itself referred only to venereal diseases, a single subcategory of the wider class of contagious diseases.[2]

## THE CONTAGIOUS DISEASES ACTS

## Contagious Diseases Act, 1864

The Contagious Diseases Act, 1864 (Act of 1864) applied to seaports and military stations in England and Ireland (eleven in all)[3] and covered the following matters:

### Hospital Certification

Empowerment of government departments (Admiralty and the War Office) to certify hospitals to treat contagious diseases, subject to a continuing inspection by a superior medical officer.[4]

## Examination Orders

A system of information, notices, and orders under which information could be laid before a Justice of the Peace (JP) by any senior police officer (superintendent or inspector) or registered medical practitioner, asserting belief, on good cause, that a woman was a common prostitute and had been, within the previous fourteen days, in a public place for the purpose of prostitution. Upon receipt of the notice:

the woman could voluntarily attend a certified hospital for examination;

if she failed to attend for voluntary examination, the JP was empowered to issue an order authorizing her apprehension by police in order to take her to such a hospital (named in the order) for involuntary examination;

such an order could be made in her absence, provided service of the notice was proved with evidence.[5]

## Detention

A woman found by a certified hospital to be infected with a contagious disease could be detained for twenty-four hours. Upon that finding:

the certified hospital was required to send a medical certificate to the JP;

the JP was then empowered to extend the period of detention, by order, for a further three months.[6]

## Offences

Refusal to submit to examination, or to obey hospital regulations (including leaving without having been duly discharged) rendered a woman who had been ordered to undergo examination liable, upon summary conviction, to up to one month's imprisonment for the first offence, and up to two months for repeat offences.[7]

## Knowing Acquiescence

Anyone who knew that a prostitute was infected with a contagious disease, but nevertheless allowed her to remain in any place for the purposes of prostitution, could also be summarily convicted and fined up to ten pounds or imprisoned for up to three months.[8]

The Act of 1864, which was passed without debate, contained a sunset clause limiting its operation to a period of three years. The Admiralty and War Office, seeking more detailed information about the pathology and treatment of venereal disease, at the same time appointed a committee to inquire and make recommendations. Its determinations included a finding that the method of uncovering the identity of women carrying venereal disease was inadequate, because it relied on information obtained from men they had infected, brothel keepers, or their companions. The committee considered the French system of periodical inspections by medical police in each town to be superior. The majority recommendations were thus for institution of a similar system, with surgeons to be appointed to examine all known prostitutes (in their homes, or at a dispensary appointed for the purpose). The surgeons would be given power to refer the women for involuntary treatment in hospital, including detention there, pending cure. One member dissented from the recommendations, on the basis that such a system was unworkable in the absence of a simultaneous system of registration. The Act of 1864 continued in operation until 1866, when it was repealed by the Contagious Diseases Act of that year.[9]

## Contagious Diseases Act, 1866

The main provisions of the Contagious Diseases Act, 1866 (Act of 1866), which was more extensive in scope,[10] included the following:

### Appointment of Visiting Surgeons

Admiralty or War Office appointments were to be made for each place covered by the Act of 1866.[11]

### Focus on Moral and Religious Instruction

While the system of certified hospitals established in the Act of 1864 system was retained, a new section provided that the Admiralty or War Office could require each hospital to provide detained women with moral and religious instruction.[12]

## Delegation of Regulatory Power

Hospital managers were empowered to make regulations governing the treatment of detained women (subject to Admiralty or War Office approval).[13]

## Periodical Medical Examinations

The JP-based system of information, notices, and orders for examination established under the Act of 1864 was retained, but it was supplemented with an organized system of periodical examinations. As before, the system incorporated voluntary examinations.[14] In addition:

Women residing within a radius of five miles beyond the limit of places scheduled in the Act could be ordered to submit to examination by a visiting surgeon for up to a year;

under regulations made by the Admiralty or War Office, visiting surgeons were empowered to prescribe the time and place of examinations;

visiting surgeons were authorized to certify a woman to be infected with a contagious disease and commit her to detention in a named hospital that had been certified under the Act;

upon receipt of a visiting surgeon's certificate the woman became liable to detention in that hospital;

a woman certified to be infected could go to hospital voluntarily, as under the previous legislation;

as before, failure to attend voluntarily could result in police apprehension;

upon voluntary or involuntary admission, the woman was required to remain in hospital for a period of up to three months and until discharged by the chief medical officer;

detention beyond that period was possible upon further certification by the hospital's chief medical officer and the inspector or visiting surgeon;

any further detention could not extend the total period of detention beyond six months;

transfer between certified hospitals was authorized upon the instruction of the inspector;

a woman whose request to be discharged had been refused by the chief medical officer could request a hearing before a JP;

a JP hearing such a matter, who was satisfied with the evidence that the woman was no longer infected with a contagious disease, was required to order the hospital to discharge her.[15]

## Offences

Compliance with the regime was enforced. Punitive measures were similar to those of the earlier Act of 1864, but more onerous for repeated non-compliance. Sanctions applied to a range of offences:

Failing to submit to examination;
   leaving hospital prior to discharge could lead to arrest without warrant;
   failing to comply with hospital regulations;
   leaving a certified hospital while still infected with a contagious disease (i.e., being subject to a current notice) and then being in any place for the purposes of prostitution;
   Summary conviction led to imprisonment (a first offence attracted a sentence of one month's imprisonment, and subsequent offences that of three months).[16]

## Release from Examination Regime

A woman who was subject to an examination regime, but not under hospital detention, could apply in writing to a JP to order her release from the regime. In such a case:

the JP was required to appoint a hearing and notify the applicant and the superintendent of police of its time and place;
   the JP was required, upon being satisfied that the applicant had ceased to be a common prostitute (or, alternatively, upon the applicant entering into a recognisance for good behavior for three months) to grant the relief sought and order her release from the regime;
   the order was subject to a condition that the woman must not, during the recognisance period, be found in any place within the prescribed limits for the purpose of prostitution; if she was found in those circumstances she would forfeit the recognisance.[17]

The Act of 1866 thereby placed a new emphasis on the role of the metropolitan police, providing for selection of suitably discreet and experienced officers. Two new places were added to those scheduled in the earlier Act of 1864.[18]

## Contagious Diseases Act, 1869

Two years after the introduction of the Act of 1866, the House of Lords debated, but did not achieve agreement on, a proposal to extend the operation of the Act of 1866 to London and other metropolitan centres requesting its introduction. A private member's bill, strongly supporting the plan, was put forth but the government of the day drew attention to its likely expense, and the plan lost its momentum and fell into abeyance. Instead, the House of Lords and House of Commons each appointed a select committee to review the operation of the Act of 1866. In 1868 the reports of these committees led to the drafting of a bill incorporating the recommended reforms, which was passed and came into effect as the Contagious Diseases Act, 1869 (Act of 1869). The new Act of 1869 amended the scope rather than the substance of the Act of 1866, building on existing provisions.

### Extended Detention Power

Women who were unfit to be examined by the visiting surgeon could be detained in a certified hospital for up to four days. A drunken woman could be detained for one day at any place named in a detention order.[19]

### Extended Residential Radius

The five-mile limit on application of the legislation to women living beyond any controlled area was increased to ten miles.[20]

### Standardization of Voluntary and Involuntary Procedures

The Act of 1869 now applied in the same way to women who had voluntarily complied with the examination procedure and to those who were the involuntary subjects of an order by a JP.[21]

*Extended Detention Period*

The maximum detention period was extended from six months to a total of nine.[22]

*Release from Examination Regime*

The procedure for release upon application to a JP was retained, but a simpler procedure was added— a visiting surgeon now had power to release a woman from the system after consulting a superintendant of police.[23]

*Expansion of Scheduled Places*

Six new places were added to those already scheduled under the legislation.[24]

The Acts, as progressively amended, were largely uncontroversial. They were seen, if they drew public attention at all, as a response of the defence force to internal requirements (regulation of matters affecting the health of soldiers and sailors). This remained the case until 1869.[25]

## THE EFFECT OF THE ACTS

By the time of the enactment of the Contagious Diseases Act, 1869, the system had almost universal application. While there were variations in different jurisdictions, the gist of the system, in each country, was control. Maintenance of a register of women known to be engaged in prostitution enabled such women to be singled out for police attention. Once documented, they could be subject to a regime of periodic medical examinations and detention for treatment pending cure if an infectious venereal disease was found during an examination. Registration generally brought with it a denial of some measure of legal rights.[26] However, the Act of 1869 became a catalyst for negative public reaction in Britain. The extended operation of the Act—in particular when its more onerous examination regime came into force—generated resistance, which found expression in campaigns opposing the legislation. The strongest campaigners were women. Hostility to the regime mounted, and the upshot was that the Acts were eventually repealed.[27]

However, in 1869, a national association dedicated to the abolition of the legislation was formed.[28] Josephine Butler, the founding secretary, led the campaign and organized the reform movement to challenge the entire regime of State regulation.[29] Female supporters of the movement for repeal of the legislation, who became associated with Josephine Butler included Florence Nightingale, Harriet Martineau, and Lydia Becker. The male members included Jacob Bright, John Stuart Mill, Sheldon Amos, and a senior political figure from Gladstone's first government, Sir James Stansfield, who had held several ministerial portfolios, but was prepared to prejudice his own further advancement by throwing his political weight behind the campaign.[30]

Other countries were not immune to the upheaval; the English reformers had considerable influence overseas as well.[31] In France, Yves Guyot and Victor Hugo gave the movement their support.[32] By 1875, an international federation, colloquially known as the International Abolitionist Federation (IAF) had been formed at Liverpool. Its full name was the British, Continental and General Federation for the Abolition of the Government Regulation of Prostitution,[33] and its aim was to achieve system-wide abolition of regulation of prostitution.[34] It held its first international congress in 1877.[35]

## The Snagge Inquiry

One argument strongly put by those seeking an end to State regulation of prostitution in England held that State regulation in fact encouraged trafficking in prostitutes in both national and international contexts.[36] In 1880 the force of this argument was felt when a scandal concerning trafficking in English girls to brothels on the Continent came to public attention. An inquiry was at once called by the British Government.[37] Headed by T.W. Snagge,[38] a barrister of some eminence, the inquiry confirmed the existence of the active trade in its report, handed down in 1882. The report stated:

I find it to be a fact established beyond all doubt that for many years a trade or traffic has been carried on whereby a very large number of English girls—many, if not most of them, under the age of 21 years—have been enlisted to become inmates of brothels in Continental cities in consideration of fees or commissions paid by the keepers of the houses to the persons procuring the girls ....

I find that fraud was frequently and successfully practiced, that girls under age were easily enrolled, that in the case of English girls false certificates of birth were the rule rather than the exception, and that the girls entered upon a life, presently to be described, to which they were almost inevitably committed, before they could possibly become aware of its true nature and condition. I find that in several cases misrepresentation, falsehood and deceit marked every stage of the procedure, from the moment that the girl was first accosted by the *placeur* in England to that of her installation in the *maison de debauche*.[39]

## Criminal Law Amendment Act, 1885

The Snagge report prompted a reform in the shape of the Criminal Law Amendment Act, 1885,[40] which imposed criminal liability for a number of offences.[41] In relation to girls these were:

### Procurement for the Purposes of Carnal Connection

This offence was age related. It prohibited procurement for carnal connection (or its attempt) of any girl aged less than twenty-one, who was not a common prostitute or of immoral character (within the jurisdiction or beyond it).[42]

### Procurement for the Purposes of Prostitution

This offence prohibited procurement (or its attempt) of any girl to become a common prostitute (again, within the jurisdiction or beyond it, but without any element related to age).[43]

*Procurement to Leave the Jurisdiction*

This offence prohibited procurement (or its attempt) of any girl to leave the jurisdiction, with the intention that she become an inmate of a brothel for the purposes of prostitution in some other place.[44]

*Procurement to Leave a Place of Abode*

This offence prohibited procurement (or its attempt) of any girl to leave her usual place of abode within the jurisdiction (not being a brothel), with the intention that she may become an inmate of a brothel for the purposes of prostitution (within the jurisdiction or beyond it).[45]

The legislation drew a distinction between carnal connection (which was age limited) and the other instances of procurement, for which there was no limitation of age.[46] The reforms introduced by the creation of these offences of procurement in the Criminal Law Amendment Act, 1885 were novel at the time. The Criminal Law Amendment Act, 1885 provided the impetus for later international discussions[47] as well as the founding of several protection societies.

## The Rise of the Protection Societies

Sexual exploitation of English women and girls by forcing them into prostitution in Continental Europe ('the White Slave Traffic'),[48] took commercial advantage of those who had few options, notably the young, the destitute, and the homeless. A protest movement formed around a core of voluntary social protection organizations that had emerged—in this case with the object of protecting and assisting girls and young women, working for the suppression of trafficking, rescuing prostitutes, and sheltering those homeless and destitute.[49] Again, Josephine Butler's early leadership was instrumental. With her initiative another new organization—this one dedicated to combating the White Slave Traffic[50]—had been established even before the Snagge Inquiry. Called the International Union of the Girls' Friendly Society (IUGFS), it was founded in 1877. It worked for the protection of girls by addressing some of the problems they faced in new or unfamiliar situations. These included vulnerability while traveling (addressed by appointing representatives to meet girls arriving at railways stations, and making accommodation available); vulnerability while living aboard (addressed by providing homes at reasonable prices); and vulnerability while seeking work (addressed by establishing employment agencies and information centres to compete with, and preferably drive out, exploitative agencies and their abuses).[51] Another such organization, The Jewish Association for the Protection of Girls (JAPG), was established a few years after the IUGFS, in 1885, as a result of the scandal attendant upon the Snagge Inquiry which had led to enactment of the Criminal Law Amendment Act that year. During the hearings it had become apparent that many victims of trafficking were Jewish girls who had been enticed away from their homes in central Europe (Russia, Poland and Romania) on the pretence of a better and more prosperous life overseas. In the course of transit to South America, Africa, and Egypt, for the purpose of prostitution, these girls were sent via England.[52]

Enticement of Jewish girls was facilitated by the anti-Semitism of the time, which extended to restrictive legislation, harshly enforced, which affected the daily lives of Jews in Central and Eastern Europe. The objectives of the JAPG organization were directed at the rescue of girls who had succumbed to entrapment, protection of girls in danger, assistance for lonely girls travelling without friends, punishment of wrongdoers, and assistance of various kinds from advice to material help, wherever it was needed by a girl or woman. Stationing the organization's workers at docks and central railway stations in London and other centres, and taking premises nearby to serve as shelters for girls rescued from traffickers, were two of the positive measures taken.[53]

Yet another organization, the National Vigilance Association (NVA), was founded in 1885 also in the wake of the inquiry leading to the Criminal Law Amendment Act. Its objectives included location of missing girls, and in the course of carrying out this work, it provided further substantiation of matters raised in the course of the inquiry and confirmed the veracity of its findings. The NVA was able to demonstrate that lack of employment was the central issue that made girls vulnerable to enticement abroad—almost all of the missing girls had been promised lucrative employment, but were in reality decoyed abroad for immoral purposes. The traffickers were profiteers—women as well as men—who literally traded in girls, buying in one country and selling in another. The buyers were brothel keepers, and they were most prevalent in countries where the statutory control regime remained in place.[54]

A network of Catholic protective organizations was established in 1897. It was called the International Catholic Association for the Protection of Girls (ICAPG), and was established at Fribourg in Switzerland, to link with Catholic agencies and work centres throughout the world. ICAPG was established in response to the discovery that several Swiss girls from Fribourg had gone to Hungary on their own, and had become enmeshed in prostitution rackets there. The organization fought trafficking in a number of ways. These included making good use of the distinctive yellow and white livery of the organization for what these days would be called brand recognition: public notices that caught girls' attention (in railway carriages, on steamers, and indeed anywhere vulnerable girls might be when travelling) warning of the dangers and offering information about safe havens; ICAPG agents dressed in the same colours, meeting girls at risk and watching for traffickers; safe havens in the form of waiting rooms and premises for accommodation; employment agencies with the overarching objective of promoting girls' moral welfare; arrangements with hoteliers to alert the agency to incidents involving traffickers (attempts at subornation of staff, for example); a separate branch of the agency dedicated to the rehabilitation of victims of the trade; and systematic monitoring of newspaper advertisements to detect decoy promises made in advertisements placed by traffickers.[55]

## The Fifth International Penitentiary Congress, 1895

The protection societies were not fighting a lone battle, however. Legislatures were also responding to calls for action from the public at large, and the strongest feelings against trafficking were aroused where minors were concerned. More stringent legislation was enacted in several jurisdictions and enforcement was even more pronounced—police determination to pursue traffickers, and strict application of the law, were seen as critical. Informed policy makers were also aware that the problem had an international dimension, making piecemeal responses by individual countries less effective. But there was an even more significant jurisdictional problem as well: elements of offences committed across national boundaries (trans-border crime) were incapable of sustaining a prosecution in any one of the jurisdictions involved.[56] The need for international co-operation was pressed at the Fifth International Penitentiary Congress held in June 1895.

Would it not be desirable for an understanding to be arrived at between the different States with a view to preventing the prostitution of young women living abroad, and all too often dragged into vice by the maneuvers of certain individuals and certain agencies? What should be the repressive measures to be adopted against those who, by means of dishonest devices, persuade young women to go abroad with a view to forcing them to become prostitutes?[57]

The recommendation was that a multi-national conference be convened, its delegates tasked with formulating international measures against White Slave Traffic.[58] Led by Alexander Coote, Secretary of the NVA,[59] and Senator Berenger of France, the pressure for action began to build internationally.[60] Coote toured the country interviewing victims, and found many of them hospitalized, ill, or dying. This fuelled his determination to garner the public opinion necessary to galvanize authorities into action, enforcing existing regulation and strengthening it in whatever ways were necessary to eradicate this predatory trade.[61] This agenda, as told in his words, was:

To go to every capital in Europe, find some leading person in each and tell him the horrors of the White Slave Traffic, ask him to call together the leading men and women and government officials to hear an address on the matter, the objects being:

To form a national committee to deal with the question from a national and international point of view; to arouse strong public opinion throughout Europe concerning the traffic; to hold an international congress in London on the subject; from that congress to approach the European Governments asking them to hold an official conference to deal with the question from an international legal point of view; to make the national committee the means in the different countries of bringing all this to pass.[62]

In pursuit of this agenda, Coote began an extended tour of the Continent. He went first to Germany, in October 1898,[63] where his efforts were rewarded by swift action from local officials who were aware of the issues and keen to establish a national committee. After Berlin came, in turn, Holland, Denmark, Sweden, Russia, Belgium, France, Switzerland, and Austria. In each country a national committee for the suppression of the White Slave Traffic was established. Countries that could not be included in the schedule were not forgotten. Coote ensured that he corresponded with relevant authorities and by that means ensured that national committees were established throughout such countries.[64]

## The London Congress, 1899

Six months before the close of the nineteenth century, a mere four years after the Conference of 1895, and less than a year after Coote's tour to press the campaign case, London hosted an international congress of delegates. The congress drew the delegates from the national committees established as a result of Coote's efforts.[65] The London Congress—a first in this arena—established a permanent International Bureau[66] to promote and co-ordinate the efforts of the national committees already established, and encourage an expansion of the system as broadly as possible, supporting new conferences and congresses in other jurisdictions.[67]

The London Congress was an ideal arena to bring together what had been piecemeal evidence, scattered across the political landscape. Now it could be seen just how precise and consistent the large quantities of evidence really were, and how grave the problem throughout Europe. A sustained network of criminal procuring had grown. This was no longer something that informed law enforcement could hope to control with punitive local sanctions. The vulnerable, mostly underage, were offered lucrative posts that did not exist. With no idea of what was in store, they travelled to foreign countries, where they had no friends or contacts, no financial resources and no language skills, and were tossed into bawdy houses—brothels—where they had to earn their keep to stay alive.[68]

Confronted with the scale of the problem and the depth of depravity of the predatory operators of the networks, the London Congress resolved to work towards an international agreement whose signatories would take uniform action—first, a prosecution regime to deal with traffickers; and second, a protection regime for potential and actual victims.[69] The French Government was requested by the International Bureau to host a formal meeting to discuss the form of the agreement, and the members duly met in Paris in 1902.[70] The Paris meeting produced an International Agreement for the Suppression of the White Slave Traffic.[71] This International Agreement was signed on 18 May 1904, and came into force on 18 July 1905.[72]

## The International Agreement for the Suppression of the White Slave Traffic, 1904

The International Agreement for the Suppression of the White Slave Traffic, 1904 (Agreement of 1904) formulated in Paris in 1902 and signed in 1904 provided the first co-operative international effort directed at suppression of the White Slave Traffic. One of the objectives of the Agreement of 1904 was to secure for women and girls underage effective protection against the White Slave Traffic.[73] Its provisions were largely administrative,[74] drafted to facilitate member States' implementation of their own programmes to detect trafficking and to repatriate and generally assist victims.

In relation to girls, the structure of the administrative machinery of the Agreement of 1904 took the following form:

**Central Authorities:**[75] Each member State was to establish its own authority to co-ordinate information flow concerning procurement of girls, for immoral purposes, abroad. That authority was also responsible for co-operation and liaison with its counterparts in other member States (Article 1).[76]

**Monitoring Ports and Railway Stations:**[77] States undertook to maintain a watch at transport embarkation hubs (railway stations and ports) and within transport systems, for suspicious activity suggesting movement of girls destined for the trade.[78] Monitoring was to be conducted by officials and their delegates, along with other qualified persons,[79] and their task was to obtain whatever information they could, using legal means, that might lead to the detection of trafficking. Furthermore, States were required to notify competent authorities such as diplomatic or consular agents upon the detection of the principals, accomplices in, or victims of trafficking (Article 2).[80]

**Repatriation of Prostitutes:**[81] Articles 3, 4, and 5 concerned the repatriation of prostitutes[82] who (1) wished to be repatriated or (2) 'were claimed by persons exercising authority over them'. Article 3 obliged States in the context of repatriation of foreign prostitutes to ascertain their identity, their civil status, and who caused them to leave their origin country. In the interim, states were obliged to entrust victims who were considered to be destitute to charitable institutions (public or private) or to private individuals if the latter had capacity to offer necessary security.[83]

Before repatriation could be arranged, agreement about the victim's identity, nationality, place of arrival and date of arrival had to be ascertained.[84] The State in which the victim was currently residing would bear the cost of her return to the State of origin if she did not have the means to pay the cost of repatriation herself, or with the aid of her husband or guardian (if she had one), or other relations. Repatriation was arranged to the nearest frontier or port of embarkation in the State of origin. That State would then pay the remaining costs of repatriation.[85] These obligations (as provided in Articles 3 and 4) did not affect the operation of any private conventions existing between the States.[86]

**Employment Agencies:** The Agreement of 1904 recognized the role of unscrupulous employment agencies in the ever-present problem of prostitution (the situation in which girls without other means of support ended up) was tackled in Article 6,[87] which obliged States to supervise employment offices or agencies that offered to find employment for girls abroad.[88]

**Other Provisions:** The rest of the Agreement of 1904 concerned adhesion,[89] entry into force,[90] denunciation,[91] ratification[92] and application to colonies.[93]

## The Agreement of 1904 and Trafficking of Children for the Sexual Exploitation of Prostitution

In this context, the provisions of the Agreement of 1904 applied only to female children of the 'white' race. The Agreement of 1904 did not apply to female children of races other than 'whites' nor to male children of any race.[94]

## The Effect of the Agreement of 1904

The Agreement of 1904 had a swift and salutary remedial and preventative effect. States co-operated and their alertness had a strongly dampening effect on the trade, which steadily declined under the pressure applied by enforcement agencies, which made good use of the background liaison done by the national committees as they increased their efficiency and range of operations.[95] In Europe, several countries (among them France and Germany) assigned to their national committees the task in relation to ports and railway stations as set out in Article 2 of the Agreement of 1904. In other places voluntary organizations for the protection of girls shared the responsibility—chief among them Les Amies de la Jeune Fille and the Catholic International Association for the Protection of Girls.[96]

In Britain the National Vigilance Association carried out this work at home (in London and Liverpool) and abroad (at Buenos Aires and in Egypt). This was not the only British association of note. Various affiliated vigilance associations and the Jewish Association for the Protection of Women and Girls joined in this work in other British ports.[97]

The British Government had previously entrusted the International Bureau with the task of obtaining victims' declarations (as referred to in the Agreement of 1904). The International Bureau felt strongly that unsupervised repatriation of unaccompanied victims was likely to achieve little, and indeed do more harm than good. These victims had often been the subjects of police prosecution, and sending them back to their own countries alone and unaided would not have any morally or socially reformative effect. Therefore, they must travel in the company of an experienced and sympathetic worker, who would return them to the care of their own families or bring them to members of the national committee of their country of origin. On this basis the International Bureau applied for permission to send a worker back with each repatriated victim, and that application was successful.[98]

Even so, despite all these efforts or, rather, because of them, the traffickers themselves became more watchful, alert and devious, making the job of detection increasingly difficult.[99] Over time, the measures contained in the Agreement of 1904, which had initially proved very successful by focusing on victim protection rather than punishment of perpetrators, became increasingly less effective.[100]

## Paris Congress, 1906 and Vienna Conference, 1909

At the Paris Congress in October 1906 the decreasing effectiveness of the Agreement of 1904, in particular where punishment of traffickers was concerned, was debated by distinguished government delegates from twenty three countries. The proceedings were described as being characterized by an earnest desire to combat all the various stages of trafficking with uniform and progressive international action. The Congress of 1906 was followed by a conference in Vienna in October 1909. There Alexander Coote, representing the International Bureau, spoke urgently, appealing for a second official conference to continue the work. Again the French Government led the organization of the meeting, and a second official conference was convened in Paris in 1910. The conference achieved the drafting of the International Convention for the Suppression of the White Slave Traffic,[101] which was signed on 4 May 1910 and entered into force on 5 July 1920.[102]

## International Convention for the Suppression of the White Slave Traffic, 1910

The International Convention for the Suppression of the White Slave Traffic, 1910 (Convention of 1910) focused on the steps that needed to be taken to effectively suppress the White Slave Traffic.[103] It did so by mandating minimum legislative measures,[104] designed to prevent exploitation of 'women and girls underage' for prostitution,[105] along with administrative measures to facilitate legal co-operation between States.[106] The discussion below focuses on the application of the instrument to underage girls.

### The Legislative Measures: Articles 1 and 5

The Convention of 1910 set a legislative benchmark by establishing an offence (in Article 1) and requiring States (in Article 3) to amend the legislation within their own jurisdictions (or to bring those amendments before their own legislatures for passage in law) in order to meet the standard set by Article 1.[107]

The benchmark provision (Article 1) made it a punishable offence to procure, entice, or lead away a girl underage for immoral purposes in order to gratify the passions of another person, even with her consent. The cross-border difficulty was addressed by providing that the elements of the offence need not be committed within a single jurisdiction in order to constitute the offence.[108] The Final Protocol of the Convention of 1910 defined the phrase 'woman or girl underage' as women or girls under twenty full years of age. It was open to a State to fix a higher age limit for protection, as long as that age limit applied equally to girls of every nationality.[109] Each State was fully able to enact legislation criminalizing any number of analogous offences.[110] Prostitution was considered a matter for each State to regulate within its own internal jurisdiction.[111]

The Final Protocol of the Convention of 1910 mandated a penalty involving loss of liberty. The view taken was that in order to suppress the offence, the penalty must be seen to be heavy in every case. Breach of the trafficking law should therefore attract a term of imprisonment, with or without other penalties or offences, for principals and

accessories alike.[112] Sentencing should also take into account the age
of the victim, any aggravating circumstances (examples were set out
in Article 2),[113] and the fact that the victim's fate was in effect to be
delivered by the trafficker into an immoral life.[114]

The other legislative measure, Article 5, worked in tandem with
Article 1 by providing for extradition of those committing the offence
set out in Article 1. That offence was incorporated by reference, and
thus deemed to be included on the list of offences in respect of which
extradition could be granted under the terms of other conventions
previously entered into between States. Article 5 similarly required
States to amend existing legislation to give effect to this provision, or
to put such amendments before their legislatures.[115]

### The Administrative Measures: Articles 6 and 7

Enforcement of the offence in Article 1 of the Convention of 1910
was furthered by the legal co-operation between States promoted in
and required by Article 6, which established a system of transmission
of letters of request (by direct communication between the judicial
authorities, by way of some intermediary acting for the diplomatic
or consular agent of the demanding State, or through diplomatic
channels). Execution of a letter of request did not impose any
obligation for repayment of expenses of any kind. The diplomatic
channel was appointed as the site of settlement of any differences or
difficulties related to transmission. Unless otherwise agreed between
the States concerned, letters were to be drafted in the language of the
State on whom the demand was made.[116] Alternatively, a letter could
be sent with a translation into one of those two languages, as certified
by a diplomatic or consular agent of the demanding State or a sworn
translator of the State on whom the demand was made.[117]

Under Article 7 the States were required to share their records of
convictions relating to the Convention of 1910 where elements of an
Article 1 offence had been committed in different countries. These
records were to be forwarded to the authorities of the other contracting
States by the authorities designated to do so under Article 1 of the
Agreement of 1904.[118]

## Other Provisions

The remainder of the Convention of 1910 established provisions relating to overage females,[119] communication,[120] accession of non-signatory States,[121] the Final Protocol,[122] denunciation,[123] application to colonies, possessions, and consular judicial districts,[124] and signature.[125]

The Convention of 1910, with the expanded offence established in Article 1, came into effect with reinforced local laws in only a few signatory States.[126] In the meantime, the traffic continued. In 1908–09 the Immigration Commission of the USA conducted an investigation on the 'Importation and Habouring of Women for Immoral Purposes' and established that a large number of alien women and girls were being imported into the USA and farmed out for the purposes of prostitution across several states. Some of these were reported to be unwilling, but there was also a larger number of willing victims. They had been sourced and paid for in Europe using the postal services (letters) or agents, who travelled in Europe and Asia from time to time and obtained the women and girls for sums ranging from $200 to $2000.[127]

## The Convention of 1910 and Trafficking of Children for the Sexual Exploitation of Prostitution.

In this context, the provisions of the Convention of 1910 applied only in relation to female children (under twenty completed years of age)[128] of the 'white' race. The Convention of 1910 did not apply to female children of a race other than 'white' or to male children of any race.[129]

## The Last White Slave Traffic Conference in 1913

The International Bureau called the last international conference to consider the White Slave Traffic in 1913.[130] The various committees reported to the Conference on the manner in which the terms of the Convention of 1910 had been carried out, and the Conference considered if further legislation might be necessary to maintain the impetus.[131] Delegates came to represent twenty-four countries.

There were thirty-one of these representative delegates along with between 400 and 500 delegates attending on behalf of the national committees.[132] The Conference paid particular attention to the issue of employment aboard. Prior to the Conference the national committees had identified the lack of restriction on sending girls abroad for employment as one of the strongest contributory causes of trafficking in each country.[133]

In addition to considering the employment question, the Conference made recommendations concerning the preventative and remedial measures needed for the successful combat of trafficking.[134] A particular focus of attention was the suite of recommendations in relation to children which covered a range of matters:

### Entertainment Venues

International legislation should be enacted to prohibit employment of girls under sixteen in theatres, circuses, concert and music halls. In addition, there should be special protection of girls underage who were employed abroad to perform in such places.[135]

### Official Commissions

An official commission composed of members of both sexes should be established in each country to ascertain the extent of the White Slave Traffic and its causes.[136]

### Exclusion of Consent as a Defence

Each national committee was asked to take steps towards amendment of local legislation already on the statute books, in order to exclude the plea of consent, at least in relation to abduction of minors to foreign countries.[137]

### Places of Refreshment

Legislation prohibiting employment of minors as waitresses or barmaids in bars, cafes, taverns and inns should similarly be enacted, subject to an exception for proprietors who were parents of such girls.[138]

## Procuration Offence

Legislation should provide sanctions for third persons found guilty of procuration.[139]

## Carnal Knowledge

Legislation should also make carnal knowledge of minors a criminal offence. It should not except even girls who consented to the conduct, or girls who were already of immoral character.[140]

## Research

The national committees should carefully study the alleged traffic in children and determine its nature and extent.[141]

## Employment Agencies

Uniform international legislation was needed to control employment agencies, in particular those operating abroad.[142]

An enormous amount of work was put into achieving the final decisions made by the Conference, including years of exhaustive inquiry into the facts.[143] At the invitation of the Russian National Committee, a further congress was called for June 1916 at Petrograd, with a preliminary conference at Copenhagen to precede it in September 1915.[144] The planned 1916 congress held great promise: the discussions had been significant and far-reaching, and the reports provided a solid foundation for further progress.[145] However, World War I intervened. Neither governments nor voluntary bodies were in a position to continue with the effort in the face of Europe-wide hostilities, and no further international meetings were held.[146] The war had effectively ended—at least for its duration—any further development of international work on trafficking.[147]

# 2

# The Grounding of Protection in International Law

## The Convention of 1921

Following the conclusion of World War I, concerted efforts at the international level were made. This chapter traces the development of the International Convention for the Suppression of the Traffic in Women and Children 1921—the first international instrument to directly address the trafficking of children by a special provision.[1]

## THE COVENANT OF THE LEAGUE OF NATIONS

The League of Nations was established in 1919. Article 23(c) of the Covenant establishing the League of Nations assigned to it general control over execution of any agreements to be entered into with respect to trafficking.

Subject to and in accordance with the provisions of international conventions existing or hereinafter to be agreed upon, the Members of the League …(c) will entrust the League with the general supervision over the execution of agreements with regard to the traffic in women and children ….[2]

The Covenant's assignment was taken up in the first instance by the Brazilian Representative, M. Castao Da Cunha, who presented a report to the Council of the League of Nations (Council) as the Council sat in Rome, in May 1920. His recommendations were that the Council keep in touch with issues arising in relation to the White Slave Traffic by appointing a special attaché to the Secretary-General and that an international conference be called as soon as possible to deal with the subject.[3]

The Council considered the recommendations and appointed an attaché to the Secretariat to carry out that duty.[4] Simultaneously, the International Bureau set in train a review of the local legislation enacted in the different States since the Conference of 1910. In view of the status of international relations at the time, the International Bureau determined that it would be impractical to attempt to organize a conference of voluntary organizations.[5] The Council therefore resolved to take no steps until recommendations had been received from an international conference on the subject.[6]

In the meantime, the delegate of Romania had observed in a note to the League of Nations that in most countries, whatever had been done in relation to the White Slave Traffic had been done upon the initiative of private individuals, rather than by governments.[7] In support of the Brazilian Representative's submissions, he stressed the importance of continued international co-operation.

It seems that during the war this criminal traffic decreased, in consequence of the many formalities which the countries at war required from travelers. Still we must mention the Eastern slave markets, where women and children were sold and which we know have taken place in Armenia and Asia Minor. The women and children come from different countries but mostly from the Near East. Now with the return of peace and relaxation of passport formalities it is to be feared that the traffic will take a new lease of life. International collaboration is the only means to fight against it.[8]

Accordingly, the Romanian delegate proposed various measures. They included:

## A Survey of States

That the Asssembly of the League of Nations (Assembly) authorize and request the Secretariat to send a questionnaire to all member governments. The questionnaire should ask what legislative measures have been taken by each government to combat trafficking, and what other measures they proposed to take in the future.[9]

## A Conference

That the Assembly immediately fix a date for the holding of an international conference to consider the responses to the questionnaire and reach agreement on future united action. The conference would be attended by a committee comprising the official delegates from all signatories to the Convention of 1910, and could usefully include a Member of the Permanent Committee of Emigration (which was also considering the White Slave Traffic problem).[10]

## THE RESOLUTION TO ACT

The Assembly met on 15 December 1920 and not only adopted the measures proposed by the Romanian delegate but also mandated further measures.[11]

## Questionnaire

The Secretariat of the League of Nations was to issue a questionnaire, authorized by the Assembly to be sent to all governments, who would be asked to state the legislative measures locally taken to combat trafficking, along with the additional measures they proposed to take in the future.[12]

## Convention

Government signatories to the Agreement of 1904 and the Convention of instruments 1910 were to be urged to put such into operation forthwith.[13]

## Conference

The Assembly was to request the Council to invite the signatory countries (or other adherents to the Agreement of 1904 and Convention of 1910) to send representatives to an international conference to take place prior to the next Assembly.[14]

## Consensus

The conference would co-ordinate responses to the questionnaire received by the Secretariat with a view to reaching agreement on future co-ordinated action by the various governments.[15]

## The 1921 Questionnaire

The Secretariat, putting the resolution into effect, prepared a questionnaire to be sent to every State.[16] The covering letter of 16 February 1921 stated:

The Secretary-General of the League of Nations presents his compliments to [name] and begs to inform him that on 15th December 1920, the following resolution was adopted by the Assembly of the League of Nations:

'The Secretariat of the League of Nations shall issue a questionnaire and the Assembly shall authorise the Secretariat to send this questionnaire to all governments. The governments shall be asked what legislative measures have been taken by them to combat the traffic, and especially what additional measures they are proposing to take in the future.'

In accordance with the Resolution, the Secretary-General has the honour to request the [name] Government to give the information asked for in the following questionnaire with reference to the measures already taken or proposed to be taken to combat the Traffic in Women and Children in [place].[17]

The questionnaire embraced the subjects of the recommendations of the international congress in 1913 and provided an opportunity for each nation to report progress on the points indicated.[18]

Each State that was a signatory to the Agreement of 1904 and Convention of 1910 also received a letter urging the government, if it had not already done so, to put those instruments into immediate legislative effect.[19]

The questions asked by the Secretariat relevant to the traffic in children are set out in the box (see Box 2.1). The questions were phrased in conjunction with the trafficking of women, except for a singular question (question 10).

---

**Box 2.1    Questionnaire Sent to All States in February 1921[20]**

---

Is it a criminal offence under the laws:
(1) To procure women and girls underage whether with or without their consent?

What is the age below which the consent of the woman or girl does not constitute a defence to the charge? Are such acts punishable if committed abroad? What are the penalties prescribed? It is requested that the Secretary-General may receive copies of any legislation relative to this question and that statistics of prosecutions and convictions be communicated to the Secretary-General.

(2) Have any other legislative measures been taken by the [name] government to combat the traffic in women and children, and if so, what are they?

(3) Does the [name] government propose to take any further legislative or administrative steps against the evil?

(4) Has the [name] government taken any steps to have ports and railway stations watched for the purpose of checking the traffic in women and children? If not undertaking this duty themselves, have they delegated this responsibility, and, if so, to what agency?

(5) Has the [name] government established any form of control over offices and agencies which provide posts of women and girls in other countries?

(6) Has the [name] government taken any steps to protect women and girls travelling on emigrant steamers?

(7) Has the [name] government taken any steps to ensure protection to emigrants and immigrants against the *White Slave Traffic* and other forms of exploitation?

(8) Has the [name] government taken any steps to ensure the protection, pending their departure, of women and girls who after their arrival as emigrants, have for some reason or other to be sent back?

(9) Colonies and Dependencies—reports have been received that it is the practice in certain colonies for immigrant white men to have native women and girls procured for them for immoral purposes,

and that these women and girls are provided for them by chiefs or procurers. The Secretary-General would be glad to be informed:

What laws or administrative measures are in operation for limiting this evil if it exists in your country?

What statistics are available showing the number of prosecutions in each of your colonies or dependencies of persons procuring these women?

(10) Children—reports have been received that the practice in certain colonies of adopting, pawning or bartering children is in existence and that these children are obtained for immoral as well as industrial purposes. The Secretary-General of the League of Nations would be glad to be informed what laws or administrative measures are in operation to secure the abolition of this traffic or to limit it if it is in existence.

Adapted from the General Report of the Conference of 1921

The third paragraph of the resolution (concerning an international conference to take place prior to the next Assembly) was considered by the Council at its meeting in Paris on 22 February 1921. At the meeting it adopted the resolution to invite the signatory States to attend, along with any other State wishing to participate.[21] The Council resolved to request the Secretary-General to invite those States on its behalf, and the conference was scheduled to be held at the seat of the League of Nations during the last week of June of that year.[22]

## INTERNATIONAL CONFERENCE ON TRAFFIC IN WOMEN AND CHILDREN, 1921

The Conference of 1921 was held at Geneva between 30 June and 5 July 1921.[23] Thirty-four States attended[24]—the highest level of representation yet achieved at an international conference on this issue. Although they were not members of the League of Nations, Germany, Hungry, and Monaco were represented at the Conference of 1921.[25] On the agenda was consideration of the desirability of amending the Agreement of 1904 and the Convention of 1910 (in item 8).[26]

Agenda item 9 proposed for discussion: (a) an international extradition clause to be inserted (Articles 1, 2, and 5, Convention of 1910); (b) revisions of international legislation relating to employment abroad, in particular of minors (Article 6 of the Agreement of 1904); (c) a new clause directed at the protection of women emigrants by means of supervision during travel; (d) a clause extending the coverage of the instruments of 1904 and 1910 to all colonies and dependencies of signatory States as foreshadowed in the Declaration to the Agreement of 1904. Agenda item 10 brought before the Conference of 1921 the topic of international measures to control child traffic, in particular in colonies and dependencies, as a separate item for consideration in its own right.[27]

## Report on the Responses to the 1921 Questionnaire

The States' replies were examined by the Conference of 1921 in the form of a report on the replies to the questionnaire.[28]

The report was prepared by M. Regnault, the French delegate. Although the speed with which the answers had been compiled meant that they were in many places inadequate in scope and precision, M. Regnault compiled a general survey of the existing situation of the measures taken by the various responding States towards the goal of suppression of the traffic in women and children,[29] along with the following observations in relation to the specific questions asked.

### Responding States

The following States replied to the questionnaire:

Austria, Argentina, Belgium and the Belgian Congo, Bulgaria, Canada, Chile, China, Czecho-Slovakia, Denmark, Finland, France and her colonies, Germany, Great Britain and her colonies, Greece, Haiti, Hungry, British India, Italy, Japan, Luxemburg, Netherlands and Dutch East Indies, Norway, Romania, Serb-Croat-Slovene State, Siam, Union of South Africa, Spain, Switzerland, and Venezuela.[30]

In relation to Question 1, the general or special meaning of the word 'offence' in the various legislatures could have led to imprecision in some replies to the questionnaire, where the responses seemed to use the term in its broad (general) sense rather than its narrower, strictly legal sense. Here M. Regnault remarked that if the replies were considered together with the terms of the laws in force in the respondent States, it was possible to gain a fuller picture in relation to breaches of law committed within the boundaries of a particular jurisdiction.[31] On this point, listing the States which punish these offences, he went on to note that Switzerland had only two Cantons (Zurich and Neuchatel) in which provisions addressing the issue had been made law.[32]

The States which did punish offenders for the activities referred to in Articles 1 and 2, whether or not some elements were committed across borders, were: Austria, Belgium, Bulgaria, Canada, France, Germany, Great Britain, Greece, Hungary, Japan, Luxemberg, Romania, and Spain. Finland, however, punished only some offences committed abroad; the limits were closely defined.[33]

Italy punished offences committed abroad only in cases of abuse of trust by parents, grandparents, other relatives of direct line, or when guardians used compulsion with threats or violence to persuade children in their care to enter prostitution.[34]

Norway distinguished between offences on the basis of (1) whether or not they were punishable in the country where the offence was committed and (2) the nationality of the person who had committed the offence.[35]

The Netherlands punished only offences committed by Dutch subjects in countries where their behaviour constituted a punishable offence.[36]

Romania punished offences as provided in the legislation of the country where they were committed. Romanian nationals could not be prosecuted if they did not return voluntarily to Romania or had not been returned under extradition.[37]

Austria punished its own nationals who committed offences in other countries even if those countries did not themselves prosecute. It did not extradite foreigners unless their behaviour constituted a crime; however, foreigners who committed offences in Austria were expelled.[38]

Switzerland had no penal provisions on trafficking in the Penal Codes of the Cantons of Zurich and Neuchatel.[39]

Non-convention countries had a plethora of provisions and penalties varying with age, making it difficult to clearly ascertain how they stood in comparison with the 'age of majority' (the age of consent) provisions (Articles 1 and 2) in relation to the Convention of 1910.[40]

M. Regnault's report set out in tabular form the different 'ages of consent' as best he could ascertain from the responses.

**Table 2.1    Age of Majority or Consent in Various Countries**

| Country | |
|---|---|
| Spain | 23 |
| Belgium, France, Italy, and Czechoslovakia | 21 |
| Hungary and Netherlands | 20 |
| Denmark, Greece, and Norway | 18 |
| Bulgaria and India | 16 |
| Finland | 15 |
| Siam (now Thailand) | 12 (to be raised to 14 years in Draft Penal Code) |
| Other (includes the Netherlands and Great Britain) | No age of consent specified |

Adapted from M. Regnault's Report.[41]

In Romania consent by the woman or girl overage was a full defence (but in Austria consent was irrelevant to commission of the offence if its elements were established.[42]

## Question 2

Some States did have laws dealing with relevant questions (for example, women employed in public houses, in France (the Law of 1 October 1907); Italy (the Law of 1913 and Decree of 1914)).[43]

## Question 3

Almost every State was proposing new legislative provisions. M. Regnault noted that punishments varied widely. However, except in cases where there were extenuating circumstances, they were never less than three months of imprisonment (Bulgaria and Greece). Some legislatures provided for penalties of 'reclusion' (Luxemburg), and even for hard labour—from two to eight years in Finland, and one to ten years in Japan—or whipping in addition to imprisonment (in Great Britain, in Canada and in South Africa).[44]

Austria distinguished between seduction and procurement, which were separate offences in that country. Criminal seduction of a girl aged less than fourteen without her consent attracted a punishment of five to ten years of hard labour, and between six months and one year if there had been consent. Procurement was punishable by one to five years of imprisonment.[45]

In most States aggravating circumstances included the victim's age (11, 12, 13, 14, 15, or 16 years) and the relationship between the child and the offender (if any). For example, if they were *in loco parentis* or other positions of trust as parents and grandparents, guardians, officials, church clerics and the like.[46]

## Question 4

M. Regnault reported that almost all Contracting States, along with those adhering to Article 2 of the Agreement of 1904, had responded affirmatively to this question, saying they had taken all necessary steps to entrust supervision of ports and railway stations to special commissioners or to railway officials, or to some other functionary of their departments of emigration or immigration, and that in most cases private associations had co-operated well with the supervision regime. States which had not adopted the Agreement of 1904 had generally not put such arrangements in place to achieve supervision of this kind in their jurisdiction.[47]

## Question 5

Perusal of the replies had disclosed some omissions in responses to this question. Germany, Chile, China, and Venezuela had not responded at all, and the laws applicable in some other jurisdictions did not enable agency supervision in the manner contemplated by the Agreement of 1904. That was the case for overseas employment agencies in Argentina, Bulgaria, Greece, and the Netherlands; Denmark had no agencies of that kind.[48]

In Austria, France, Great Britain, Hungry, Italy, Japan, Luxemburg, Norway, Serb-Croat-Slovene State, and Switzerland supervision was a function of the government itself, at the level of local or municipal authorities. In most of these countries, an employment agency was required to be licensed, and employment abroad could only legitimately be arranged pursuant to some prior contractual arrangement, or with the consent of parents, or upon production of satisfactory information concerning the proposed employer (moral reputation and the like), or where all those conditions were fulfilled. That was the situation in France and in Great Britain.[49] Austrian minors (under 18 years of age) were required to obtain consent from the Court of Chancery before accepting employment abroad.[50]

### Question 6

M. Regnault noted that while some measures are prescribed by governments (as in Great Britain and Japan), more generally the steamship companies took the initiative by, for example, keeping women travelling alone separate from other passengers, putting female supervisors in-charge of the areas reserved for women, and forbidding men's access to those areas of the ship. First-class and second-class passengers were generally not permitted to visit passengers in steerage without an accompanying ship's officer.[51]

### Question 7

In all jurisdictions the private associations were a valuable adjunct to the official supervisory services such as the general police force. They included emigration societies, protection societies, and the steamship companies themselves, which had a commercial interest in safe passage on their vessels. All undertook, in one way or another, to protect emigrants or immigrants against exploitation in all its forms. In most cases they had premises dedicated to the purpose of protecting women.[52] Japan had instructed all consuls serving abroad to protect, and repatriate as necessary, Japanese emigrants.[53]

## Question 8

Most States which had contracted to observe the Agreement of 1904 had in fact done so in terms of their compliance with paragraph 2 of Article 3.[54]

Particularly in France, Great Britain, and Austria the steamship companies were a valuable adjunct to official efforts. In relation to repatriation of women and girls, in particular if they refused to disembark in another country, or had been expelled, they undertook to notify the State emigration authorities or police. The police were necessarily involved in repatriations to ensure they were effected according to law, but they were invariably assisted by private associations.[55]

## Question 9

Of the colonies and dependencies, the Dutch East Indies had observed the Convention of 1910 since May 1913, taking all measures necessary to prosecute procurers as the need arose.[56]

The British, French, and Belgian colonies had not experienced the problem of trafficking in native women and children by tribal chiefs or procurers for immoral purposes for the benefit of white emigrants, although the Permanent Committee for the Protection of Aborigines in the Belgian Congo had notified a few isolated or doubtful cases. The home and colonial governments had nevertheless responded with laws establishing punishable offences of trading or trafficking in human beings, which could be used to prosecute such cases as might in the future arise.[57]

## Question 10

As was the situation expressed in the responses to Question 9, it appeared that trafficking in children was not an evil to which the colonies had fallen prey.

While in the Far Eastern countries it was thought that cases of adoption could be found, it was not thought that immorality was likely to be involved in those cases. In addition, in French Indo-China (by Decree of 31 December 1912) and in the Dutch East Indies (under the Governor's declared regulation), laws had been passed with a view to protecting children. Trading, in the sense of pledging or exchanging children, was considered still to exist among primitive tribes, but was thought otherwise to have all but disappeared elsewhere with the imposition of colonial laws.[58]

In conclusion, M. Regnault praised the action taken to that time, remarking that he was 'chiefly struck by the valuable effects of the Agreement of 1904 and of the Convention of 1910.'[59] He noted that although there were some very particular difficulties relating specific responses, with only a few exceptions all the Contracting States had, with exacting care, carried their obligations pursuant to those instruments; and that of the States that had not yet undertaken to ratify the instruments, some had in any event harmonized their own legislation with the principles set out in those instruments, or were planning to do so. He urged those States to join their efforts with those of the Contracting Parties by formalizing their involvement.

In conclusion, therefore, one can only express the wish that these States should become, at the earliest possible moment, Contracting Parties to the Convention of May 4th, 1910, and that, under the supervision laid down in Article 23(c) of the Covenant of the league of Nations, they should take all necessary measures for rendering effective the suppression of the Traffic in Women and Children.[60]

## Resolutions of the Conference of 1921

Adopting the view set out in the report, the Conference of 1921 concluded that the Agreement of 1904 and Convention of 1910 should be applied, as they contained the principles and essential measures to be dealt with, and offered the means of remedying the situation if they were fully operationalized.[61]

The International Bureau concurred in this view, and presented a report on the condition of trafficking to the Conference of 1921.[62] That report stated:

If the concentration of the forces of good all over the world can destroy the lucrative and commercial value of the traffic, a very heavy blow will have been struck at its roots. The only object of its existence is the money to be made out of it by unscrupulous and immoral men and women. This can most effectively be prevented by uniform international legislations ....[63]

The Conference of 1921 thereupon recommended that the Council urge full adoption of the Agreement of 1904 and Convention of 1910 by all members of the League of Nations and States which had not yet ratified or fully enacted them, stressing the critical importance of doing so.[64] The Final Act of the Conference of 1921 made this recommendation.[65]

As for the instruments themselves, certain provisions of the Agreement of 1904 and the Convention of 1910 required some reinforcement, and the Conference of 1921 adopted additional resolutions and recommendations, which were also set out in the Final Act of the Conference of 1921.[66] These amended or supplemented the provisions of the Agreement of 1904 and Convention of 1910 then in force.[67] The recommendations, which in certain areas addressed the trafficking of children together with that of women, were in brief:

## Attempt

That in addition to the offences set out in Articles 1 and 2 of the Convention of 1910, the Council should request governments to provide in their legislation for an offence of attempt, and within the legal limits of *actes preparatories* in relation to the offences in Articles 1 and 2 (Recommendation 3).[68]

## Age Limits

That (with reference to Paragraph B of the closing Protocol of the Convention of 1910, where the age was set out) the age of 21 full years should be the minimum age considered 'underage' for purposes of protection, and that the Council of the League of Nations should request States which were already parties to the Agreement of 1904 and Convention of 1910 (or were ready to enact them) to extend that age to 21 years (Recommendation 4).[69]

## Extradition

That where existing treaties do not already provide for extradition in reference to Article 5 of the Convention of 1910, because of the urgent need to prosecute the offences set out in Articles 1 and 2 of the Convention of 1910, States should take all measures within their power to extradite or provide for the extradition of persons accused or sentenced in relation to those offences (Recommendation 5).[70]

## Transit Points

That, in accordance with Article 2 of the Agreement of 1904, governments should approach railway and shipping companies to display notices in railway stations and in ports, warning women and girls of the dangers of trafficking, and setting out information about sources of accommodation and assistance (Recommendation 8).[71]

## Employment Agencies

That States which had not yet enacted (by legislative or administrative measures) provisions concerning the licensing and supervision of employment agencies and offices should undertake to do so in order to ensure, by regulation, the protection of women and children seeking employment in other countries (Recommendation 9).[72]

## Terminology

That the words 'White Slave Traffic' be replaced in the texts of international instruments by the words 'Traffic in Women and Children' (Recommendation 13).[73]

Because he considered the problem of trafficking in children particularly large and difficult on the basis of the responses to the questionnaire, the Vice President of the Conference of 1921 proposed the formation of a committee to be charged with examination of the subject.[74] Further deliberation followed, with the result that the matter was referred to an existing committee for consideration.[75] That committee concluded that despite the fact that States had specifically been asked about the matter in the questionnaire, many governments had not been able to answer it, or answer it in as much detail as they would have liked to do in the time allowed for responses; more time was required for fuller investigation.[76]

The committee's conclusion led the French representative on the committee to propose, and the committee unanimously adopted, a resolution setting out its recommendation that the Conference of 1921 propose to the States that they fully investigate trafficking in children in their own jurisdictions in order to uncover traffickers and bring them to justice. It left to each jurisdiction the work of amending the civil provisions embodied in its laws to the extent necessary in relation to conditions set down for the adoption of children.[77]

The Conference of 1921 accepted the recommendation as resolved. The Final Act was amended to reflect that recommendation.

12. The Conference recommends that the governments should consider the question of the traffic in children, and should cause the necessary enquiries to be undertaken for the discovery of persons engaged in this traffic, and for their prosecution. It also recommends that the governments should amend the provisions of their civil laws regarding adoption of children, if these provisions do not afford sufficient protection.[78]

## Other Recommendations

The Conference of 1921 held at Geneva between 30 June and 5 July made other recommendations beyond the scope of amendments made to the existing instruments of 1904 and 1910. These were also incorporated in the Final Act:

### Notification of Adherence

A recommendation by the Conference of 1921, 'anxious to provide for the protection of women and children, whatever their race or colour', that the Council of the League of Nations should invite member States that were party to the 1904 and 1910 instruments on the subject of trafficking in women and children, and other States, to notify their

adherence of those instruments for themselves and on behalf of their
colonies and dependencies (Recommendation 2).[79]

## Protection While Travelling

In relation to the question of emigration and immigration, a
recommendation that all States should adopt whatever administrative
and legislative measures were required to bring trafficking in women
and children to an end. In particular, the Conference of 1921 drew
attention to the need to provide protection for women and children
who were travelling alone, and asked that governments do so not only
at points of departure and arrival, but also for the duration of travel
(Recommendation 6).[80]

## International Agreement

An observation by the Conference of 1921 that it would be desirable
for the International Commission on Emigration to attend to the
question of the traffic in women and children, with a view to framing
specific provisions concerning emigration which would ultimately
form part of an international agreement (Recommendation 6bis).[81]

## Repatriation

A recommendation that the international associations concerned
with the traffic in women and children be called upon to work to
ensure the repatriation of women or girls who had been expelled
from another country or refused permission to remain in that country
(Recommendation 7).[82]

## Reporting

A recommendation, pursuant to Article 23(c) of the Covenant of
the League of Nations, that the Council should direct the Secretariat
to request all League of Nations members, and all States that had
adopted the existing 1904 and 1910 instruments, to supply the
Secretariat with an annual report on the measures they had taken, or

contemplated, with a view to putting an end to the traffic in women and children.[83] All annual reports should be provided to all members and signatory States, in full or in summary form, in order to make the experience gained by all jurisdictions available to the others, and the Secretariat could draft a suitable questionnaire to be sent to them.[84] In addition, the Conference of 1921 recommended that similar annual reports be sought from the international associations for the suppression of the traffic, for circulation in the same manner (Recommendation 10).[85]

## Advisory Committee

A recommendation that the States appoint a committee of five or six representatives and three to five assessors, constituted as an advisory body to the League of Nations. The committee would advise the Council on 'the general supervision over the execution of agreements with regard to the traffic in women and children', as well as consider all related matters of an international character submitted before it from time to time.[86]

The committee would not have authority or direct power (Recommendation 11).[87] In addition:

The Council would be responsible for making appointments to the committee. However, the Conference of 1921 was of the view that it should make certain recommendations: that as far as it was able to do so, the Council should, in making appointments, consider the general interests of States along with geographical representation. To that end, France should be represented, because it had assumed obligations in relation to the instruments of 1904 and 1910, including undertaking to collect various information, which it would furnish to the Secretariat.[88]

The assessors should represent certain organizations that were already involved—the International Office for the Suppression of the Traffic; a women's international organization; and (together or individually) three international societies, namely the Jewish Association for the Protection of Girls; the International Catholic Association for the Protection of Girls; and/or the Federation of National Unions for the Protection of Girls.[89]

The committee should meet at the request of the Council, as and when required. Expenses of attendance should be borne by the State or association represented by the committee member. The committee itself should liaise closely with the national and international organizations through the assessors. That was seen as the best way to achieve co-ordination and co-operation of official and unofficial efforts to suppress the traffic.[90]

## Humanitarian Concerns

The Conference of 1921, having been apprised of trafficking in women and children for political or military purposes and the consequences of such trafficking, felt it must ask the League of Nations to intervene to prevent such practices, which it noted to be contrary to the laws of humanity (Recommendation 14).[91]

## Thanks and Assurances

In conclusion, the Conference of 1921 requested that its thanks be conveyed by the Secretariat of the League of Nations to organizations which had made recommendations, and that the Secretariat also inform them that their proposals had been considered by a specially formed committee prior to discussion or determination by the Conference of 1921 (Recommendation 15).[92]

# Approval of the Final Act of the Conference of 1921

By resolution, the Council unanimously approved the Final Act, with all its recommendations, on 12 September 1921.[93] The Secretary-General was given carriage of the matter in these terms:

The Council having considered the Final Act drawn up by the International Conference on Traffic in Women and Children, which met at Geneva from June 30th to July 5th, 1921, expresses its approval of the recommendations contained therein, especially those addressed to the Council, and instructs the Secretary-General to carry them into effect, to send one original copy of the Final Act to the French Government and to transmit a copy to the Assembly for its consideration.[94]

## Drafting the New Convention

The British Delegate on the Council proposed that carrying the recommended modifications to the 1904 and 1910 instruments into effect required a new convention.[95] As the need for united action was seen to be urgent,[96] he presented a draft convention[97] for the suppression of the traffic in women and children (British Draft Convention), which had been prepared by British delegates and circulated to the Council.[98] That a new instrument was intended to be created was clear from the preamble. The recitals covered the following matters:

### Prior Instruments

The purpose of facilitation of the execution of the prior instruments dealing with the same subject was stated (the Agreement of 1904 and the Convention of 1910).[99]

### Final Act

That cognizance had been taken of the Final Act of the Conference of 1921 was noted.[100]

### New Convention

A new general convention was stated to be the best way to effect the decisions set out in the Final Act, and the decision to conclude a convention for this purpose was noted.[101]

### British Draft Convention

The body of the British Draft Convention contained the following major provisions:

### Article 1

Signatory States who were not parties to the Agreement of 1904 and the Convention of 1910 declared that they accepted all the rights and obligations established under those instruments as modified by Articles 2–8 to the same extent as if those instruments were inserted in this instrument.

## Article 2

'Traffic in women and children' was substituted for 'White Slave Traffic' in the 1904 and 1910 instruments.

## Article 3

Signatories agreed to legislate to sanction the offences set out in Articles 2 and 3 of the Convention of 1910 along with attempts to commit those offences and acts preparatory to commission of those offences, to the extent permitted by the law in the local jurisdiction.

## Article 4

Signatories agreed, in relation to extradition that was not provided for by existing treaties, to take all measures within their power to extradite or enable extradition of any person accused or sentenced in relation to offences specified in Articles 1 and 2 of the Convention of 1910, as provided in Article 5 of the Convention of 1910.

## Article 5

The age of 'twenty-one completed years of age' was substituted for 'twenty completed years of age' in Paragraph B of the final Protocol to the Convention of 1910.

## Article 6

Signatories exercising supervision over offices and agencies engaged in finding employment for women and children abroad (pursuant to Article 6 of the Agreement of 1904) undertook to legislate as required to ensure their protection.

## Article 7

In relation to immigration and emigration, signatories undertook to adopt whatever administrative and legislative measures were required to check the traffic in women and children. This included legislating as necessary to protect women and children traveling alone on emigrant ships, at points of departure and arrival and during the journey, as well as arranging exhibition of warning notices in railway stations and in ports to apprise women and girls of the danger posed by traffickers and advertise places where they are able to find help and accommodation.[102]

## French Amendments to the British Draft Convention

The British Draft Convention was amended at the suggestion of the French Government,[103] which recommended substitution of the preamble and seven articles (French Draft Convention). The substitutions were to the following effect:

### Purpose

To conclude a convention supplementary to the 1904 and 1910 instruments that secure suppression of the traffic in women and children (described as 'White Slave Traffic' in the preambles to the 1904 and 1910 instrument(s), taking into account the recommendations of the Conference of 1921 and set out in the Council's Final Act (Preamble).[104]

### Agreement to Prior Instruments

Contracting States that had not already agreed to the 1904 and 1910 instruments agreed to ratify them immediately, and further agreed that ratification of the new convention would operate as ratification of the earlier instruments for any State that proved unable to meet this stipulation (Article 1).[105]

## Prosecutions

Contracting States agreed to do everything they could ('take all measures') to bring before the law anyone engaged in trafficking children of either sex who commit an offence as defined by Article 1 of the Convention of 1910 (Article 2).[106]

## Preparatory Offences

Contracting States agreed to similarly prosecute inchoate (preparatory or incomplete) offences to the extent permitted by law, where they were made as contemplated by Articles 1 and 2 of the Convention of 1910 (Article 3).[107]

## Extradition

Contracting States agreed to co-operate to secure the extradition of offenders under Articles 1 and 2 of the Convention of 1910 where trans-jurisdictional offences involved countries which did not share extradition conventions (Article 4).[108]

## Age of Protection

Contracting States agreed to amend Final Protocol Paragraph B of the Convention of 1910 by changing the age of consent/majority from twenty to twenty-one 'completed years of age' (Article 5).[109]

## Employment Protection

Where employment for women and girls was being supervised or arranged in another country (pursuant to Article 6 of the Agreement of 1904), Contracting States agreed to require the offices or agencies under their supervision to make enquiries directed at securing their protection, and take whatever actions were required for their protection (Article 6).[110]

## Immigration and Emigration

Contracting States agreed to enact whatever administrative and legislative measures were needed to stop the traffic in women and children.

Specifically, States undertook to regulate emigrant ships in order to protect women and children travelling as passengers and at the points of departure and arrival, and to arrange for warning notices and statements (about resources offering help including sources of accommodation and information) at railway stations and ports (Article 7).[111]

## The Amended Draft Convention

The Council accepted the amendments proposed by the French Draft Convention and incorporated them into an Amended Draft convention.[112] At that point, the British delegate proposed, unless the Council wished to consider the Amended Draft Convention at once, that it be referred to the Assembly. There it would be examined by a committee before being signed by members of the League of Nations during the Assembly's current session. To that end, the British delegate moved a Council resolution to the effect that the Council, cognisant of the terms of the Amended Draft Convention, refer it to the Assembly with the Council's recommendation for its examination and signature.[113]

### The Fifth Committee, 1921

The Fifth Committee of the Assembly discussed the Amended Draft Convention.[114] Discussions related to the conformity of the Amended Draft Convention with the recommendations of the Final Act; the accuracy and precision of the French and English texts of the Amended Draft Convention; and whether specific clauses were needed to incorporate age reservations made by States. The delegates of India and Siam (Thailand) argued here that in countries where adulthood was deemed to be reached at an earlier age than applied in Europe, the age of protection was inappropriate. Japan, through its delegate, indicated that its existing legislation placed it in a position where it would be unable to conform at once.[115]

### Drafting Committee

At this stage three eminent jurists were appointed as members of a Drafting Committee to consider these issues.[116] The Drafting Committee compared the French and English texts and suggested minor alterations in the French text in order to render them identical in effect. It also compared the Amended Draft Convention with the recommendations of the Final Act and suggested omission of the second paragraph of Article 1 as well as amendments to Articles 1, 4, and 6 to make them adhere more closely to Recommendations 1, 5, and 9 of the Conference of 1921.[117]

In summary, the jurists' recommendations were:

## Preamble and Articles 3, 5, and 7

No alteration to the Amended Draft Convention.

## Article 1

New wording 'they will transmit with the least possible delay' replaced the draft wording 'they will transmit forthwith after the signature of the present Convention' and Paragraph 2 was omitted.[118]

## Article 2

The plural 'offences' replaced the singular 'offence'.[119]

## Article 4

Wording refining the statement relating to measures to extradite offenders under Articles 1 and 2 of the 1910 instrument.[120]

## Article 6

Wording that increased the precision of the terms of the agreement regarding supervisory agencies to include legislative or administrative measures regarding licensing and supervision where the Contracting State had not already done so.[121]

The amendments were designed to achieve closer adherence to the recommendations contained within the Final Act without going beyond it. In relation to the age related questions, the Drafting

Committee was of the opinion that the reservations suggested could be made without special additional clauses in the instrument itself, if ratifying States made reservations to that effect at the time of signing.[122]

## Final Wording for Resolution

The Fifth Committee made the alterations as recommended approving the instrument, in that final form. It included a recommendation in the report it submitted to the Assembly. The recommendation was for speedy adoption of the instruments by the Assembly, and that accordingly, all duly authorized delegates should sign the instrument, and those without such authorization should obtain it from their governments forthwith.[123]

The Assembly voted to pass that resolution on 29 September 1921 with 22 abstentions. The next day the International Convention for the Suppression of the Traffic in Women and Children was declared open for signature.[124] It entered into force on 15 June 1922.[125]

## INTERNATIONAL CONVENTION FOR THE SUPPRESSION OF THE TRAFFIC IN WOMEN AND CHILDREN, 1921

The International Convention for the Suppression of the Traffic in Women and Children 1921 (Convention of 1921) was intended to supplement the Agreement of 1904 and Convention of 1910.[126]

In brief, the new measures were as follows:

## Article 2

Had its origins in Recommendation 12 of the Conference of 1921. It required States to take all measures available at law to detect and prosecute trafficking offences within the meaning of Article 1 of the Convention of 1910, for those trafficking in children of either sex.[127]

## Article 3

Obliged States to punish attempts and preparatory acts connected with the offence, as set out in Article 1 of the Convention of 1910.[128]

This was an advance on the terms of the Convention of 1910, and had been added pursuant to Recommendation 3 of the Conference of 1921.

## Article 4

Supplemented States' extradition powers by providing that in the absence of extradition conventions already entered into between States, States would take all measures within their power to extradite or provide for the extradition of accused or convicted offenders under Article 1 of the Convention of 1910.[129] This gave effect to Recommendation 5 of the Conference of 1921 in relation to Article 5 of the Convention of 1910.

## Article 5

Had its origins in Recommendation 4 of the Conference of 1921. It made the new age limit twenty-one completed years of age in place of twenty years, which had applied pursuant to the Convention of 1910.[130]

## Article 6

Required States that had not yet taken legislative or administrative measures in relation to the licensing and supervision of employment agencies and offices to do so, legislating as necessary to protect all children seeking employment in another country.[131] With its origins in Recommendation 9 of the Conference of 1921, this provision enhanced the effect of Article 6 of the Agreement of 1904, which had related only to female children.

## Article 7

Gave protection to child emigrants. It required States to legislate and establish administrative measures to check the traffic in children. In particular, States undertook to legislate for the protection of children travelling on emigrant ships at points of departure and arrival, and during the journey, and to place warning notices in railway stations and ports alerting children to the danger and listing sources of help and accommodation.[132] This measure had its origins in Recommendation 8 of the Conference of 1921 and supplemented the terms of Article 2 of the Agreement of 1904.

## Other Provisions

Related to becoming a party to the Agreement of 1904 and Convention of 1910,[133] signature,[134] ratification,[135] accession,[136] entry into force,[137] denunciation,[138] record of Contracting States,[139] and application to colonies, overseas protectorates or territories under sovereignty or authority.[140]

### The Convention of 1921 and Trafficking of Children for the Sexual Exploitation of Prostitution

In this context, the provisions of the Convention of 1921 applied to female and male children (under 21 completed years of age)[141] of any race.[142]

### The Effect of the Convention of 1921

Although the Convention of 1921 did increase the scope of the protections first established by the earlier instruments (the Agreement of 1904 and Convention of 1910), the illegal trade did not cease as a result. Cross-jurisdictional exploitation of underage girls for the purposes of prostitution in a foreign State continued.[143]

# 3

# Expanding the Scope for Action

## The Convention of 1933

This chapter traces the development of the International Convention for the Suppression of the Traffic in Women of Full Age, 1933, during the decade 1923–33.

## THE SPECIAL BODY OF EXPERTS

### Constituting the Special Body of Experts

The Advisory Committee on Traffic in Women and Children (Advisory Committee) appointed by the League of Nations pursuant to Recommendation 11 of the Final Act of the Conference of 1921,[1] met for its second session in March 1923.[2] The USA, through its representative, Grace Abott, submitted a challenging recommendation for a sensitively handled investigation of the trafficking in women and girls by the League of Nations.[3]

An investigation be undertaken through the Secretariat of the League of Nations in order to ascertain the following facts with reference to international traffic in women and girls; (1) whether there is international traffic in women and girls for the purposes of prostitution; (2) between what countries the traffic is being carried on and the methods used in procuring and transporting women and girls; (3) the effectiveness of national measures undertaken to eliminate the traffic.

In this investigation, the acts as to (1) adult women who willingly and with full knowledge of the purpose for which they are being recruited as well as (2) young girls and (3) adult women who by force or fraud are imported or exported for purposes of prostitution should be ascertained. Geographically the investigation should include, if possible the principal cities of the world, but, if this is not possible, typical cities should be selected from where there is reason to believe the traffic is or is not being carried on, those in which regulated houses and those in which abolition is the policy, those situated in countries in which prostitutes and all those who live or benefit by prostitution are excluded from admission, and those whose laws regulating immigration make no or inadequate provisions for excluding immoral persons.

From official sources, the facts as to the administration of laws designed to eliminate the traffic can be learned; to secure the information as to the traffic itself, it will be necessary to send to the cities included in the survey, agents of high standing with special training and experience to make personal and unofficial investigations. It is recognised that such investigations are difficult, not to say dangerous, but they are absolutely necessary to secure the facts to refute sensational exaggerations or general denials as to the traffic and – what would seem to be for the Committee of supreme importance – an intelligent basis for a sound programme for international co-operation for the suppression of the traffic, if it is to be found to exist.[4]

The Advisory Committee could only acknowledge that the information it already had was limited; thus more information would materially assist the anti-trafficking effort. In addition, the majority proposed to appoint experts charged with going to the countries concerned and making enquiries (on-the-spot study). This would require the governments of the States involved to co-operate. A majority (five votes to three) resolved to accept the recommendations. First, the Advisory Committee noted its reasons for making the recommendation: it recognized the soundness of the USA recommendation and declared such a study to be a valuable source of information that would greatly benefit its work in determining the best way to counteract the traffic in women and children. Second, that the Council should appoint experts to undertake an on-the-spot study. Third, that the Council should consider alternative funding sources if the League could not meet the expenses itself.[5]

The Council duly approved the proposal on 19 April 1923, noting that it recognized the Advisory Committee's need for the information that could be gleaned from such a study. Knowing the conditions under which the traffic was carried on was important for the Advisory Committee's work, and the Council agreed it could best be collected in a study by Council-appointed experts with the consent and collaboration of the relevant governments in the jurisdictions being inquired into.[6]

The methodology suggested by the Council was a questionnaire, to be drawn up by specialists as soon as possible, then sent to interested States by the Secretary-General. The experts would be authorized to make their enquiry on-the-spot, with the consent of the governments concerned, then draw their conclusions from those replies along with the reports on the results of the enquiry obtained from each jurisdiction.[7]

During its twenty-fifth session (7 July 1923), and subject to satisfactory financial resources being available, the Council appointed the expert body to enquire into the current situation internationally.[8] However, the geographical scope of the study was limited to Continental America, Europe, the Near East, and some southern Mediterranean countries. Its determinative scope was to ascertain the existence and nature of the traffic, its volume, location, and characteristic features, in addition to probing the effectiveness of existing measures.[9]

The Fifth Committee was gratified to have obtained Council adoption of the Advisory Committee's recommendation. It noted that it expected the study to prove 'of the greatest value in indicating whether the measures now being undertaken are sufficient or whether further action is required' and noted that the success of the enquiry clearly depended on 'the goodwill and collaboration' of the jurisdictions in which enquiries were to be made. The Fifth Committee expressed the earnest hope that each country would give that assistance in full.[10]

The Fifth Committee passed a resolution to the same effect,[11] as did the Assembly on 15 September of that year. The Assembly similarly expressed itself to attach 'great importance' to the expert enquiry and repeated the language of 'earnest hope' that the States involved would fully facilitate whatever investigations the experts considered warranted.[12]

As for the financial support required, by letter dated 5 October 1923, the USA informed the Secretary-General that the American Bureau of Social Hygiene would carry the cost of the enquiry to the extent of $75,000.[13] This sum appeared sufficient to enable the enquiry to be undertaken without cost to League of Nations funds; as the Council had approved the enquiry and appointed the experts, the Secretary-General obtained authorization from the Acting President of the Council to accept the offer on behalf of the League of Nations, and gratefully did so.[14]

## The Special Body of Experts Report

The Special Body of Experts submitted its report to the Council on 18 February 1927.[15] The report made clear that there was an issue of some concern; although girls of minor age (under twenty-one) who were procured with or without fraud were protected under Article 1 of the Convention of 1910, there was still 'a good deal of traffic in girls, some of whom are little more than children'. The Special Body of Experts estimated that at least 10 per cent of the traffic, and probably more, was made up of girls of minor age. That figure had been based on statements made by *souteneurs* (literally, 'supporters', that is, pimps) and by the girls themselves, along with age records made when prostitutes were registered in foreign countries. Mexican souteneurs made it clear that only young girls were wanted for this trade. Argentine information similarly stated that the foreign girls were always young. European souteneurs interviewed during the inquiry were taking to South America, for every adult women procured, at least one minor (at the rate of at least 50 per cent). Foreign prostitutes registered in Paris between 1919 and 1923 and aged between eighteen and twenty-one years constituted between 10 and 36 per cent of the total (registrations were, in each of those years, 36, 29, 10, 12, and 25 per cent respectively). In Portugal, 40 per cent of all registered prostitutes (a figure which included foreigners) were between sixteen and twenty years of age. All this went to suggest that a figure of 10 per cent under twenty-one was significant under-representation.[16]

In addition, while very young girls could be seen openly at work in many places, they were often licensed or registered as prostitutes; this was possible because the procurer or *madame* had used false birth certificates in order to effect the registration. Moreover, even larger numbers were found to be practising prostitution clandestinely. The Special Body of Experts reported that the resorts frequented by young semi-professionals often supplied the souteneur or the international trafficker with a ready recruiting ground.[17]

The Special Body of Experts had found it difficult to determine the real ages of the girls, particularly the foreign prostitutes, because their passports never showed them to be minors: and their exploiters had always coached the girls to add five, six or seven years to their true age.[18]

As for the existing instruments themselves, the Special Body of Experts was of the view that its provisions were 'clear and comprehensive'. The problem lay with implementation. If the instruments were carried fully into effect that would make a significant difference to the exploitation of women and girls for prostitution in a foreign country. But exploitation occurred even in countries that were parties to the existing instruments. Yet, the legislation of many States was still below the standard set in the instruments they had adopted. The Special Body of Experts instanced one country where girls of fourteen, fifteen or sixteen were quite often registered as prostitutes in circumstances that left little room for doubt that they had in fact been procured for that purpose. In several other countries, girls in that age range could be found in licensed houses and clandestine brothels.[19] The Special Body of Experts believed the question to be intertwined with the wider matter of the age of consent to sexual intercourse (below which age a defence of consent cannot be sustained).[20] That age was as low as twelve in some countries (in at least one case as low as ten) if a defendant could prove in evidence that the girl was 'not previously chaste'.[21]

The Special Body of Experts suggested, because the number of girls of minor age who were exploited on pretence of majority was so large, the Advisory Committee should consider ways of modifying the established instruments to overcome that difficulty.[22]

## ADVISORY COMMITTEE SESSIONS, 1927–30

The Advisory Committee took full cognisance of the Special Body of Experts findings concerning minors. In April 1927, at its sixth session,[23] the Advisory Committee considered the report, taking particular note of the finding concerning minors being among the victims of trafficking. It then adopted a resolution to the effect that it would place the issue on its agenda for the next session in order to consider whether it was desirable to remove the age-limit from the Convention of 1910 as amended by the Convention of 1921.[24]

At its subsequent session (its seventh, held in March 1928),[25] the Advisory Committee did indeed discuss that matter. However, although the Advisory Committee heard various arguments made by different parties, it was made aware that to propose such a modification to the existing instruments would further delay their ratification by certain States. The Advisory Committee therefore adopted a resolution requesting the assessor for the Jewish Association for the Protection of Girls and Women, Mr Cohen, to report on the desirability of abolishing the age limit in the existing instruments.[26] At the Advisory Committee's eighth session, held in April 1929,[27] Mr Cohen duly reported on the matter in some detail, informing the Advisory Committee that he had consulted the national committees for the suppression of the traffic, who recommended removal of the age limit; that the recommendation was supported by various international conferences and congresses, and that all the assessors of the Advisory Committee and the women's organizations also supported the move. Mr Cohen therefore enquired whether it would be possible for the Advisory Committee to obtain the support of States for the following provision:[28]

Any person who procures or attempts to procure any woman or girl for purposes of prostitution within or without the country, shall be liable to a penalty of ....[29]

Mr Cohen informed the Advisory Committee that the abolition of the age limit in the existing instruments of 1910 and 1921 would make it possible to punish offences connected with trafficking much more effectively.[30] This was because false documents and statements were often tendered to authorities, giving them the impression that girls had reached their majority (twenty-one years) as provided in the instruments (the Convention of 1910 as amended by the Convention of 1921). This made the girls appear, falsely, to be beyond the reach of those provisions.[31]

However, Mr Cohen warned against premature action and proposed a preliminary step, ascertaining the opinion of the various States to ensure that no modification was proposed which could not be incorporated into all systems of law. During the discussions the French delegate noted that France favoured elimination of the age limit in the instruments. The German and Spanish delegates also advised that in their countries, new criminal codes had been proposed or adopted which abolished the age limit.[32] The trend seemingly being towards abolition, the Advisory Committee unanimously adopted a resolution making the point that the time had come to reconsider the matter. The resolution stated that the Advisory Committee had considered the views expressed to it on the question, and requested that the Council authorize the Secretariat to obtain the views of all governments on the proposal to eliminate the age of twenty-one in the Convention of 1921 and to submit a report to the next session of the Advisory Committee.[33]

In June 1929 the Council approved the Advisory Committee's resolution. The Secretary-General sent a letter (dated 1 August 1929) to the States requesting their opinion on the matter of the age of majority. The Advisory Committee was duly advised of the responses from States as they were received during that year, and the Advisory Committee took cognisance of the answers at its next session (the ninth, held in April 1930).[34]

Not all States had replied by the time of the meeting. The Advisory Committee noted that fact,[35] but proceeded to examine the replies it had received. Although the Advisory Committee considered that the age limit frequently hindered suppression of trafficking because it encouraged the use of false documentation or statements, it thought that to make a decision at that point would be premature. It preferred to await more replies.[36] It resolved to that effect, stating that most of the replies it had received were in favour of elimination of the age of twenty-one years from the instruments (the Convention of 1910 as amended by the Convention of 1921) and that it was 'inclined to the view that this step should be taken' but it thought that 'it would still be more desirable to emphasize the fact that the offences covered by the Convention of 1921 are more serious when committed against those of minor age.' It therefore preferred to secure further replies before expressing its definite opinion, and called for a further report to be submitted to its meeting the following year.[37]

## COMPLETION OF CONSULTATION AND SECRETARIAT REPORT

Following the Advisory Committee's 1930 resolution, the Secretariat finalised its consultation and submitted a supplementary report to the Advisory Committee in 1931.[38] At its tenth session (in April 1931) the Advisory Committee examined the replies.[39]

The report disclosed that twenty-six States were, in principle, in favour of abolition of the age limit. However, several States expressed particular reservations. France wished studies to be conducted in order to find ways to permit the countries which had retained the earlier system of licensed houses to comply with the future convention. Denmark had just framed a new penal code that conformed with the Convention of 1921 as it stood. The Danish delegate considered that Denmark might accept the proposed amendment because in that country every act of aiding, assisting or abetting prostitution, for purposes of gain, was already a criminal offence.[40] The Advisory Committee was pleased to note, as compared with the previous year, the marked increase in the number of replies received that were in favour of abolishing the age limit. But it requested that the question be reconsidered the following year in relation to other amendments to the existing instruments,[41] in view of the reservations made by some States.[42]

## ADVISORY COMMITTEE ELEVENTH SESSION, 1932

The eleventh session of the Advisory Committee was held in April 1932.[43] At that meeting the matter was duly re-examined, and three main arguments were advanced in favour of abolition of the age limit of 21 in the existing instruments:[44]

First, the great difficulty experienced in giving minors protection under Article 1 of the Convention of 1910 as a result of the frequent use of false papers.[45]

Second, in most cases women were not fully aware of the adverse situation in which they were to be placed. Such consent should be considered nugatory, even if the woman was no longer a minor and had freely consented to being made the object of traffic; it should not provide a defence or be a bar to prosecution of the traffickers.[46]

Third, even where victims were overage and had previously been prostitutes, the law should not permit traffickers to derive financial benefit from that situation.[47]

The existence of licensed houses appeared to be a source of great difficulty in the matter of the age limit—indeed the chief source. Abolishing the age-limit according to the proposed amendment could have the result of rendering managers of those legally licensed premises, and the recruiters who supplied women to ply their trade there, liable to punishment. However, several countries who did in fact have a legal licensing scheme for such premises were nevertheless in favour of pursuit of the question of abolition of the age limit, and expressed their view that the Advisory Committee should not take the existence of licensed premises to be a bar to amending the existing instruments (the Convention of 1910 and Convention of 1921) in that way.[48]

The Advisory Committee received from the Secretariat the report consisting of the States' answers to the circular letter together with a comparison of the laws and regulations in force in countries that had an existing criminal regime that punished trafficking in women who had achieved their majority and had consented thus demonstrating the various stances adopted in each country and the constraints imposed by existing legislation.[49]

## Abolition of the Age Limit

Of the 40 States who were parties to the existing instruments, 31 States (listed below) responded that in principle they were in favour of abolishing the age limit, with or without limitations.[50]

# Proposed Abolition of Age Limit: Responses from States

## States in Favour of Abolition in Principle

Albania, Australia, Austria, Belgium, United Kingdom, Bulgaria, Canada, China, Cuba, Czechoslovakia, Estonia, Finland, France, Hungary, India, Italy, Japan, Lithuania, Luxemburg, Netherlands, New Zealand, Norway, Panama, Poland, Romania, Siam, South Africa, Spain, Sweden, Switzerland and Yugoslavia.[51]

## Additional Observations

### Denmark

Responded that it had certain objections concerning the expediency of the measure contemplated.[52]

### India and Siam

Advised that while they were in a position to agree to eliminate the age limit in relation to international traffic, they must reserve an age limit for purely national traffic. Later, India was removed from the list of countries in favour. It had stated, by letter dated 7 November 1929, that its own Age of Consent Committee recommended an age of consent outside marriage of 18 years— a proposal that was under current consideration. For that reason, India was not at that time prepared to give a definite opinion on the proposed age limit abolition, except to say that it was unlikely to object to that abolition as far as the international trade was concerned.[53]

### Italy

Favoured abolition of the age limit as long as the offences continued to specifically refer to commission of offences upon persons under age. The Italian government was of the view that trafficking in minors should attract heavier penalties than trafficking in victims over the age of majority.[54]

### France and Belgium

Were in favour of abolition of the age limit being studied in principle. Belgium, noted that it reserved a final decision pending clearer specification of the proposal by the Advisory Committee.[55]

### Other States

While responding in favour of the proposal, indicated that their own local legislation had in one way or another already achieved abolition of the age limit, and they therefore assumed that the proposal conformed with what was already in place in their own jurisdictions.[56]

Of the States which already had a criminal law regime sanctioning trafficking in women overage with their consent, only a few had legislated to punish the traffic of women and girls overage without qualification.[57] Various provisos affected the operation of the suppression laws. One variant punished only trafficking for profit. That added an evidentiary burden to the prosecution, which had to establish intention as an element of the offence.[58] Another variant suppressed only international trafficking in women and girls overage. In such cases the prosecution had to prove international transit of the victim to make out the offence.[59] Another variant punished trafficking in women overage with their consent where the victim was a member of the offender's family.[60] Another variant distinguished between victims of good and bad character.[61] In such cases traffickers could raise character as a defence and go unpunished if they could show that the victim was a prostitute or a person of loose morals. Another variant added the element of 'habitual' trafficking in women and girls overage with their consent;[62] yet another distinguished between procuration for immoral carnal connection and leading the victim into prostitution, with trafficking in women overage with their consent punishable only where the victim was to be put to work in a brothel or otherwise serve as a prostitute.[63]

Discussions at the Advisory Committee level proceeded at some length on the matter of whether trafficking in women who had attained their majority and consented should be punishable only in limited circumstances (in particular, punishing traffickers of victims for the trade abroad). Some country delegates sought criminal sanctions without exclusions, arguing that the traffickers would use the provisos as defences and thereby avoid punishment. Others contended that extension of the current provisions of the Convention of 1910 and Convention of 1921, without limitations, to women overage, might result in injustice in some cases. They noted, in that context, that only a few States who already had these sanctions in place had enacted them without any limitations.[64]

Accordingly, the Advisory Committee had to determine, in considering this matter of the proposed amendment to the provisions of the existing instruments (the Convention of 1910 and the Convention of 1921):

The manner in which it proposed to effect abolition of the age limit for punishment of the traffic in women and girls;

whether trafficking, carried out with consent, should be made punishable in restricted or unrestricted form (with or without provisos); and

if it resolved in favour of restrictions, what their nature should be.[65]

## Advisory Committee Resolution, 1932

Having considered the matter and duly noted the answers received from the signatory States to the Conventions of 1910 and 1921, the Advisory Committee resolved to the effect that variations currently existed between the laws in different jurisdictions: some countries already punished trafficking in women overage, without limitation; others had no such sanctions in their penal legislation; and others punished the traffic with certain limitations or provisos such as adding an international element.[66]

The Advisory Committee declared that it considered the traffic to be 'always and in all circumstances a profoundly immoral and anti-social act' and also considered that experience had shown that 'impunity as regards traffic in women who are overage and who consent is hampering the effective suppression of traffic in minors.' It therefore resolved that that trafficking in women should be punished, even if that trafficking was carried out on consenting victims who were overage. On that basis it requested the Council to seek approval from States to introduce modifications in their national legislation as necessary to achieve that effect, and to amend the two conventions concerned (1910 and 1921) to reflect that decision.[67]

Subsequently, upon the request by the Council, the Secretary-General transmitted the resolution to the States. The question of the abolition of the age limit in the two conventions (1910 and 1921) was referred to the Assembly by the Council in May 1932.[68] In October of that year the Assembly approved the resolution.[69]

## AMENDING THE CONVENTIONS OF 1910 AND 1921

Consequent upon that approval, the Fifth Committee commenced an examination of the action needed to amend the instruments. The Fifth Committee was of the opinion that abolition of the age limit in the conventions (1910 and 1921) would best be achieved at the time when States were asked to enter into an international agreement to criminally sanction souteneurs. This possibility was at that time being canvassed by the Legal Sub-Committee of the Advisory Committee. The Fifth Committee thought that this same body should be asked to consider the age abolition question at its next meeting, thereby combining due consideration of both the age limit and the punishment of souteneurs. It recognized, however, that some delay in amending those instruments was inevitable. It therefore expressed its hope that the members of the League of Nations and the signatories to the two conventions (1910 and 1921) would take action, in the meantime, to amend their national legislation to abolish any age limit in their laws against trafficking in women and children, as soon as possible, without waiting on changes in the conventions (1910 and 1921) themselves.[70]

France submitted a draft instrument that provided for punishment of any person who, in order to gratify the passions of another, procured, enticed, or led away, even with her consent, a woman of full age for immoral purposes in another country.[71] The French delegates noted that the instrument referred only to traffic in women overage who had given their consent and were sent to a foreign country, and explained the form of the drafting in this way:

The States which had maintained the system of regulation could go no further at present, and, indeed, the abolitionist States themselves, could hardly agree upon a text acceptable to all, in view of the diversity in their penal legislation on the question as regards women overage. Almost all these countries have numerous and varied reservations in their legislation. In these circumstances, it appeared difficult to draw up the text of a convention which could be accepted by a reasonably large number of signatories.[72]

While many of the delegates and representatives of voluntary organizations involved in deliberation as members of the Advisory Committee found this proposal disappointing, to the extent that it did not go as far as they would have liked (their preference being for sanctions against all cases of trafficking regardless of age or consent, they nevertheless appreciated that the pro forma was a step in the right direction, would fill the gap in the conventions (1910 and 1921) pending their amendment, and had the practical virtue of being capable of immediate action.[73]

Accordingly, the Advisory Committee agreed to the text of a Draft Protocol,[74] (AC Draft Protocol) the main provisions of which covered the following:

A recital to the effect that authorization was established on behalf of the countries represented (Preamble).

A provision to the effect that any person who procured, enticed or led away a woman or girl of full age for immoral purposes in another country, in order to gratify the passions of another person, would be guilty of an offence, notwithstanding that the woman consented, or that the elements of the offence had been committed in different jurisdictions (Article 1).

A provision to the effect that States whose laws were insufficient to deal with the offences in Article 1 would take whatever steps were necessary, or propose those steps to their home legislatures, to ensure that those offences were punished in accordance with their seriousness (Article 2).

A provision to the effect that States undertook to liaise with each other in relation to the commission of cross-border offences, or their attempt, by any person, male or female, as referred to in the Protocol and the two conventions (1910 and 1921). The following information was to be shared, to the extent that it was legally possible to supply it:

Official notice of sentence;

A notice containing all useful particulars of offenders along with their civil status, description, finger-prints, photograph and police record and an indication of their *modus operandi*; and

Particulars of any measures of refusal of admission, or of expulsion.[75]

These documents and particulars were to be sent forthwith, straight to the authorities of the countries concerned by the authorities named in Article 1 of the Agreement of 1904. Where possible, they were to be sent in all cases where it had been established that the offence, sentence, refusal of admission or expulsion had occurred (Article 3).[76]

## Advisory Committee Resolution, 1933 and AC Draft Protocol

In April 1933, by resolution, the Advisory Committee requested the Council to communicate the AC Draft Protocol to States, asking them to respond to the Secretary-General with any observations. The Advisory Committee further hoped that if there were no serious objections to the AC Draft Protocol, it would be possible for the delegates of States attending the 1933 Assembly to sign an international agreement bringing the AC Draft Protocol into effect.[77]

In addition, the Advisory Committee requested the Council to prepare a draft of the standard clauses required to legally constitute the proposed instrument, and to communicate those to the States along with the articles.[78] The Council approved that resolution in May 1933, and the Secretary-General duly submitted the AC Draft Protocol to the States on 29 June 1933. As regards procedure, the Council adopted suggestions proffered by the representative of Panama in order to bring the instrument into force.[79]

The representative of Panama, in the light of the Advisory Committee's unanimous approval of the AC Draft Protocol and the fact that governments had previously been consulted on abolition of the age limit in the Conventions of 1910 and 1921, hoped it might be possible to open the new instrument for signing in autumn 1933.[80]

In relation to procedural aspects, the representative of Panama suggested:  ask  governments to meet in a special conference in September 1933 to sign the instrument during the meeting of their delegates at Geneva for the Fourteenth Assembly when submitting the AC Draft Protocol, the Secretary-General should invite States to give their delegates the necessary full powers; and the Assembly itself should decide whether the special conference should be convened after the State's observations on the AC Draft Protocol had been received.[81]

## Responses to AC Draft Protocol

Some States sent brief responses to the AC Draft Protocol as summarized in the box below. The Netherlands, Hungary, and the United Kingdom provided more substantial responses.

## Brief Responses by States to AC Draft Protocol

### Belgium

No objection to the adoption, in principle, of the AC Draft Protocol.[82]

### China

China was in favour of signing an international agreement on this subject, but its detailed observations would be presented by its delegation at the conference finalizing its provisions.[83]

### Colombia

Colombia, through its Ministry for Foreign Affairs, communicated its satisfaction with the AC Draft Protocol, which it considered effective and practical and entirely consonant with the underlying principles against the traffic. However, it had not yet ratified the Convention of 1921. However, the legislative bill approving the convention and empowering the Colombian Government to accede to the prior instruments of 1904 and 1910 had been submitted to its National Congress for the third time, with a special recommendation. Upon approval, Colombia would advise the Secretary-General and deposit its instruments of accession.[84]

## Danzig

The Senate of the Free City of Danzig reserved the right to comment on the AC Draft Protocol but did not intend to send a representative to the drafting conference.[85]

## Denmark

Denmark raised one point of objection which prevented it agreeing to the AC Draft Protocol on that point, but it otherwise had no objection to the instrument. The point in contention was that the AC Draft Protocol proposed that contracting parties should undertake to punish 'whoever has procured, enticed or led away, even with her consent, a woman or girl of full age for immoral purposes in another country'. However, Denmark's Criminal Law provided (in Article 228, paragraph 2, as at 15 April 1930) an age limit of 21 years, beyond which age prosecution would not stand unless the abductee was unaware of the purpose of the abduction. The Danish authorities were reluctant to propose amendments to that Danish provision.[86]

## Egypt

The Egyptian Government declined to participate in the drafting conference, with regret.

## Estonia

Estonia supported the AC Draft Protocol and advised that it would give its permanent delegate to the League of Nations full powers to participate and sign the AC Draft Protocol.[87] It informed the Secretary-General that it would take part in the drafting conference.[88]

## Greece

The Hellenic Government supported the Draft Protocol and invested its permanent delegate to the League of Nations with full powers to participate in the proposed drafting conference.

## Hungary

Hungary advised that it would be represented at the drafting conference.

## Italy

The Italian Government demurred, in part on the basis of the complexity of the topic. It advised that although it appreciated factors and intentions that guided the Advisory Committee that drew up the AC Draft Protocol, it considered the complexity such that the problem required more careful study. It suggested that further examination might demonstrate the desirability of a coordinated body of measures to attack the problem. It therefore could not support a hasty adoption of the AC Draft Protocol. Italy considered, in principle, that, it was impractical and unsatisfactory to entrust the conclusion of such international agreements to special conferences held during the session of the Assembly.[89]

## Lithuania

Lithuania approved the AC Draft Protocol and advised that its delegates to the fourteenth Assembly would have power to sign it.[90]

## Monaco

The Principality of Monaco was supportive, and noted that it had acceded to the instruments of 1904, 1910 and 1921 on trafficking.

Monaco considered that adoption of the terms of the AC Draft Protocol could only be advantageous. It had no difficulty adopting the system of complete protection that the AC Draft Protocol contemplated.[91]

## Norway

Norway had no observations to make on the AC Draft Protocol. The Norwegian Government advised that it would be represented at the drafting conference.[92]

## Poland

Poland had no objection to signing an international agreement on the subject and advised that it was willing to take part in the drafting conference.[93]

## Romania

Romania had no objection to delegations to the fourteenth Assembly of the League of Nations having full power to establish the final text of the AC Draft Protocol, and would sign it if that was the decision of the conference.[94]

## Sudan

Sudan did not wish to be represented at the drafting conference and because it considered the problem remote from issues affecting the Sudan, it was not in a position to offer useful observations on the AC Draft Protocol.[95]

## Switzerland

Switzerland had no particular observations to make about the AC Draft Protocol. Adopting it would not necessitate amendment of the Swiss law.[96]

### Czechoslovakia

The Czechoslovak republic had no objection to the provisions of the AC Draft Protocol, but considered a simpler solution to be available: amendment of Article 1 of the Convention of 1910 by deleting the words 'underage'. Czechoslovakia would in any case be represented at the drafting conference.[97]

### Yugoslavia

The Royal Government of Yugoslavia had no objection to the AC Draft Protocol and advised that it would be represented at the drafting conference.[98]

### Union of South Africa

A representative would be sent to the special conference to be held to draw up the final form of the AC Draft Protocol.[99]

### Cuba, Mexico, Uruguay, and Venezuela

These countries acknowledged receipt of the Secretary-General's request and stated that they would respond to the AC Draft Protocol at a later date.[100]

### Comprehensive Responses

**The Netherlands** responded that at the Conference of 1921 it had proposed abolition of the age limit in the Convention of 1921.[101] Subsequently, it had, more than once, expressed the same view.[102] Thus, it was pleased to see that an AC Draft Protocol had emerged from the Advisory Committee's research concerning age-limit amendment of the Conventions of 1910 and 1921. However, the limited scope of the AC Draft Protocol was a matter of regret.[103] The preference of the government of the Netherlands would be for a more general solution than merely suppression of the traffic in women of full age sent abroad.[104] While a solution that made trafficking in women of full age punishable in all cases would have been ideal, the Netherlands accepted that the AC Draft Protocol was a step in the right direction– correcting a very serious defect in the existing instruments (the Conventions of 1910 and 1921).[105] The Netherlands' detailed observations in relation to the AC Draft Protocol were:

It recommended insertion of a new article: 'the High Contracting Parties agree to take the necessary steps to secure the punishment of attempts to commit, and, within legal limits, of acts preparatory to the commission of, offences specified in the present Protocol' (Article 3 of the Convention of 1921 referred only to offences mentioned in the Convention of 1910.)[106]

It recommended replacing the words 'of the present Protocol' in Article 4 (on settlement of disputes)[107] with the words 'of the present Protocol and the Conventions of 1910 and 1921'. Article 4 dealt only with the interpretation and application of the instrument.[108] The 1910 and 1921 Conventions did not contain any article on settlement of disputes.[109] The Netherlands foresaw objections that such wording would be outside the special scope of the instrument, but contended that it would be sufficient to refer to Article 3 of the instrument, which established rules concerning offences referred to in the Conventions of 1910 and 1921.[110]

It recommended inserting, alongside Article 8 (dealing with the coming into force of the instrument),[111] an article to the effect of Article 31 of the Convention of 13 July 1931 for limiting the Manufacture and regulating the Distribution of Narcotic Drugs. Its reason was that some of the final clauses were incomplete, compared with others appearing in conventions recently concluded under the auspices of the League of Nations. By way of example, it noted the absence of any stipulation as to the date of coming into force of the instrument after ratifications or accessions had been deposited.[112]

**Hungary** recommended including in the Preamble to the AC Draft Protocol a recital to the effect that the representatives of the States concerned had met with the purpose of extending the prevention and punishment of the traffic in women, and that, to that end they had decided to amend the existing instruments (the Conventions 1910 and

1921). This would link the AC Draft Protocol with the conventions in the Preamble itself. In addition, it suggested:

To improve the clarity of Article 3, paragraph (b), the words 'his police record' could be replaced by the words 'judicial antecedents' or something similar (on the basis that it was intended to refer to sentences previously passed on the offender.)[113]

No provision was made in Article 5[114] to show the date to which the instrument could be signed. It considered that the instrument should be open for signature until at least 1 January 1924.[115]

It recommended insertion of a clause by which States could accede 'after the entry into force of the Protocol'. Article 7(1) provided only that the instrument could be acceded to from the date of the closure of the signatures.[116]

It noted that a country might accede to the instrument immediately after the term fixed for signature (when, failing sufficient ratifications, the Protocol had not yet come into force). An international convention could not, in principle, be acceded to until it had come into force. For that reason it would be preferable to allow accession only from the date on which the instrument came into force.[117]

Article 8 provided that the instrument would come into force after the Secretary-General had received two ratifications or accessions. But the instrument would automatically come into force if two States had acceded to it, even if no State had ratified it. That meant the instrument could come into force by accession independently of the signatory States, which should be avoided because only a convention already in force can be acceded to. The solution was to delete the words 'or accessions' in Article 8(1) and make the entry into force of the instrument subject to its ratification by two signatory States. The entry into force of the instrument would also be better set as the sixtieth or ninetieth day after the second ratification had been lodged, to enable the Secretary-General time to notify all the States concerned of the date.[118]

Further the amendment of Article 8 would be required for the Secretary-General to notify all States concerned of the date of receipt of the second ratification and the date of the entry into force, which, if the previous recommendation was accepted, would depend on that event.[119]

**The United Kingdom**, also, was fully supportive of the general object of the AC Draft Protocol, but had some observations to make about the draft.

It recommended changes to the title of the instrument and its Preamble, as it doubted that the term 'Protocol' was altogether suitable, unless the instrument was to be regarded as definitely supplementary to the existing series of instruments (the Agreement of 1904 and the Conventions of 1910 and 1921).[120] If the intention was to link the document to those instruments (particularly the Convention of 1910, which dealt with persons underage) that link should be explicitly stated in the Preamble.[121] It recommended something resembling paragraph 2 of the Preamble to the Convention of 1921.

In addition, Article 8 of the Convention of 1910 and Article 1 of the Convention of 1921 had no counterpart in the AC Draft Protocol.[122]

It noted that while Articles 1 and 2 were more limited in scope than the original proposals for abolition of the age limit (as to trafficking in women within the jurisdiction as well as across borders), it concurred with the provisions in general. However, it considered the words 'propose to their respective legislature' in Article 2 unnecessary, because it was clearly every government's duty not to ratify a convention without legislative power to enforce it. It was inadequate for an international instrument of this kind to be adopted by an undertaking to propose the measure to a home legislature in circumstances where that legislature could refuse to pass it.[123]

It observed that Article 3 would involve establishing elaborate international machinery for international exchange of police information. A great deal of that machinery was incompatible with UK policing practice. In addition, the article had no provision for discretion: the full penal record and personal description of offenders were to be circulated irrespective of the circumstances of the case (For example, being a first, or young, offender, or where the offence was merely attempted). Circulation of such information could in some cases prevent the offender from in future obtaining a visa to a foreign country for genuine purposes, or be permanently blacklisted in police registers in various jurisdictions. The United Kingdom therefore suggested that the article be deleted and replaced by Article 7 of the Convention of 1910.

The Contracting Parties undertake to communicate to each other the records of convictions in respect of offences covered by the present Convention where the various acts constituting such offences have been committed in different countries. These documents shall be forwarded direct by the authorities designated in conformity with Article 1 of the Agreement concluded at Paris on May 18th, 1904, to the corresponding authorities of the other Contracting States.[124]

Generally, the United Kingdom considered the form of the AC Draft Protocol not to be ideal. A clause providing that information was to be sent to 'the countries concerned' was ambiguous as to whether it covered the countries 'concerned in an individual case' or all countries 'concerned in cases of traffic in women and children'. If *all* countries were included, large quantities of paperwork of peripheral interest would burden police and waste time and expense on translating information and filing large quantities of data. In addition, some of the formal articles and the Preamble did not follow the usual structure of League of Nations instruments. The United Kingdom presumed that redrafting would be done to make these conform.[125] It suggested:

**Amendment of Article 4** to provide for reference to the Permanent Court of International Justice at The Hague in all cases, unless the disputing parties agreed on referral to some other court. Suggested text to that effect was supplied. It provided that if disputes arose concerning interpretation or application of the Protocol, it was, in the absence of other agreement, to be referred to the Permanent Court at the request of any party if all the parties to the dispute were parties to the Protocol of 16 December 1920 relating to the Statute of the Court; if not, referral would lie to an arbitral tribunal constituted in accordance with the Hague Convention of 18 October 1907 for the Pacific Settlement of International Disputes.[126]

**Amendment of Article 8** to insert the words 'on the day' or 'on the ... day' should be inserted between the words 'come into force' and the words 'after the Secretary-General' and that, for practical reasons, the number of ratifications or accessions required to bring the Protocol into force should be increased from two to five or six.[127]

**Amendment of Article 9**[128] by removal of the last sentence of paragraph 1 and its insertion in Article 10 as a third paragraph in amended form. The redrafted wording was supplied, to the effect that any High Contracting Party could at will declare that the present Protocol was to cease to apply to 'all or any of his colonies, protectorates, overseas territories or territories under suzerainty or mandate' and that it would thereupon cease to apply one year after receipt by the Secretary-General of the declaration. All such declarations received were to be communicated by the Secretary-General to all the members of the League of Nations and to non-member States referred to in Article 5.[129]

## Fifth Committee's Draft Protocol

The Fifth Committee considered the States' responses to the AC Draft Protocol and heard statements from delegates, then prepared a revised draft Protocol (FC Draft Protocol) and adopted a resolution. That resolution recommended that the Assembly convoke a diplomatic conference to draw up the final text of the FC Draft Protocol for signature. The Fifth Committee also adopted a recommendation to the Assembly requesting transmission of the FC Draft Protocol to the diplomatic conference.[130]

The FC Draft Protocol included some new material along with numerous changes to the text. The major modifications included a Preamble containing recitals concerning the purpose of the instrument (better securing the suppression of trafficking in women and children); the form of instrument decided (a convention supplementary to the instruments of 1904, 1910, and 1921); the background information considered (the recommendations contained in the report to the Council of the League of Nations by the Traffic in Women and Children Committee on the work of its twelfth session); and formal parts (appointment for this purpose the Plenipotentiaries who had full authority and duly agreed to the terms of the instrument). The specific provisions amended by the FC Draft Protocol were:

In **Article 1** a paragraph was added to the effect that the term 'another country' included the colonies and protectorates of the High Contracting Party as well as territories under his suzerainty or mandate. Every such country was covered even if it had been excluded from the application of the instrument by a declaration under Article 11. The words 'to be carried out' were added to paragraph 1 of Article 1, being inserted after the phrase 'immoral purposes'.

In **Article 2** the words 'or propose to their respective legislatures' were removed.

In **Article 3** the words 'present Protocol or' were replaced with the words 'present Convention and' in the first paragraph of Article 3. The provision then covered (a) records of conviction, useful and available information about offenders such as civil status, description, fingerprints, photographs, police record, *modus operandi* and the like; and (b) particulars of any measures of refusal of admission or of expulsion. The words 'in each particular case' were added to the final paragraph; the words 'they shall be sent' were replaced with the word 'and'; and the word 'sentence' was replaced with the word 'conviction'.

A new **Article 4** was added to the effect that the High Contracting Parties agreed to take the steps necessary to punish attempted offences and, within legal limits, preparatory acts.

## Assembly Resolution, 1933 for Diplomatic Conference

The Assembly met on 7 October 1933. At that meeting it adopted a resolution convening a diplomatic conference to draw up the final text of the Convention for the Suppression of Traffic in Women of Full Age.[131] The diplomatic conference duly met between 9 and 11 October of that year.[132]

### States Represented at the Conference of 1933

Australia, Austria, Belgium, China, Czechoslovakia, Denmark, Estonia, Finland, France, Free City of Danzig, Germany, Greece, Hungary, Irish Free State, Italy, Japan, Lithuania, Netherlands, Norway, Poland, Portugal, Spain, Sweden, Switzerland, Union of South Africa, United Kingdom of Great Britain and Northern Ireland, and Yugoslavia.[133]

## Conference of 1933 Discussions on FC Draft Protocol

The Conference of 1933 discussed the FC Draft Protocol,[134] focusing on Articles 1 and 2 at its first meeting.[135] The deliberations on each major provision are summarized below.

### Article 1, Paragraph 1[136]

Portugal, through its delegate, expressed a preference for offences to be described in standard criminal law terminology rather than the existing wording. Switzerland proposed deletion of the words *de la pratique* and be replaced by *en vue de la debauche* as in the text originally drafted by the Advisory Committee; this would harmonize the text with the Convention of 1910. France agreed, its delegate citing the purpose of the instrument (combating procuration) and noting that it would take effect in those terms whether or not immorality was cited as a motivating force later. While it also agreed, the United Kingdom submitted, through its delegate, that in English, retaining the words 'to be carried out' clarified the meaning. The Irish Free state preferred substitution of the words 'immoral practices' for the words 'immoral purposes to be carried out' for reasons of euphony; if the Conference of 1933 really did wish to qualify the expression 'immoral purposes'– a well understood phrase that had been used in earlier instruments. Regardless of that decision, the Irish delegation considered the words 'to be carried out' superfluous. Observing that under Article 6 both texts were authoritative, the Conference of 1933 agreed to accept the suggestion to delete the words 'de la pratique' from the French version and retain the words 'to be carried out' in the English text.[137]

### Article 1, Paragraph 2[138]

Here Germany sought a clearer distinction between a suzerainty and a mandate. Its delegate suggested substitution of 'and countries for which a mandate has been entrusted to a High Contracting Party' for the words 'or mandate'. It also wanted Article 4 embodied in Article 1 or, alternatively, inserted between Articles 1 and 2.[139] The Austrian delegate proposed four amendments:

Replacement of the words 'the present Article' with the words 'the present Convention' (because that provision applied to all the articles of the convention without exception).

On this point the Swiss delegate submitted that a sentence intended to apply to the whole convention should appear at the head of the convention and not in the middle of Article 1.[140] The UK delegate, while not expressing an opinion on the desirability of the amendment itself, observed that adoption of the change would have the effect of making Article 3 apply to colonies which had been excluded under Article 11.[141] At the suggestion of the president, M.J. Limburg of the Netherlands,[142] provisional agreement was reached: the text would be left as it stood, but if the Conference of 1933 thought it appropriate to make the change after discussion of Article 3 it could make the change later.[143]

Deletion of the word 'another' from the expression 'another country' (because, if Paragraph 2 remained unchanged, paragraph 1 could be understood as meaning 'for immoral purposes to be carried out in a colony', which would make the traffic punishable even if the offender was guilty of procuring in a colony for immoral purposes to be carried out in the same colony).[144]

Here the Portuguese delegate agreed that the drafting could be tightened, noting the intention that the convention should apply all over the world; the only reason colonies, protectorates and territories under mandate had specifically been mentioned was that conditions in such territories varied enormously. The final text must make it clear that a sovereign state had a right to punish procurers even when the immoral practices in which they were involved occurred in the colony or protectorate of a mother-country which had no wish or occasion to punish the offence in its colony. Considering the Austrian amendment reasonable, the President thought use of the word 'country' alone presented an added advantage (because it covered both mentions of the word 'country' in paragraph 1).[145] The UK delegate did not consider the amendment an improvement (because if the word 'country' stood alone in Paragraph 2, Paragraph 1 could be understood as meaning 'for immoral purposes to be carried out in another colony' or 'another protectorate', thus having the effect of excluding the mother-country).[146] The Italian delegate concurred with the UK view, but the delegate of the Irish Free State and the delegate of Poland agreed with the President. Ultimately, the amendment was adopted.[147]

Deletion of the words 'of the High Contracting Party concerned' (because the provision applied equally in every colony and protectorate).[148] This amendment was also adopted.[149]

Addition of 'of overseas territories' in the same manner as Article 11, such that the first sentence read 'the term 'country' includes colonies, protectorates and overseas territories as well as territories under suzerainty or mandate'.[150] Here the Portuguese delegate submitted that, since the reference to the High Contracting Party had been removed the term 'overseas territories' was now unclear. The French and UK delegates concurred with this view. It was therefore agreed to refer the sentence to a Drafting Committee along with the amendments suggested by the German delegate.[151]

## Article 2[152]

Here the President considered the text originally drafted by the Advisory Committee to be superior to the FC Draft Protocol. In the original the High Contracting Parties agreed to propose the matter to their respective legislatures. That version presented two advantages: (1) it was inadvisable, in psychological terms, to 'agree to take the necessary steps' without making any reference to the consultation of the legislature; and (2) countries were able to ratify the convention before the passage of the requisite legislation (a slow process). The President noted, in this context, a similar provision in the Versailles Treaty relating to the International Labour Office. The delegate of Greece supported the President in this view, considering that early ratification would facilitate early exchange of the information provided for in the convention even before legislative changes had been effected. France preferred to keep the text as it was, on the basis that adopting the President's suggestion posed a serious risk that, while ratifications might be received earlier, legislative changes would not follow, ultimately rendering the convention a dead letter. The French delegate pointed out that this had occurred with the International Labour Office with regard to Article 408 of the Versailles Treaty cited by the President earlier. The UK delegate agreed, noting that while the phrase preferred by the President had indeed been employed in the Convention of 1910, it had not persisted in the Convention of 1921. While the President did not agree with the French delegate's position, he withdrew his amendment and Article 2 was accordingly adopted.[153]

## Appointment of Drafting Committee

As the discussions of the Conference of 1933 drew to a close, the President proposed the appointment of a Drafting Committee to make amendments. That committee, made up of delegates of United Kingdom, France, Austria, and the members of the International Bureau, was appointed.[154] The Drafting Committee duly completed a new draft convention[155] (DC Draft Convention) after considering the amendments recommended to the Conference of 1933 and in the Drafting Committee.[156]

When the Conference of 1933 met for the second time, the rapporteur of the Drafting Committee, the delegate of France, explained the changes that had been made to the FC Draft Protocol. Certain articles in DC Draft Convention had been reordered to make the structure of the text more logical. As it now stood, Articles 1 and 2 related to the obligation to punish particular acts; Article 3 established provisions for communication of information; and Article 4 and the following articles contained general and formal provisions relating to dispute settlement, ratifications, and accessions.[157]

In relation to the main provisions, the DC Draft Convention made the following changes to the FC Draft Protocol:

### Preamble

Reordering the recitals concerning purpose (better securing suppression of the traffic in women and children); background information (recommendations made in the report to the Council by the Traffic in Women and Children Committee setting out its twelfth session conclusions); decision to supplement the Agreement of 1904 and Conventions of 1910 and 1921 (relating to the suppression of the traffic in women and children) with a further convention; agreement in accordance with authorized powers, as follows.

## Article 1

Adding the ambit of Article 4 in Paragraph 2; deleting the word 'another' in the expression 'another country' and replacing the phrase 'territories under his suzerainty or mandate' with 'territories under his suzerainty and territories for which a mandate has been entrusted to him' in Paragraph 3; omitting the words 'this term includes every such country even if it has been excluded from the application of the convention by a declaration made in accordance with Article 11.'

## Article 2

Was left unchanged.

## Article 3

Replacing 'and' with 'or' in the expression 'referred to in the present convention *and* the Convention of 1910' in Paragraph 1; and adding the words 'which may have been applied to him' after the word 'expulsion' in Article 3(b).

## Examination of DC Draft Convention

The Conference of 1933 examined the DC Draft Convention prepared by the Drafting Committee, again focussing upon adjustments to the text.[158] Of the substantive provisions, Article 1 was reconsidered; Articles 2 and 3 and the Preamble were adopted.[159]

In relation to Article 1, Paragraph 1, the delegate of Italy requested a definition of the term 'woman or girl of full age' in the instrument to prevent any misunderstanding. The President thought that unnecessary, as Article 5 of the Convention of 1921 defined minors as being up to 'twenty one completed years of age'; further, such an addition would create a problem, because the legislation of almost every jurisdiction provided that a married woman under twenty-one years was regarded as being of full age. In relation to Article 1, paragraph 3, the Italian delegate requested that 'overseas territories' be added to the list, which he argued was otherwise defective. The French delegate explained why the term had been omitted by the Drafting Committee: it was geographically local, rather than universal, and the principle of uniformity suggested that it did not belong in a list of legal and political terms. It had for those reasons opposed the addition. Article 1 was then adopted unanimously.[160]

## States Voting to Adopt Article 1

Australia, Austria, Belgium, United Kingdom, China, Czecho-slovakia, Estonia, France, Germany, Greece, Hungary, Japan, Lithuania, Netherlands, Norway, Poland, Portugal, Spain, Sweden, Switzerland and the Union of South Africa.[161]

Finland, Irish Free State, and Italy abstained.[162] The Free City of Danzig and Yugoslavia were absent.[163]

## New Provision for Extradition

One notable proposal made at this meeting was for a new article relating to extradition in the DC Draft Convention. The delegate for Switzerland proposed, and the meeting agreed, to include an article that mirrored provisions in Article 5 of the Convention of 1910 and Article 4 of the Convention of 1921. The Conference of 1933 adjourned briefly, and on reconvening approved the following text, which the Drafting Committee had presented for inclusion in the DC Draft Convention as Article 4.

The provisions of Article 5 of the Convention of May 4th, 1910, and of Article 4 of the Convention of September 30th, 1921, relating to extradition are also applicable to the offences specified in Article 1 of the present Convention.[164]

## Finalizing the Text

At its third meeting the Conference of 1933 concentrated on perusal and approval of the DC Draft Convention's final form. In relation to the issue of extradition, several delegates reported that they had sought instructions from their governments. Some had as a result been instructed that they were authorized to sign the final text only if the instrument did not include the proposed extradition provision. To preserve the passage of the bulk of the instrument, the President proposed that the Conference of 1933 withdraw the article concerning extradition and pass a further resolution. The resolution would be to the effect that the Conference of 1933 considered that an additional provision should be added to the Convention of 1933 (signed on 11 October 1933) in relation to the offence set out in Article 1, and that the Council should invite the Advisory Committee to propose that governments sign such a provision.[165]

The French delegate advised that despite his own authorization to sign the instrument in a form that included the extradition article, he would accede to the President's proposal and appreciated the reasons for it. The Swiss delegate had no objection to the article being omitted. He did not think it essential, and observed that adoption of the proposed resolution would merely postpone adoption of the extradition provision. Accordingly, the Conference of 1933 agreed to delete the new article.[166]

After resolving the issue of the extradition provision, the President announced a vote on the final text of the instrument in its entirety, because the Conference of 1933 had thus far adopted each article separately.[167]

Italy abstained from voting. Its delegate stressed that the Italian Government was not indifferent to the problem of the traffic in women. Indeed, Italian law as it stood demonstrated Italy's interest and commitment, and was manifest in the activities of its administrative authorities and the work of its delegate on the Advisory Committee.[168] Nevertheless, this was a complex and delicate matter, and one which needed to be dealt with holistically, rather than on a piecemeal basis.[169]

Japan abstained from voting as its delegate was not yet in receipt of instructions. The delegate had felt obliged to seek further instructions as a result of the considerable changes made to the text. The Japanese Penal Code was undergoing amendment at the time, as the Japanese delegate noted, and it was intended that the code would mirror the provisions of the instrument. The delegate was therefore hopeful that the Japanese Government would soon be in a position to sign the instrument.[170]

The Irish Free State had also not yet given its instructions, so its delegate was unable to take part in the vote. He assured the Conference of 1933 that his government had great sympathy with the objects of the instrument, and expressed his hope that it would be in a position to accede to it in due course.

The President stressed to the Conference of 1933 that delegates' votes on the form of the text itself were quite distinct from the decision to sign. He thought, therefore, that some delegates might be able to vote in the affirmative even though they were not yet in a position to sign.[171] Finally the vote was taken.

## Result of Votes

**In Favour:** Australia, Austria, Belgium, United Kingdom, Czechoslovakia, Free City of Danzig, France, Germany, Greece, Hungary, Lithuania, Netherlands, Poland, Portugal, Spain, Sweden, Switzerland, Union of South Africa.[172]

**Abstentions:** Irish Free State, Italy, Japan.[173]

**Absent:** China, Estonia, Finland, Norway, Yugoslavia.[174]

The President announced that eighteen delegates had voted in favour of the convention, three had abstained and five votes were absent, and that the convention was therefore unanimously approved.[175]

## THE INTERNATIONAL CONVENTION FOR THE SUPPRESSION OF THE TRAFFIC IN WOMEN OF FULL AGE, 1933

The International Convention for the Suppression of the Traffic in Women of Full Age, 1933 (Convention of 1933) completed by a new convention, the Agreement of 1904 and Conventions of 1910 and 1921.[176]

## Legislative Measures

Signatory States were required by Article 2 to move to amend local laws to sanction the offences set out in Article 1 in proportion to their gravity.[177]

Article 1 imposed a requirement to sanction, irrespective of consent, any person who, in order to gratify the passions of another person, procured, enticed or led away a woman or girl of full age for immoral purposes to be carried out in another country. The offence was made out even if the acts constituting its elements were committed in different countries. The scope of the term 'country' encompassed not only the State but also its colonies, protectorates, territories under suzerainty, and territories for which a mandate had been entrusted.[178]

Signatories undertook to sanction attempted offences, but the Convention of 1933 gave further scope to punish acts preparatory to offences, again binding States 'within the legal limits'.[179]

## Administrative Measures

Under Article 3, States were obliged to undertake to share information with each other concerning offences or attempts to commit offences referred to in the Conventions of 1910, 1921, or 1933, by any person of either sex, where the elements of the offence were accomplished in different countries. The requirements were subject to the laws of the jurisdiction concerned. They included provision, without delay, of records of convictions, any useful and available information concerning the offender (for example, fingerprints, photographs, and police records) along with particulars of any measures of refusal of admission or of expulsion applicable to the offender. Authorities named in Article 1 of the Agreement of 1904 were to send these straight to the authorities of the countries concerned in each case where an offence, conviction, refusal of admission or expulsion had been properly established.[180]

The Convention of 1933 also introduced a dispute settlement provision. Any dispute of any kind relating to the interpretation or application of the Conventions of 1910, 1921, or 1933 which was not amenable to diplomatic settlement was required by Article 4 to be settled in accordance with any agreements in force between the States which provided for settlement of international disputes. If no such agreement was in force, the dispute was to be referred to arbitration or judicial settlement. If the choice of tribunal was contested, Article 4 provided that the dispute was to be referred to the Permanent Court of International Justice at the request of any one party, where all States involved were parties to the Protocol of 16 December 1920 regarding the statue of that Court. Where one or more of the States was not a party to the Protocol, the dispute was to be referred to an arbitral tribunal constituted in accordance with the Hague Convention of 18 October 1907 for the Pacific Settlement of International Disputes.[181]

The remainder of the Convention of 1933 provided for signature,[182] ratification,[183] accession,[184] entry into force,[185] denunciation,[186] and application to colonies, protectorates, overseas territories, territories under suzerainty or territories for which a mandate exists.[187]

### The Convention of 1933 and the Trafficking of Children for the Sexual Exploitation of Prostitution

In this context, the provisions of the Convention of 1933 applied only to female children, however, those children could be of any race. The Convention of 1933 did not apply to male children whatsoever.

# 4

# Unification and Progressive Development in the Convention of 1949

This chapter traces the development of the final instrument enacted in the period, 1864–1950, the Convention for the Suppression of the Traffic in Persons and of the Exploitation of the Prostitution of Others, 1949.

## FIRST DRAFT CONVENTION

### The Special Body of Experts

The Special Body of Experts as well as considering the issue of girls of minor age, also examined the subject of traffickers and their associates. On this question, Special Body of Experts, in its report concluded:

In most cases which have come under our notice, the movements of the women and girls were controlled by third parties for the sake of the profits attached to the business. Some measure of fraud or deception, direct or indirect, is usually a feature of the business. The traffickers include *madames* who manage houses of prostitution; *souteneurs* who are mainly responsible for securing the girls and controlling their movements; principals who are financially interested in vice-districts or brothels and lend money to *madames* and *souteneurs*; and intermediaries who sometimes secure and transport girls for the *souteneurs* and *madams*.

There is no regular organisation of traffickers, but these persons play into one another's hands when it suits them to do so and conspire to defraud their victims. There are recognised resorts in big cities where *souteneurs* and their friends meet and exchange information and advice as to their prospects. Associated with traffickers are various other disreputable persons of the underworld.[1]

Accordingly, the Special Body of Experts set out its view as follows:

It is the 'third-party' element which makes the traffic so tragic an affair in its worst aspects. If the third party could be eliminated, the battle would be largely won. Some countries realise this principle and punish severely *souteneurs*, *madames* and others who live on the proceeds of prostitution. Instances have been given of effective legislation dealing with this point. There are many countries where no such action is taken. Foreign *souteneurs*, procurers, *madames* and other persons of the kind should be excluded or deported as a preventative measure. Governments will be well advised to review their laws relating to living on the earnings of prostitution and, if necessary, to strengthen them.

The difficulty of eliminating the third-party element becomes greater in countries where the keeping of brothels is legal, where licensed houses exist and where the system of registering prostitutes is maintained.[2]

## Advisory Committee Sixth Session, 1927

At the sixth session of the Advisory Committee in 1927,[3] the recommendation of the Special Body of Experts on the topic of traffickers and their associates was considered. The Advisory Committee recommended refusal of entry to such criminals, along with expulsion from States in whose territories they were found to be operating, and requested a comprehensive compilation, for the Advisory Committee's perusal, of all laws and regulations in each country relating to the offence of living wholly or partly on the earnings of prostitutes. The resolution adopted by the Advisory Committee were to the effect that:

A recommendation that States should take strict measures against foreign procurers and soutenuers, refusing them entry or, if they were apprehended after admission, they should be deported in addition to any punishment to which they are liable.[4]

A request that the Secretariat compile a review of the laws of different countries about which it held details, concerning criminal sanctions for persons living on immoral earnings and present it to the Advisory Committee at its next session.

A statement that after perusal of the compilation the Advisory Committee would be in a position to study the question, and if appropriate make further enquiries concerning the effectiveness of the laws listed there, or the difficulties met with in their application.[5]

## Advisory Committee Seventh Session, 1928

The focus of the seventh session in 1928,[6] was on the need to ensure that the provisions in place to bring the operations of souteneurs to an end were effective. To this end, Advisory Committee members and assessors detailed the applicable regulations within their own jurisdictions.[7] Having deliberated about the relative penalties to which traffickers were subject, the Advisory Committee unanimously resolved[8] to the effect that, having noted the large volume of work and substantial expense involved in making the full compilation of laws it had sought, it requested the Secretariat to make a brief study of the laws and penalties affecting souteneurs.[9]

The Fifth Committee was of the same view as the Advisory Committee and fully approved of the request that the Secretariat produce a concise study.[10]

The Council approved the resolution on 5 June 1928. On 30 June the Secretariat wrote to all State representatives on the Advisory Committee requesting them to communicate the laws and penalties relating to the souteneur in their respective States.[11]

## Advisory Committee Eighth Session, 1929

At its eighth session the Advisory Committee perused the Secretariat's brief report.[12] The Advisory Committee noted the report's limitations (it covered only some points of practical importance, only some systems of law, and focused on souteneurs rather than with the wider aspects of procuration).[13]

Particular matters that the Advisory Committee considered included the definition of the offence and the difficulties experienced by authorities tasked with making arrests of souteneurs. Many of these offenders had broken laws in different jurisdictions; the Advisory Committee considered that these prior convictions should be taken into account at sentencing. Having heard explanations from several delegates concerning the laws that were operative in their own jurisdictions, the Advisory Committee resolved, at the suggestion of the delegates of Belgium, France, and Great Britain, to request the Council to bring the study to the special notice of States, emphasizing the importance of ensuring that the regulations in place, and their application in practice, were effective to apprehend and punish souteneurs.[14] The need to grant powers enabling speedy arrest of souteneurs was a key element, along with penalties appropriate to the nature of the offence and its international reach, and provision for repeat offenders.[15] The Council accepted the Advisory Committee's resolution and instructed the Secretary-General to inform States about the report.[16]

The Fifth Committee agreed that this new focus on apprehending and punishing souteneurs was the best way to attack the trafficking problem. It accordingly recommended that the Advisory Committee establish a sub-committee tasked with considering this approach in order to generate more precise and comprehensive measures.[17]

## Advisory Committee Ninth Session, 1930

The proposal for a sub-committee was dealt with at the ninth session of the Advisory Committee in 1930.[18] Delegates' discussions led to the conclusion that the sub-committee should not be composed entirely of lawyers.[19] A broader committee that included members with some knowledge of the problem in its practical aspects, including enforcement—in particular, from the police point of view—was preferred.[20] Delegates stressed the desirability of the sub-committee having power to call upon expert assistance if that appeared, in the sub-committee's view, to be expedient.[21]

With those matters in mind, the Advisory Committee unanimously adopted a resolution to the effect that it had considered the report of the Advisory Committee, and the report of the Fifth Committee, which had stressed the need to focus on suppressing and penalizing the actions of souteneurs, and therefore recommended that a sub-committee of the Advisory Committee be appointed to enquire into that issue.[22]

The resolution also set out the Advisory Committee's view that the sub-committee to be formed should consist of the government representatives serving on the Legal Sub-Committee of the Child Welfare Committee, and that its task would be to report to the Advisory Committee at its next session, having studied the laws and regulations 'tending to the more effectual punishment of souteneurs, and especially the nature of their penalties which could be imposed for this purpose'.[23]

## Advisory Committee Tenth Session, 1931

At its tenth session, in 1931,[24] the Advisory Committee took cognizance of the draft protocol prepared by its Legal Sub-Committee to supplement the Convention of 1921[25] (LSC Draft Protocol). The LSC Draft Protocol had been prepared at the Legal Sub-Committee's session in December 1930 at Paris.[26] There had been detailed discussion about the way the word 'soutenuer' should be defined. The issue was that laws in some jurisdictions were structured in a way that presupposed the elements of aiding and abetting of prostitution, habitually or for personal profit. Other jurisdictions structured the offence around the element of living wholly or partly on the prostitution of another person. In some places, suppression of the activities of souteneurs would be enhanced if both formulations were included in the provisions criminalizing trafficking.[27] The Advisory Committee accordingly adopted a dual definition which incorporated these elements in a manner that permitted authorities to act pursuant to the particular legislative provision applicable in each country.[28]

The Advisory Committee agreed that the penalties provided for those who exploited the prostitution of another person should not, in principle, be more lenient than those that applied in other cases of procuring or trafficking.[29] It also dealt with the matter of provisional release, with or without bail.[30] In principle, the Advisory Committee felt that offenders should not be granted provisional release, as their offence, as souteneurs, was continuous in nature; in addition, implicit in the offence itself was a resource (the victim's earnings) which gave offenders a ready means of raising bail or other security bond from the illegal activity itself. In addition, souteneurs were, by the nature of their occupation, streetwise and cunning, thus to effectively address this aspect, the Advisory Committee thought that enforcement agencies needed an effective investigative regime that would disclose the true picture concerning the living being made, and at the same time supply evidence that could support a successful prosecution.[31]

The Advisory Committee, having revised the LSC Draft Protocol,[32] adopted it in the revised form, which it entitled 'Draft Additional Protocol to the International Convention for the Suppression of Traffic in Women and Children from September 1921' (Draft Additional Protocol). The Advisory Committee then requested the Council to submit the Draft Additional Protocol to all interested parties (States, Members of the League of Nations and signatories to the Convention of 1921) for their comments.[33] The Draft Additional Protocol provided for undertakings by signatories.

To punish souteneurs of either sex who were guilty of aiding or assisting the prostitution of another, habitually or for personal gain, or were guilty of exploiting others by deriving the whole or part of their livelihood from such prostitution (Article 1).[34]

To uphold the severity of sanctions against souteneurs. Since a souteneur was guilty of a special offence, the penalties should not be more lenient than those provided for procuring and trafficking, and should include loss of civil and political rights to the extent permitted by the legislative system of the country (Article 2).[35]

To increase penalties wherever the victim was a minor, or the souteneur was the husband, linear ascendant relation, or close relation of the victim; or where the offender employed violence, threats, false pretences, abuse of authority or power; or where the offender had prior convictions for the same offence (Article 3).[36]

Not to permit a person charged with Article 1 offences to be granted provisional release, with or without bail (Article 4).[37]

To make souteneurs liable for penalties or special administrative measures and measures of security in addition to the primary penalties. Such additional measures included denial of a permit of residence or passport, compulsory residence, local banishment, police translocation, detention in compulsory labour institutions and houses of correction, and deportation, where souteneurs were foreigners (Article 5).[38]

Article 1 offences were to be deemed extraditable offences pursuant to conventions already existing between contracting parties, and in the absence of such conventions, all measures within State parties' powers were to be taken to facilitate extradition (Article 6).[39]

All authorities were empowered to arrest and punish a souteneur, whether the authority was within the same country as the accused or in the country in which any one of the acts constituting the offence had been committed (Article 7).[40]

In this revised form, the Draft Additional Protocol was submitted to all interested parties as the Advisory Committee had requested.[41]

## Advisory Committee Eleventh Session, 1932

By the time the Advisory Committee reconvened in 1932,[42] one-third of the States had submitted their responses in time to be considered by the Advisory Committee at its Eleventh Session.[43] The Advisory Committee noted that the great majority of replies made no objection to the proposal to add provisions for the punishment of souteneurs to the international instruments (has recommended by the Advisory Committee). Indeed, the answers suggested that an agreement might be reached on the definition of souteneurs, the question of extradition, and competency of tribunals. However, the articles which dealt with levels of punishment and criminal procedure created greater difficulty.[44] The responses suggested a present inability to reach international agreement.[45]

Rather than discussing the situation on the strength of the replies that had been received, the Advisory Committee preferred to wait until a majority of States had communicated their views. However, to hasten the process, the Advisory Committee decided to submit all responses to the Legal Sub-Committee as they were received, at the same time instructing this body to prepare a report for the next Advisory Committee session. In addition, the Advisory Committee resolved to send its Draft Additional Protocol to voluntary international organizations with a request to submit their views to the Secretariat.[46] The Legal Sub-Committee would then consider those opinions along with the answers received from States.[47]

## Advisory Committee Twelfth Session, 1933

The Legal Sub-Committee had met in January 1933 to peruse the States' responses to the Draft Additional Protocol.[48] The Advisory Committee was informed in its twelfth session that the Legal Sub-Committee had met with difficulty in amending the Draft Additional Protocol to cohere with the responses. The Legal Sub-Committee had particular difficulty formulating the elements that were to constitute the offence.[49]

It was impossible to take effective measures to suppress the activities of souteneurs without a uniform definition of the offence across all jurisdictions, yet the legislative situation in different States varied markedly.[50] The Advisory Committee was well aware that this was an issue.[51] Some delegations required a definition of the offence wide enough to accommodate their countries' system of licensed houses, but this would not satisfy all parties.[52] The Advisory Committee could not see a solution to this problem being found at the current session.[53] It observed that ideally, any person living off the immoral earnings of women would be punished, so any progress towards abolition of licensed houses would be of great assistance in resolving States' differences over the terms of the Draft Additional Protocol.[54] Here it noted that a joint committee had already asked the Secretariat to investigate further and prepare, in readiness for the thirteenth session, a paper on the abolition of licensed houses. Meanwhile, some delegates were hopeful that the system of licensed houses would in time be abolished in jurisdictions where it remained in use, because that would make their efforts to resolve the terms of an international agreement directed against the activities of souteneurs considerably easier.[55]

The Advisory Committee, while observing that, at least for now, it seemed impossible to make much progress, nevertheless resolved to keep the matter on its agenda and to continue to study it in future sessions. It recommended that until then, since the activities of souteneurs presented grave dangers to society, that States which had not yet legislated to sanction activity by souteneurs should institute penal provisions carrying exemplary punishments. In addition, the Advisory Committee requested that the Council, when it considered and adopted the Advisory Committee's report, should make a point of apprising States of that recommendation.[56]

## Advisory Committee Thirteenth Session, 1934

The Advisory Committee, at its thirteenth session in 1934,[57] noted in its records a resolution made at the Fifth International Conference for the Unification of Criminal Law, held in Madrid in 1933, in relation to harmonization of legislation as it pertained to souteneurs.[58] The Advisory Committee discussed the resolution with great interest, as it noted the difficulties which might arise in connection with its own efforts, and possible ways to avoid that problem by ensuring that collaboration occurred between the Advisory Committee and the International Bureau for the Unification of Criminal Law.[59]

The United Kingdom delegation proposed that the question be referred to a sub-committee for consideration, and in collaboration with the Secretary-General of the International Bureau for the Unification of Criminal Law drafted a resolution. This resolution had noted with interest the discussions at the Madrid conference the year before; had taken cognizance of its efforts to harmonize legislation dealing with souteneurs; noted the resolution of the fourteenth Assembly that collaboration with the International Bureau for the Unification of Criminal law be instituted; and the need for such collaboration to tackle problems with which both bodies were concerned.[60] It therefore requested the International Bureau for the Unification of Criminal Law to adopt as its objective 'the most complete and stringent legislative provisions for the suppression of all forms of activity on the part of souteneurs'. Further, that the

Advisory Committee would at its next session consider the matter of an international convention for the punishment of souteneurs.[61]

The Advisory Committee duly adopted that resolution.[62] The Fifth Committee noted this progress and expressed its satisfaction; it noted that the Advisory Committee had, in collaboration with the International Bureau for the Unification of Criminal Law, been considering drafting an international convention covering the punishment of souteneurs, and was pleased that the Advisory Committee would consider the matter at its next session.[63]

## International Bureau for the Unification of Penal Law, Paris, 1935

The International Bureau for the Unification of Penal Law met in Paris in 1935, where it drafted a convention (IBUPL Draft Convention) directed at the suppression of exploitation of the prostitution of others.[64] The IBUPL Draft Convention was amalgamated with clauses proposed by the Legal Sub-Committee and compiled as a single document. To this, the Secretariat added the clauses needed to constitute the document as a proposed convention for the consideration of the Advisory Committee at its fourteenth session.[65]

## Advisory Committee Fourteenth Session, 1935

When the Advisory Committee met in 1935,[66] a general exchange of views about the proposed IBUPL Draft Convention took place. The delegate of the United Kingdom doubted that an effective solution could be found before there had been progress on the matter of abolition of licensed houses; he thought the Advisory Committee should ask the Secretariat to prepare a statement for the next session, based on the information the Secretariat had on file about the situation in each jurisdiction to deal with commercialized vice.[67] Different measures had been taken in different countries—some regulatory, some abolitionist—and the delegate of the United Kingdom thought it useful to consider whether, in light of that variability, agreement could be reached.[68]

Some delegates wanted the Advisory Committee to decide the question at the present session, and felt it was in a position to do so. These delegates felt that the IBUPL Draft Convention could meet the needs of abolitionist States because under its terms, every form of exploitation of another person's prostitution was made a punishable offence.[69] A few members of the Advisory Committee felt the text could be accepted as it was.[70]

Following these discussions, the Advisory Committee made its determination. It decided that several matters were yet to receive the exhaustive examination they felt was necessary. It therefore appointed a sub-committee[71] for that purpose. The sub-committee would be assisted by experts from the International Bureau for the Unification of Penal Law, the International Criminal Police Commission, and the Social Questions Section and Legal Section of the Secretariat. The Advisory Committee instructed the sub-committee, with assistance from the Secretariat, to make a legislative study of the question and prepare a preliminary draft convention that reflected its findings ready for consideration at the Advisory Committee's next session.[72]

The sub-committee duly studied the laws in force and in preparation in the various jurisdictions, and in light of those provisions drafted an international convention dealing with the exploitation of prostitution. The draft contained thirteen articles, and was followed by three recommendations (Sub-Committee of Experts Draft International Convention).[73]

## Advisory Committee Fifteenth Session, 1936

In 1936 the Sub-Committee of Experts Draft International Convention was considered by the Advisory Committee at its fifteenth session.[74] A majority of Advisory Committee members considered that the Advisory Committee, having considered various aspects of the matter for several years, could not postpone the matter any longer, and was now obliged to frame an international convention. The Advisory Committee wanted to solve the problem in a manner that would permit and encourage as many countries as possible to become parties.[75] The Advisory Committee's deliberations were for the most part concerned with an article in the Sub-Committee of Experts Draft International Convention which read:

The High Contracting Parties agree to punish, to the fullest extent compatible with their national laws, any person who exploits immorality either by aiding, abetting or facilitating the prostitution of third parties, or by deriving any material profit therefrom.[76]

By unanimous vote the Advisory Committee deleted the words 'to the fullest extent compatible with their national laws', and decided to base the convention without question on the abolitionist principle.[77] The resulting document was the International Convention for Suppressing the Exploitation of Prostitution (First Draft Convention)[78] as recommended by the Advisory Committee.[79] The main articles included:

Parties agreed to punish any person who, by any means whatsoever, incited, enticed or led a person of either sex away for the purpose of exploiting immorality (Article 1).[80]

Parties agreed to punish any person who exploited immorality by aiding, abetting or facilitating the prostitution of third parties, or by deriving any material profit from those activities (Article 2).

Aggravating circumstances were defined as: (1) victim being under twenty-one years of age, infirm, or feeble-minded; (2) offence being committed with coercion, violence, threats, abuse of authority or power, false pretences, trickery, or toxic substances or narcotic drugs; (3) offender being a spouse, relative in direct lineal ascent, or by adoption or marriage, or the sibling or guardian of the victim. Aggravating circumstances were to have the effect determined by national laws (Article 3).[81]

Participatory acts were deemed to be separate offences in cases where they could be tried only in different jurisdictions (Article 4).[82]

Prior convictions for related offences in foreign jurisdictions, where these were recognized in local law under the principle of international recognition, would be taken into account for the purpose of establishing habitual criminality; they would also be used, with or without special proceedings, to impose incapacities, disqualifications or interdictions under applicable public or private law (Article 5).[83]

To the extent that victims were permitted by local law to be a party to criminal prosecutions, foreigners would be able to exercise that right on the same terms as nationals (Article 6).[84]

Any State observing the principle of non-extradition of nationals could on that ground refuse to hand over one of its nationals accused or convicted of an offence under the present instrument, but was required to prosecute the offender in its own courts, in the same manner as if the offence had been committed in the local jurisdiction.[85] However, the penalty was not to the maximum penalty provided by the law of the jurisdiction in which the offence took place (Article 7).[86]

The three recommendations were:

In cases of exploitation of immorality under Article 2, whether or not there were aggravating circumstances under Article 3, deriving profit from immorality should be presumed of anyone who lived with or was habitually in the company of a prostitute, or exercised control, direction, or influence over the movements of a prostitute in such a way as to show that they were aiding or abetting or compelling her prostitution with any other person (Recommendation 1).

Where clear evidence of the character of persons exploiting immorality was available, legislation should be enacted to facilitate police searches in disorderly houses (Recommendation 2).

Appropriate rehabilitative measures should be taken along with ordinary penalties, in order to lead to their improvement and protect the community (Recommendation 3).[87]

The Advisory Committee considered that countries in which prostitution was still regulated should be permitted to sign the instrument subject to certain reservations, in particular in relation to Article 2.[88] It therefore unanimously adopted the following resolution:

The Traffic in Women and Children Committee requests the Council to recommend to Governments the conclusion of an international convention for the punishment of persons who exploit the prostitution of others.

The Committee, acting in conformity with its previous decisions, considers that this convention should be based on the principles of the legislation in force in the abolitionist countries.

Being desirous, however, of securing the largest number of accessions to this convention, the Committee contemplates the possibility for States which see fit to do so to make certain reservations, particularly with regard to Article 2 of the draft recommended by the Committee.

Accordingly the Committee requests the Council to refer the attached draft convention to the government members and non-members of the League of Nations as a basis for study.[89]

The Council approved this resolution, and the Secretary-General accordingly sent the First Draft Convention to States as resolved.[90] In doing so, the Secretary-General asked States to submit their observations by 1 November 1936.[91]

Cognizant to the fact that the system of licensed houses was one of the chief contributing factors to trafficking, the Fifth Committee observed that the Advisory Committee had made this clear through its various resolutions and reports, and said it should be an immediate aim of the Advisory Committee to achieve abolition of these houses.[92]

## Discussion of Replies to First Draft Convention

During its first session[93] the Advisory Committee reviewed and discussed responses to the First Draft Convention[94] from 37 States.[95] Nearly all replies indicated approval of the object and main principles of the First Draft Convention.[96] Nevertheless, numerous amendments were proposed,[97] and the issue of permitting States to become parties to the instrument with reservations was, as a matter of principle, raised as a concern.[98]

The number of suggested alterations led the Advisory Committee to appoint two experts to consider them. Professor J.A. Roux and M.F.E. Louwage were appointed, the former representing the International Bureau for the Unification of Criminal Law, the latter representing the International Criminal Police Commission.[99] These experts recommended several amendments to the First Draft Convention, and the Advisory Committee was of the view that these would answer many, though not all, of the objections.[100] The issue of reservations was not new; during discussions of the First Draft Convention in the previous year, the Advisory Committee had considered that possibility, with Article 2 being a particular focus of attention. However, several of the delegates at this session were anxious about the potential effects of reservations of the kind contemplated.[101]

In this regard, regulationist States in particular would be required, as a matter of policy, to make reservations on articles of central importance to the operation of the instrument, the result of which would be major deviations from the unanimously agreed purpose and intent by the Advisory Committee.

This would be a particularly regrettable result, as some states with regulationist policies were actively reconsidering them but would be unable to achieve changes in the local laws in time for them to accept such an instrument.[102] Reservations that dealt with such a central aspect of the operation of an international instrument were a serious departure from the general rule in international agreements, that is, signatories to conventions were expected to be in a position to apply them, and should only support instruments they were willing and able to implement.[103]

A plan for an alternative approach was therefore mounted. It was proposed that, rather than accepting such wide reservations to operative articles, States which were willing to sign the instrument, but unable for policy reasons to ratify their signatures shortly thereafter, should formally declare that to be the case in a document such as a final act appended to the instrument. That document would make clear their in-principle support for the instrument and willingness to adapt local systems in a manner that would permit ratification in the future, and might even define some period within which the necessary local changes would be brought about.[104]

The idea appealed to the Advisory Committee, which considered it a possible means of avoiding wide reservations.[105] It resolved to appoint a sub-committee to examine the plan from a legal perspective.[106] Delegates were duly appointed from France, the Netherlands, Poland, Romania, the United Kingdom and the USA, to meet in Paris within two months of the end of the Advisory Committee's current session.[107] Generally a sub-committee of this nature would report to the Advisory Committee, but because of the instrument's importance and the need to proceed without delay, the sub-committee was instructed to report directly to the Council. The Swiss delegate demurred on the basis that the First Draft Convention should go first to a diplomatic conference.[108]

Being hampered in any detailed consideration of the terms of the First Draft Convention by the various amendments proposed by the States, the Advisory Committee decided to entrust that task, also, to the sub-committee, on the basis that it would not make amendments that might affect the character of the main principles on the First Draft Convention.[109] A resolution in those terms was adopted. The resolution noted that the Advisory Committee had considered the responses received from governments to the First Draft Convention; had observed that most responses were in favour of an international convention on suppression of exploitation of prostitution; had taken into account an expert report that had canvassed the many suggestions made by various governments; and had considered the matter of widely drawn reservations to the First Draft Convention and alternatives that avoided the need for them, so as to gain adherence to the instrument by as many States as possible. The Advisory Committee further resolved that it was of the opinion that the discussions already held would enable the sub-committee to formulate a definitive draft for the proposed instrument. It requested the sub-committee to meet promptly to consider the issue of reservations and present a definitive draft along with its report to the Council for consideration at the Council meeting in September 1937.[110]

The sub-committee's report to the Council was to include requests to the Council first, to submit the definitive draft to States (members and non-members) for fresh consideration, and second, to instruct the Secretary-General to enter an agenda item at the Assembly's ordinary meeting in 1938 on the matter of convening an inter-governmental conference for the conclusion of the instrument.[111]

## SECOND DRAFT CONVENTION

As directed, the appointed sub-committee met in Paris on 15–19 June 1937 to prepare a definitive draft of the First Draft Convention (Second Draft Convention).[112] The main articles of the Second Draft Convention were, in substance:

Parties undertook to impose criminal sanctions against any person who, in order to gratify the passions of another and for the purposes of gain, procured, enticed, or led away by whatever means, irrespective of consent, a person of either sex of full age for the purpose of exploiting that person's prostitution (Article 1).[113]

Parties further undertook to impose criminal sanctions for keeping or managing a brothel; exercising, for gain, control or influence over a person of either sex in such a way as to compel or aid their prostitution with another; or in any other way exploiting the prostitution of another person of either sex (Article 2).[114]

Participatory acts related to the offences defined in the instrument would be treated as separate offences, in cases where offenders could only be tried in different countries, subject to the constraints of the domestic law (Article 3).[115]

In jurisdictions that recognized the principle of international recognition of previous convictions, subject to the constraints of the domestic law, foreign convictions for the offences defined in the instrument (in Articles 1, 2, and 3) were to be taken into account as evidence of habitual criminality, or for the purpose of imposing incapacities, disqualifications or interdictions, whether in the sphere of public or private law, with or without special proceedings (Article 4).[116]

The sub-committee found its task of framing Articles 1 and 2 difficult and complex. It observed in its report that before it could settle the terms of those articles the stated purpose of the proposed instrument had to be defined, and it needed to deal with the manner in which prior conventions had already dealt with related issues.[117]

The Convention of 1910 contemplated an offence of procuring, in order to gratify the passion of another person, a woman of full age when there is fraud, violence or any measure of compulsion.[118] The Second Draft Convention, directed at suppression of the traffic in persons and exploitation of the prostitution of others, contemplated a similar offence of procuring a woman under the age of twenty even with her consent.[119] The Convention of 1921 had raised the age of protection to twenty-one and extended the protection to all minors, male or female. The offence in the Convention of 1933 applied to procuring of a woman or girl of full age, even with her consent, for immoral purposes in another country.[120]

These various provisions had created a gap which the sub-committee unanimously agreed should be filled by the Second Draft Convention. It considered that the way to do this was to protect persons of full age of either sex against procuration for profit, irrespective of consent, and whether or not the person concerned was taken abroad and also other forms of exploitation of their prostitution.[121]

It was thought that the Second Draft Convention should retain as far as possible the language of previous conventions. One form of words that would meet that requirement was noted:

Whoever, in order to gratify the passions of another person, procures, entices or leads away, even with her consent, a person of full age of either sex, for immoral purposes inside a country, shall be punished.[122]

However, the sub-committee felt that this formulation would be at once too far-reaching and too restrictive.[123] Its breadth was excessive in that it would punish even participants in actions connected with prostitution who had not sought gain, and the person was a consenting adult.[124] Since prostitution in those terms was not an offence in most countries it was not feasible to legislate for sanctions against those who procured prostitution in those terms without seeking remuneration. The sub-committee considered a motive of gain to be fundamental to the new offence.[125]

In addition, the phrase 'immoral purposes' appeared to take the instrument beyond the intention of the parties for whom the instrument was being framed. The expression 'immoral purposes' in a document that imposed legal consequences on consenting victims of full age would take the proposed instrument far beyond the subject matter of trafficking in women and children. The sub-committee was therefore of the view that the word 'prostitution' should be used rather than 'immoral purposes'.[126]

Aware that imposition of criminal sanctions needed to be justified, the sub-committee was of the view that the object of the offence, which was framed in terms of the elements or actions of *procuring, enticing* and *leading away* must be the *exploitation* of the prostitution of a victim either by the person doing the procuring or by some third person.[127]

The sub-committee observed that the formula was narrow in scope in that it would not apply to all types of exploitation of the prostitution of others. In any event, it felt that the provisions should deal specifically with two particular species of exploitation, which could not be always assumed to be caught by the formula, but should be punished. They were first, all persons who kept or managed brothels, and second, the souteneurs who exploited prostitution. The sub-committee made particular reference to those activities in its draft, along with a general stipulation that criminal sanctions should be imposed for any form of exploitation of the prostitution of another.[128]

Some States had, in their responses, enquired about the matter of male prostitution and whether it was necessary to bring it within the purview of the Second Draft Convention.[129] The sub-committee was of the opinion that as male prostitution was severely punished as a form of vice in most countries, there was no reason why its exploitation should not also be punishable under the instrument.[130]

Taking all these matters into account, the sub-committee suggested the adoption of a form of words in Articles 2 and 3 as follows:

Article 1—each of the High Contracting Parties agrees to provide for the punishment of the following, namely: whoever, in order to gratify the passions of another and for the purposes of gain, procures, entices or leads away by whatever means, even with consent, a person of either sex of full age for the purpose of exploiting that person's prostitution.[131]

Article 2—each of the High Contracting Parties further agrees to provide for the punishment of the following, namely (a) whoever keeps or manages a brothel; (b) whoever, for the purposes of gain, exercises control or influence over a person of either sex and in such a way as to compel or aid that person's prostitution with another, or (c) whoever, in any other way, exploits the prostitution of another person of either sex.[132]

The sub-committee noted that the expression 'exploiting' or 'exploit' in these articles had been included in part to exclude the servants or members of the family of a prostitute, or other persons who might derive material profit from the prostitute's immoral earnings but do not exploit that prostitution.[133] This met the request of several governments not to make such association punishable.[134]

The sub-committee also observed that the wording of Articles 1 and 2 was a compromise. Sub-committee discussion had disclosed a structural tension between the views of members who would have preferred a single, general clause intended to cover all cases. The sub-committee settled on the more defined wording so as to satisfy the stipulation of other members that the activities of the brothel-keeper and the souteneur be specifically addressed.[135]

Substantial attention was also paid to the search for a formula suitable for insertion in the final act of a diplomatic conference—the approach that had been suggested as a way to avoid reservations on operational parts of the instrument (Articles 1 and 2).[136] The sub-committee proposed the insertion of a declaration whose recitals stated that the conference recognized that in States where regulation of prostitution was maintained, legislation would be required, under Article 19 of the instrument, to enable them to become parties, and that the possibility of changing the local system to secure passage of amending legislation was largely dependent on public opinion.[137] The conference therefore declared that all members, including those from regulationist countries,

are in full agreement with the principles underlying this abolitionist Convention and are convinced that its elaboration by them will be of material assistance in enabling those States whose practice and legislation are not at present in harmony with the principles of the Convention, to secure the necessary changes which the Members of the Conference desire earnestly to see secured within the next few years.[138]

The sub-committee was of the view that the conference should recommend in the final act that States should forthwith, even before ratification of the instrument, enact whichever provisions could be made operational in domestic law without a formal ratification, since some time was expected to elapse between signature and ratification of the instrument in many cases. It accordingly suggested insertion of a declaration to that effect in the final act.[139]

## Submission to Council and State Responses

The Second Draft Convention was duly submitted, along with the sub-committee's report, to the Council. On 14 September 1937 the Council instructed the Secretary-General to place on the agenda of the Assembly's ordinary meeting in 1938 the question of the convocation of an inter-governmental conference to conclude the instrument.[140] Under Council instructions the Secretary-General sent the Second Draft Convention and the sub-committee's comments on it to all members of the League as well as non-member States,[141] with the request that they respond with their observations on the Second Draft Convention by 1 May 1938.[142] The various States replied as set out below.

## General Remarks Concerning Second Draft Convention, 1937

### Union of South Africa

No observations to add.

### Belgium

No observations to add. Belgium also stated that a draft law abolishing official regulation of prostitution in Belgium and making criminal the exploitation of others persons' immorality had been submitted to its Chamber of Representatives. Belgiam was unable for legal reasons to sign the Second Draft Convention until its legislature had considered that new law. However, Belgium reserved the right to accede later to any instrument adopted by an inter-governmental conference on the matter.[143]

### United Kingdom

No observations on the main principles of the articles in the Second Draft Convention as prepared by the sub-committee. The United Kingdom was willing to accept the report as a basis for an instrument.[144]

## Bulgaria

No objections or reservations. Bulgaria held that the Second Draft Convention was a most satisfactory solution to a problem of great moral importance. It accepted the draft as it was, as the basis for discussion at a future conference.[145]

## Egypt

Egypt paid tribute to the efforts made by the League of Nations and its various bodies but wished to suspend examination of the Second Draft Convention until it had reached a final decision on its own approach to suppression of prostitution, and had promulgated adequate legislation locally.[146]

## United States of America

The USA considered the Second Draft Convention to afford a satisfactory basis on which to call an international conference on the subject.[147]

## France

France approved the underlying principles and noted its wish to move amendments to its laws to enable it to participate in conventions of that kind.[148]

## Greece

Greece, through its Ministry of Justice, was in complete accord with the fundamental principles embodied in the Second Draft Convention and noted that it believed their application necessary as a supplement to prior instruments. There was no objection to the criminalization of exploitation of males for purposes of prostitution even if the offence appeared to be rare.[149]

## Guatemala

Guatemala was in full agreement with the Second Draft Convention and the principles embodied in it. Its government had no objections to the Second Draft Convention and was happy either to attend the conference to discuss the instrument or in any case accede to the instrument in due course. Guatemala drew attention, however, to the large number of Spanish-speaking countries involved, and suggested Article XVII enabling the instrument to be drawn up in Spanish as well as the usual French and English, because each Spanish-speaking country would otherwise make its own translation and thereby affect the uniformity of the convention and its application.[150]

## Iceland

Denmark reported that the matter had no practical relevance to Iceland, so it was not prepared to submit any observations.[151]

## Latvia

Latvia's previously favourable standpoint was maintained (as described in the letter of 11 November 1936, which said 'that the competent authorities had stated that they had no observations to make on the subject and were in favour of the conclusion of an international convention on the basis of the draft in question').[152] It had no objection to the Second Draft Convention.[153]

## Lithuania

Lithuania had no observations to make about the Second Draft Convention.[154]

## Monaco

Monaco had no objections to the Second Draft Convention.[155]

## Norway

Norway referred to its memorandum of 29 July 1937 but otherwise had no observations to make on the Second Draft Convention.[156]

## Romania

Romania found the Second Draft Convention acceptable as it stood, without any reservations, since most of the principles and provisions contained in it were already embodied in Romanian legislation.[157]

## Siam

Siam had no observations to make beyond those contained in its communication of 22 March 1937.[158]

## Sweden

Sweden submitted the Second Draft Convention to its competent authorities to be considered, and found that, as with the First Draft Convention, the principles set out in the proposed instrument were essentially in conformity with Swedish law on the subject.[159]

## Switzerland

The Swiss authorities found that the Second Draft Convention called for similar observations to those it had made to the Secretariat of the League of Nations in a note dated 1 December 1936. The Swiss Federal Criminal Code was required to be voted on by the Swiss people before it could come into force. Article 173 of that Code contained provisions for systematic prevention of incitement to, or exploitation of, the prostitution of others. However, some provisions of the Second Draft Convention were at odds with Federal legislation, in particular in relation to protection of male persons of full age (as provided for in Article 1). Switzerland would therefore not be able to amend its legislation to comply with the proposed instrument once the Federal code came into force.[160]

## Venezuela

Venezuela stated itself to be in one sense in favour of the adoption of the Second Draft Convention, as the acts contemplated by the proposed instrument for suppression were undoubtedly worthy of punishment, but the Venezuelan Penal Code did not deal with matters which were covered by the instrument. Venezuela's penal legislation was governed by a principle of prior legal definition of crimes and punishments, and the proposed instrument would necessitate a reform of the Penal Code, introducing an article defining certain acts as crimes, and providing appropriate penalties for them.[161]

However, Venezuala was precluded by its national constitution from legislating for sanctions that were not provided for in Venezuelan law itself. All Venezuelans citizens enjoyed constitutional rights including a right of personal security, by virtue of which no person could be tried for any act whatsoever unless an existing legal text defined the offence and specified the penalty (paragraphs (b) and (c), Guarantee 17, Article 32 of the National Constitution).[162]

The present Penal Code only punished acts committed by persons who, in order to gratify the passions of another, persuaded minors to engage in prostitution or acts of debauchery, or abetted or encouraged their prostitution or debauchery (Chapter 3, Articles 388–391). Thus the state of the legislation in Venezuela meant that the instrument could be of no effect even if a situation arose in which it would be appropriate to apply the proposed penalties for the exploitation of the prostitution of persons of full age.[163]

## Yugoslavia

Yugoslavia had no observation to make about the Second Draft Convention as a whole.[164] However, in relation to Article 1, its authorities felt it might have been advisable to include procurers who exploit the prostitution of other persons from habit. Article 1, if supplemented in this way, would read, 'each of the High Contracting Parties agree to provide for the punishment of the following, namely: whoever, in order to gratify the passions of another and for the purposes of gain, or from habit, procures, entices, or leads away by whatever means, even with consent, a person of either sex of full age for the purpose of exploiting that person's prostitution.'[165]

## Chile

Chile was unable to accept the terms of the instrument as set out in the Second Draft Convention. Chile stated its reasons in a memorandum as follows:

(1) the health authorities of Chile provisionally tolerate brothels, because up to the present, in the existing economic and social conditions, it has been possible, in virtue of special regulations, to supervise the state of health of prostitutes, to provide treatment for them and look after them in hospital; (2) with regard to treatment, the institution in Chile of compulsory medical inspection twice a week at certain hospitals and a system, of inspection of licensed houses make it possible to provide adequately for the large majority of syphilis cases and to treat, the relatively high number of women found to be in a contagious condition; (3) the authorities hope shortly to have their own hospital service for the treatment of contagious cases, this being compulsory under the Code. The carrying-out of this scheme, together with the campaign now being waged by the health authorities in the prevention of disease, should enable them without difficulty to close down completely, within a reasonable period, all licensed houses, which for the moment, from an epidemiological point of view, facilitate the treatment of women suffering from venereal diseases.[166]

## Denmark

Denmark had no objection to raise about the Second Draft Convention.[167]

## Estonia

Existing Estonian legislation was in complete accordance with the Second Draft Convention. The Estonian authorities were therefore of the opinion that, taking into account the social conditions in Estonia, an international convention was unnecessary as far as Estonia was concerned.[168]

## Hungary

Hungary was in full agreement with the principles underlying the Second Draft Convention and wished to abolish the system of regulation of prostitution, but was obliged to take into account the present situation in its own country. The existing Hungarian system was regulatory, supplemented by a series of measures to protect women. As long as the current social and economic conditions (in particular the latter) continued, Hungary felt itself unable to change that system, saying it would not be possible to consider a transition towards an abolitionist system until a sufficient number of anti-venereal dispensaries had been provided across the country, and every patient was able to obtain free medicine and treatment. The Hungarian Government therefore preferred to state at once that it would be impossible for it to sign the Second Draft Convention, even with the reservations provided, or to take part in an intergovernmental conference held to conclude that instrument.[169]

## Turkey

Turkey replied that under its Penal Code it was a punishable act to lead away or entice a person of either sex under twenty-one years of age in order to gratify the passions of another (Article 436). Procuring of girls or women over twenty-one years of age by their brother, husband, or parent was a punishable offence under that Article, which also provided for punishment of any person who led away girls or women under twenty-one completed years, or procured, enticed or conveyed them from one place to another, even with their consent. The same article provided for the punishment of any person who, in order to gratify the passions of another and for the purposes of gain, procured, enticed or led away a woman of full age by means of violence, coercion, ruse or influence. Apart from those offences, Turkish law tolerated the existence of licensed houses, subject to the proprietors having obtained a permit from the authorities. The Second Draft Convention in question was therefore to some extent incompatible with the existing laws of Turkey, and the Turkish Government considered it unnecessary to submit further observations on the matter.[170]

The Fifth Committee noted that from the answers received by the League regarding the First Draft Convention and the answers received regarding the Second Draft Convention, that it appeared that the majority of States were, in principle, in favour of concluding such an instrument. The Advisory Committee noted that observations were made in relation to individual articles.[171] In discussion on how to conclude such an instrument the sense was that proceeding too quickly to a conference may be counterproductive despite the instrument's main objects and purposes not attracting a dissenting voice during the deliberations. Given this, the Advisory committee made an in principle determination that 1940 might be the most suitable time for the convocation of a conference to conclude such an instrument. This procedure, the Advisory Committee felt achieved two outcomes: firstly it provided States that were considering abolitionist legislation the opportunity to take further steps along that path and secondly, it enabled the Secretary-General to make a provision in the draft budget for 1940 to be submitted to the next Assembly for the convocation of such a conference.[172]

Given this, the Fifth Committee submitted a resolution to the Assembly with recitals to the effect that it noted that a majority of the countries responding to the two drafts had agreed to the proposed instrument's object and main principles; that it considered that the instrument would fill gaps left in prior instruments relating to trafficking in women and children; that it noted that several countries with a policy of regulating prostitution were in a difficult legislative position that threatened to prevent their participation in the instrument, however, legislation which might address the difficulties was being considered; that it was in favour of the convocation of a conference for the conclusion of an instrument whose object was suppression of exploitation of prostitution. It therefore recommended convocation of such a conference by the Council in 1940 and instructed the Secretary-General to make financial provision for it in the draft budget for 1940.[173] In 1939 the Second World War broke out, and the planned conference did not take place.

## POST-WAR REVIVAL OF UNIFICATION EFFORTS

After the end of the Second World War, the United Nations (UN) was established and the UN Economic and Social Council (UN ESCOR) during its fourth session in 1947 passed a resolution instructing the Secretary-General to take up once more the examination of the Second Draft Convention on the subject of exploitation of the prostitution of others, and

make any necessary amendments in order to bring it up to date and introduce any desirable improvement in view of the changes in the general situation since 1937, ascertain from governments whether the conventions as amended is likely to meet their approval, and to submit the draft convention together with any amendments made therein to the Social Commission for the subsequent approval of the Economic and Social Council.[174]

The Secretary-General did as requested, and the resulting document was sent to all member States as well as a number of international organizations, requesting comments.[175]

## UN ESCOR Fifth Session, 1947

The Fifth Session took place in 1947,[176] and UN ESCOR considered whether the earlier instruments (the Agreement of 1904, Convention of 1910, Convention of 1921, Convention of 1933 and Second Draft

Convention) should be amalgamated. The close connection between those instruments, including the Second Draft Convention, which was lying fallow, led UN ESCOR to request the Secretary-General of the United Nations to present a report on such unification to the Social Commission. The Social Commission was asked to consider the proposal and advise UN ESCOR at a future session about what would be required to effect it.[177]

## UN ESCOR Seventh Session, 1948

At its seventh session in 1948,[178] UN ESCOR passed a resolution naming the instruments to be consolidated (the earlier instruments of 1904, 1910, 1921, and 1933 and the Second Draft Convention of 1937), and in further recitals noted that it took into account Council resolution 43(IV) of 29 March 1947, which instructed the Secretary-General to take up the Second Draft Convention for amendment in ways that would update and improve it and the Council resolution 83(V) of 14 August 1947, which requested the Social Commission to consider the possibility of consolidation of instruments.[179] UN ESCOR considered that developments in general conditions since 1937 made feasible an 'immediate formulation and conclusion of a new and comprehensive convention for the suppression of the traffic in women and children and the prevention of prostitution.' It was therefore of the opinion that all instruments should be consolidated, updated and improved, and requested the Secretary-General to prepare a new consolidated draft, seek the views of governments and specialist international organizations on it, and then submit the draft and any responses to the Social Commission at its fourth session. It further requested the Social Commission to treat the draft as a matter of priority and respond to it not later than the ninth session of the Council, and suggested that if the Social Commission was unable to complete its task in that time, it should submit instead a revision of the Second Draft Convention, including any necessary formal amendments and additional amendments that were likely to be approved, but omitting any the Social Commission felt were unlikely to attract general agreement.[180]

UN ESCOR made a further recommendation in anticipation of a satisfactory conclusion of the instrument, asking that States that had not already done so, to provide in their public and voluntary social welfare services for preventive and rehabilitative measures directed against prostitution, including free and confidential treatment for venereal disease where this was not already available under general medical care. It also suggested that States that had not already done so should legislate to empower re-educative and rehabilitative measures in regard to children and young persons in need of care who were, or might become, prostitutes.[181]

The Secretary-General accordingly supplied a draft instrument (SG Draft Convention) to member States, specialized bodies and non-governmental organizations, and submitted it to the fourth session of the Social Commission.[182]

## Social Commission Fourth Session, 1949

The SG Draft Convention was considered as a matter of priority at the fourth session of the Social Commission in May 1949. The Secretariat and nine non-governmental organizations with consultative status were first heard.[183]

Several provisions were modified at this session,[184] and the Social Commission also added a Final Protocol to the effect that the now revised instrument (Social Commission Draft Convention) set out minimum obligations, beyond which States were free to legislate. In addition, it drew to UN ESCOR's attention the fact that voting on a provision relating to abolition of registration or supervision of prostitutes, which the Social Commission had considered the most controversial element of the revised draft, had been very close.[185]

The Social Commission also drew attention to clauses governing disputes about the interpretation and application of the instrument, for which contingent reference to the International Court of Justice was provided, and other provisions concerning trust territories and non-self-governing territories, along with jurisdictional matters concerning an issue arising in States in which treaties became automatically applicable, and a question concerning the appropriate organ of the

UN to be empowered to invite non-member States to become parties to the instrument. The Social Commission recommended that UN ESCOR approve the Social Commission Draft Convention and submit it to the General Assembly (UN GAOR) recommending the conclusion of an international convention in accordance with this revised draft.[186]

## Social Commission Draft Convention

The Social Commission Draft Convention consisted of thiry-two articles and a Final Protocol:

### Summary of Provisions of the Social Commission Draft Convention

#### Preamble

Recitals stated that the trafficking that accompanied prostitution was an evil, and that both prostitution and trafficking were inconsistent with human dignity and worth, and endangered welfare at the level of the individual, the family, and the community. The instruments in force on the subject of trafficking in women and children were named (the Agreement of 1904 as amended by the Protocol of 1948; the Convention of 1910 as amended by the Protocol of 1948; the Convention of 1921 as amended by the Protocol of 1947; and the Convention of 1933 as amended by the Protocol of 1947). The Second Draft Convention extending the scope of those instruments was noted, along with a statement concerning the feasibility of now concluding a consolidating instrument encompassing all the existing instruments and the Second Draft Convention.[187]

#### Article 1

Parties agreed to punish any person who, to gratify the passions of another:

(1) procures, entices or leads away, for purposes of prostitution, another person, even with the consent of that person; (2) exploits or is an accessory in the prostitution of another person, even with the consent of that person, provided these offences are committed for the purposes of gain. Any person who commits or is an accessory in the commission of any of the above-mentioned offences, shall, however, be punished regardless of motives of gain: (a) if the person procured, enticed, led away or exploited is less than twenty-one years old at the time of the offence; (b) if the person is procured, enticed, led away or exploited for the purpose of being sent abroad; (c) if the person is procured, enticed, led away or exploited by the use of fraud, deceit, threat, violence, or any other means of duress.[188]

## Article 2

Criminal sanctions were to be imposed upon any person who kept, managed, knowingly financed or took part in financing a brothel, or knowingly let a building, part of a building or other place for the purpose of the prostitution of others.[189]

## Article 3

Attempts and preparatory acts related to offences referred to in Articles 1 and 2 also attracted criminal sanctions, subject to the constraints of local law.[190]

## Article 4

Participation in an offence provided for under the instrument would be treated as separate offences, subject to requirements of domestic law, even when those offences must be tried in different countries or territories.[191]

## Article 5

Where victims were entitled under local law to be parties to criminal proceedings related to instrument offences, foreigners would also be entitled to be parties on the same terms and conditions.[192]

## Article 6

Parties agreed to take all necessary steps to repeal or abolish laws or administrative provisions that regulated prostitution by requiring registration, a permit system or other exceptional requirements for supervision or notification of prostitution.[193]

## Article 7

Prior convictions for instrument offences committed in foreign jurisdictions were to be taken into account in establishing recidivism or disqualifying the offender from the exercise of civil rights, subject to the requirements of domestic law.[194]

## Article 8

Instrument offences defined in Articles 1 and 2 were to be treated as extraditable pursuant to existing or future extradition treaties, and jurisdictions where extradition was not conditional on the existence of a treaty, were to recognize those offences as themselves extraditable between jurisdictions. Extradition was to be granted pursuant to the domestic law of the jurisdiction requested to extradite an offender.[195]

## Article 9

In cases of jurisdictions that did not recognize the principle of extradition of nationals who committed instrument offences abroad, they were to prosecute and punish those returning nationals as if the offence had been committed locally, even when the offender had acquired nationality after committing the offence. Article 9 was not to apply in cases where extradition of a foreigner could not be granted on the same basis.[196]

## Article 10

Foreigners who were in a country party to the instrument, having committed an instrument offence abroad, were to be prosecuted and punished as though the offence had been committed in that country: if extradition had been demanded and could not be granted by the country of refuge for reasons unconnected with offence itself; or if the courts in the jurisdiction of refuge had jurisdiction over offences committed abroad by aliens; or if the offender's home jurisdiction gave courts power to try offences committed aboard by aliens.[197]

### Article 11

Articles 9 and 10 were not to apply when the offender had been tried in a foreign jurisdiction and had been convicted and served the sentence imposed or had the sentence remitted or reduced according to the law of that jurisdiction.[198]

### Article 12

The instrument was not to be interpreted as determining a State's attitude towards the general operation of the limits of criminal jurisdiction under international law.[199]

### Article 13

The instrument was not to alter the principle that instrument offences were to be defined and sanctioned by each jurisdiction according to its domestic law.[200]

### Article 14

Parties undertook to execute letters of request relating to offences referred to in this instrument in accordance with their domestic law and practice.[201] Transmission between countries was to be effected by direct communication between their judicial authorities, their Ministers of Justice, or between another competent authority and the Minister of Justice, or through diplomatic or consular representatives, who were to send letters of request directed to the competent authority and were to receive papers constituting the execution of the letters of request direct from that authority. Except where letters were sent to the Minister of Justice, copies were to be sent to the superior authority of jurisdiction requested to execute the letter. Letters were to be drawn in the language of requesting authority unless otherwise agreed, and the requested authority could require a certified translation in its own language. Parties were to notify all other parties of the methods of transmission it was prepared to recognize; existing procedures were to apply in the meantime. No claim for reimbursement of charges or expenses incurred in relation to execution of letters of request would lie, other than for expenses of experts. Article 14 was not to be construed as an undertaking to adopt evidentiary processes in criminal matters contrary to the domestic laws of States.[202]

## Article 15

Parties were to operate services charged with collection, compilation and centralization of data about instrument offences, to facilitate prevention and punishment of those offences, and liaise with their counterparts in other jurisdictions.[203]

## Article 16

Parties undertook, subject to the requirements of domestic law in their own jurisdictions and to the extent the data-management authorities referred to in Article 15 deemed desirable, to furnish to their counterparts in other jurisdictions particulars of any instrument offences or attempted offences, searches, prosecutions, arrests, convictions, refusals of admission and expulsions, and in general any useful information about persons guilty of instrument offences, including their movements, description, fingerprints, photographs, methods of operation, police records, and records of conviction.[204]

## Article 17

Parties undertook to support and undertake measures to prevent prostitution and rehabilitate prostitutes, through public and private educational, health, social, economic and other related services.[205]

## Article 18

In relation to immigration and emigration, parties undertook to take whatever steps were necessary to meet their obligations under the instrument to prevent the traffic in persons of either sex for the purposes of prostitution. This included legislating as necessary to: protect women and children as immigrants or emigrants, at places of arrival and departure and while en route, and maintaining systems of public warning about the dangers of trafficking; supervision of railway stations, airports, ports of embarkation and en route, and other public places; and notifying appropriate authorities of the arrival in their jurisdictions of any person who appeared to be involved in trafficking, whether as principal, accomplice or victim.[206]

## Article 19

Subject to the requirements of domestic law, parties undertook to obtain declared statements from foreign prostitutes in order to establish their identity, their civil status, and the identity of any person who had caused them to leave their own country. That information was to be communicated to the authorities in the country of origin, for the purpose of facilitating their eventual repatriation.[207]

## Article 20

In relation to repatriation of trafficked persons, parties undertook; as far as possible, and subject to the requirements of domestic law, to provide temporary care and maintenance for destitute persons who had been trafficked for purposes of prostitution while they waited to be repatriated; and to repatriate any persons from whom declarations had been taken under Article 19 who wished to be repatriated or was claimed by those responsible for them.[208]

Repatriation was to take place after agreement about relevant records (data concerning identity, nationality and places and dates of arrival at frontiers) had been reached between the jurisdictions concerned. Parties undertook to facilitate the passage of persons being repatriated. If they were destitute or could not themselves or with the help of relatives repay the cost of repatriation, the cost was to be borne by the country of present residence as far as the nearest frontier or port of embarkation or airport, and the remainder by the country of origin.[209]

## Article 21

Parties undertook to supervise employment agencies to reduce the risk of exposure to the dangers of prostitution of those seeking employment.[210]

## Article 22

Parties undertook to communicate to the Secretary-General of the United Nations what laws and regulations relating to the instrument were already in force in their jurisdictions, and to report annually thereafter any new laws and regulations, along with measures they had taken in relation to the matters dealt with in the instrument.[211] The Secretary-General of the United Nations was to publish that information periodically and send it to all States, members and non-members, to which the instrument had been officially communicated pursuant to Article 24.[212]

## Article 23

Unresolved disputes about the interpretation or application of the instrument were to be referred to the International Court of Justice.[213]

## Article 24

Signature or acceptance of the instrument was open to members of the United Nations and non-members invited by the UN ESCOR, and on behalf of UN-administered trust territories, and the Free Territory of Trieste. The word 'State' included any such territory for the purposes of the instrument. To become parties to the instrument, States could sign without reservation, sign subject to later acceptance, or accept. Instruments of acceptance were to be deposited with the Secretary-General of the United Nations.[214]

## Article 25

The instrument was to come into force ninety days after two or more States had signed without reservation, or accepted, pursuant to Article 24.[215]

## Article 26

States were to become parties ninety days after they signed without reservation, or accepted, pursuant to Article 24, provided the instrument was then in force, or when it did come into force, if that had not yet occurred.[216]

## Article 27

Parties were able, by notifying the Secretary-General of the United Nations, to extend the operation of the instrument to territories for which they held responsibility for international relations; application of the instrument to that territory was to occur ninety days after receipt of the notification.[217] Parties agreed to act under this article as soon as possible, and the Secretary-General of the United Nations was to communicate the instrument to all States referred to in Article 24 for transmission to the responsible authorities of their non-self-governing territories, trust territories or other non-metropolitan territory for which they were responsible.[218]

## Article 28

Parties would be able to formally denounce the instrument for themselves, or for territories to whom it had been extended pursuant to Article 27, after five years of its entry into force, by depositing a formal instrument to that effect with the Secretary-General of the United Nations. The denunciation was to take effect one year after its receipt by the Secretary-General of the United Nations.[219]

## Article 29

All States referred to in Article 24 (members and non-members) were to be informed by the Secretary-General of the United Nations of the date of entry into force of the instrument along with details of all signatures, acceptances, notifications and denunciations received in accordance with Articles 24, 27, and 28.[220]

## Article 30

States were to become parties to the instrument on the understanding that if they signed without reservation as to acceptance or accepted, they were in a position to give effect to the terms of the instrument pursuant to their own domestic law.[221]

## Article 31

Parties that were also parties to the instruments referred to in the Preamble (the Agreement of 1904 as amended by the Protocol of 1948; the Convention of 1910 as amended by the Protocol of 1948; the Convention of 1921 as amended by the Protocol of 1947; or the Convention of 1933 as amended by the Protocol of 1947) were, as between themselves, to treat those instruments as abrogated by this instrument, and each of those instruments would be deemed to be terminated when all parties to it had become parties to the present instrument.[222]

### Article 32

On the day it came into force, the Secretary-General of the United Nations was to register the instrument pursuant to Article 102 of the Charter of the United Nations.[223]

### Final Protocol

The Final Protocol formally stated the parties' agreement that Article 1 offences were minimum offences which States were free to sanction more broadly, in the absence of intention of gain, even where Article 1(a), (b) and (c) did not apply, or to punish other similar offences. Articles 24, 25, 26, 27, 28, and 32 were to apply to this Final Protocol.[224]

## UN ESCOR Ninth Session, 1949

The Social Commission Draft Convention was considered by UN ESCOR at its ninth session,[225] and again during discussions at the meetings of its own Social Committee,[226] held in 1949.[227] The Social Committee was exploratory and did no more than canvass members' views; it did not vote on amendments to the Social Commission Draft Convention provisions.[228]

Several issues concerning the Social Commission Draft Convention were raised by the representatives of various states. The USSR, Brazil and France saw a potential difficulty with Article 1, which could be seen as defining the elements of the offence too narrowly.[229]

France argued that Article 6 should be redrafted to include socio-medical records;[230] Belgium, the United Kingdom, and United States endorsed Article 6 in its original form, and Turkey considered that a reasonable transition period should be allowed before Article 6 came into effect.[231]

France also thought Article 17 required redrafting to emphasize re-education and adjustment to normal social life. The United Kingdom disagreed since, as its representative observed, different countries would adopt different measures under Article 17 and it would be better not to seek to define these too closely.[232]

The USSR representative suggested, with reference to Article 23, that an arbitrator selected by mutual agreement by the parties was preferable to resolution of disputes by the International Court of Justice.[233]

The representatives of Poland and the USSR considered, as far as Article 27 (the 'colonial clause') was concerned, that the instrument should apply automatically to territories that were not self-governing. The United Kingdom and France disagreed on the basis that this was impracticable; the clause should be retained.[234]

The Social Committee, having discussed these matters, approved the recommendation made by the Social Commission to submit the Social Commission Draft Convention to UN GAOR.[235]

UN ESCOR passed a resolution at its ninth session,[236] submitting the Social Commission Draft Convention to UN GAOR with the recommendation that an international convention be concluded on the basis of the current draft.[237] The resolution set out the matters UN ESCOR considered necessary to be stated and taken into account. It was to the effect that UN ESCOR had considered the instruments then in force along with the 1947 and 1948 resolutions to resume study of the Second Draft Convention, and to update, improve and consolidate all instruments, and that having considered the Social Commission Draft Convention submitted after the fourth session of the Social Commission, it recommended conclusion of an international convention 'on the basis of the proposed draft, taking into account the views expressed at the ninth session of the Council' and submitted the Social Commission Draft Convention, along with the record of Council proceedings, to the UN GAOR with the request that member governments and parties to the various instruments be informed of the recommendation.[238]

The UN ESCOR resolution, along with the Social Commission Draft Convention, was submitted to UN GAOR in its fourth regular session, then referred by UN GAOR to the Third Committee.[239]

## Third Committee Meetings, 1949

The Third Committee considered the Social Commission Draft Convention during meetings 237 to 269, held between 30 September and 28 November 1949. At meetings 237 to 248, held between 30 September and 12 October 1949, Articles 1 to 6, 14, 15, 17, 18, and 21 to 24 were considered along with the preamble and the Final Protocol.[240]

At meeting 238 the Third Committee resolved to delete certain paragraphs in Article 1 concerning the purposes of gain.[241]

The revised text was adopted by twenty-five votes to five with two abstentions. At meeting 248 a vote to delete Article 27 was carried (25:19 with four abstentions). In addition, a proposal from Ukraine was adopted by a roll call vote (23:22 with five abstentions). That proposal was to delete the phrase in Article 24 relating to trust territories and the meaning of the word 'State', and replace them with words to the effect that 'State' in the present convention, which included members and invited non-members, was to include 'all the colonies and trust territories of a State signatory to or accepting the convention, and all other territories for which such State is internationally responsible.'[242]

Articles 8 to 10, 12, 25, 26, and 28 to 32 were of precise legal import, so any amendments could be substantive and have unforseen legal implications.[243] The Third Committee therefore requested the Sixth Committee to consider these and make recommendations, and to advise in particular upon the legal effects of deleting or retaining the phrase 'subject to the requirements of domestic law' in Articles 4, 7, 16, 19, and 20.[244]

The Sixth Committee duly considered these matters at its meetings during 1949[245] and offered its conclusions in a memorandum from the Chairman.[246] It was of the opinion that the phrase under consideration had an indeterminate meaning that was subject to interpretation. The best course of action would therefore be to replace that wording with the phrase 'to the extent permitted by domestic law' as the qualifier of obligations in Articles 3, 4, 7, and 16, and the phrase 'in accordance with the conditions laid down by domestic law' as the better qualifier in Articles 19 and 20.[247]

The Sixth Committee recommended deletion of Article 10 in its entirety.[248] The reason was that many countries recognized only territorial jurisdiction, or jurisdiction based on the nationality of the offender, for criminal offences.[249] The Sixth Committee made a number of other suggestions including replacement of the words 'country or territory' with the word 'State', since deletion of Article 27 by the Third Committee had removed the reason for use of that phrase.[250] In addition, it thought provision of a definition of the term 'prostitution' was desirable, and it recommended deletion of Articles 26 and 32.[251] All recommendations made by the Sixth Committee were examined and approved[252] at meetings 268 and 269 of the Third Committee.[253]

When the Third Committee met on 28 November 1949 for its 269th meeting, it voted (34:0 with eight abstentions) to adopt the revised version of the Social Commission Draft Convention (Third Committee Draft Convention) and sent it in its entirety for approval to the UN GAOR.[254] That Third Committee Draft Convention was duly sent and considered on 2 December 1949 by UN GAOR at plenary meetings 263 and 264, with representatives from ten countries participating. They were Belgium, Egypt, France, India, Pakistan, Poland, Sweden, Ukrainian SSR, USSR, and the United Kingdom.[255]

During the discussion the United Kingdom delegation submitted five amendments to the Third Committee Draft Convention. The first concerned addition to Article 1 of the paragraphs previously deleted by the Third Committee. The objection to deletion of the reference to purpose of gain was based on the argument that this widened the scope of offence, and thus the instrument, and could lead to various legal anomalies. The wording was now vague and unsatisfactory; but could be remedied by restoring the definition of procuration by including 'for the purposes of gain' in the clause. The Swedish delegation agreed with the United Kingdom's position. India and Pakistan disagreed, saying the primary aim was to safeguard human dignity and worth, and provide an avenue for progress in dealing with the social evil of prostitution and its associated activities.[256] On this basis, the instrument should not be narrowed in its scope; it was preferable that the legal systems in jurisdictions that tolerated prostitution and associated activities for traditional reasons should be brought within the purview of the instrument standards.[257] On a vote the United Kingdom's proposed amendment was rejected (14:24 with nine abstentions).[258]

The United Kingdom also proposed deletion of the final paragraph of Article 23[259] concerning signature and ratification of the instrument.[260] It argued for reinstatement of the text deleted by the Third Committee. UN GAOR considered this second United Kingdom proposal along with its third, to amend by including a new Article 24A that had the effect of reintroducing Article 27, as deleted by the Third Committee. It would read:

Any party to this convention may, at the time of ratification or of accession or at any time thereafter, declare by notification addressed to the Secretary-General of the United Nations that the present convention shall extend to all or any of the territories for the international relations of which it is responsible. This convention shall extend to the territory named in the notification as from the ninetieth day after the day of receipt by the Secretary-General of the United Nations of such notification.

Each party to this convention agrees to take as soon as possible the necessary steps to extend the application of this convention to such territories, subject, where necessary for constitutional reasons, to the consent of the governments of such territories.

The Secretary-General of the United Nations shall communicate the present Convention to the States referred to in Article 23 for transmission to the responsible authorities of (a) any non-self-governing territory administered by them; (b) any trust territory administered by them; (c) any other non-metropolitan territory for the international relations of which they are responsible.[261]

The United Kingdom's representative explained the intention in moving the amendment to Article 23 (its second proposal) as being to restore the text to its form prior to amendment by a slim majority (one vote) in the Third Committee, and its third proposal as designed to reintroduce the text of Article 27 as it originally stood.[262] In this the United Kingdom had support from France and Belgium, whose delegates said that they could not concede that the instrument should automatically apply to non-self-governing and trust territories, for constitutional reasons. This argument was opposed by India, Pakistan, Poland and the Ukrainian SSR, whose delegates argued for automatic application to dependent territories, including colonies, because colonial powers had responsibility for progress in their dependencies. In the end, both the second and third amendments proposed by the

United Kingdom were rejected by roll call votes (the second, 14:33 with four abstentions and the third 14:34 with three abstentions). The United Kingdom thereupon withdrew the fourth and fifth proposed amendments, since both were consequential upon adoption of the proposed Article 24A.[263]

Article 6 also generated some differences of opinion. That article provided that States were to abolish laws and regulations for the registration of prostitutes. France saw immense difficulties in attempting to effect such wide-ranging changes all at once, rather than gradually undoing a problem by adapting an old society to new conditions of life. Its delegation accordingly argued for temporary medical supervision of prostitutes as a transitional measure.[264] India was determined not to grant prostitution any kind of legal status, and its representative argued that medical examinations necessarily involved medical registration, and in so doing, tacitly legitimized prostitution.[265]

Finally, the UK amendments having been dealt with (defeated or withdrawn), at the 264th plenary meeting of the UN GAOR on 2 December 1949, the vote was called.[266] The President put the text to the vote by roll-call.[267] The Convention for the Suppression of the Traffic in Persons and of the Exploitation of the Prostitution of Others was adopted by thirty-five votes to two, with fifteen abstentions.[268]

## CONVENTION FOR THE SUPPRESSION OF THE TRAFFIC IN PERSONS AND OF THE EXPLOITATION OF THE PROSTITUTION OF OTHERS, 1949

The Convention for the Suppression of the Traffic in Persons and of the Exploitation of the Prostitution of Others, 1949 (Convention of 1949) was premised on the recognition that trafficking in human beings for the purpose of prostitution was incompatible with human dignity and the worth of the person.[269] It endangered individual, family and community welfare alike.[270] The Convention of 1949 consolidated and unified the instruments that preceded it (the Agreement of 1904, the Conventions of 1910, 1921, and 1933) and encapsulated the tenor of the principles of the Second Draft Convention.

The provisions were minimum requirements, rather than constraining States from making even stronger legislative provisions concerning human trafficking and exploitation for the purposes of prostitution.[271]

## Summary of Provisions of Convention of 1949

The measures contained in the Convention of 1949 are summarized below.

### Article 1

The elements of the offence were defined independently of consent, and were stated in terms of procuring, enticing or leading away any person for the purposes of prostitution to gratify the passions of another.[272]

Article 1 also introduced criminal sanctions which applied to any person who 'exploited the prostitution of another person', even with their consent, for gratification of the passions of another person.[273]

### Article 2

Article 2 required signatories to sanction (1) keeping or managing or knowingly financing or agreeing to take part in the financing of a brothel; (2) knowingly letting or renting a building, part of a building or other place for the purpose of the prostitution of others.[274]

### Article 3

Attempts and preparatory acts were also punishable, to the extent permitted by domestic law.[275]

### Article 4

Intentional participation in relation to Articles 1 and 2 were punishable, to the extent permitted by domestic law.[276]

## Article 5

Article 5 obliged States to ensure that where victims were entitled under local law to be parties to proceedings related to instrument offences, foreigners would also be entitled to be parties on the same terms and conditions.[277]

## Article 6

States undertook to take all necessary measures to repeal or abolish any law or administrative provision that subjected any person engaging in prostitution, or suspected of doing so, to special registration, document production or other exceptional requirements for supervision or notification.[278]

## Article 7

This provision related to previous convictions entered in foreign States for offences under the Convention of 1949.[279] States undertook, to the extent permitted by the law of their own jurisdictions, to take such previous convictions into account in establishing recidivism or disqualifying offenders from exercising civil rights.[280]

## Article 8

This article dealt with extradition. Under it, the offences defined in Articles 1 and 2 were to be regarded as extraditable offences pursuant to any extradition treaty in force between States. States that did not require the existence of a treaty in order to make extraditions undertook to recognize those offences as extraditable as between themselves. Extradition was to be granted in accordance with the law of the State requested to make an extradition.[281]

## Article 9

Article 9 provided that nationals who had committed the offences set out in Articles 1 or 2 while abroad, and had then returned to their own States, were to be prosecuted in and punished by the courts of their own States. In States that did not permit extradition of nationals, Article 9 would not apply if in a similar case between the States to the Convention of 1949 the extradition of an alien could not be granted.[282]

## Article 10

Article 9 would also not apply if the offender had been tried in a foreign State and served the sentence imposed (if convicted) or been granted remission or reduction under that jurisdiction's law.[283]

## Article 11

The instrument was not to be interpreted as determining a State's attitude towards the general operation of the limits of criminal jurisdiction under international law.[284]

## Article 12

This article specified that the Convention of 1949 had no effect on the principle that the offences to which it referred should be defined, prosecuted and punished according to the domestic laws applicable within each State.[285]

## Article 13

This article concerned transmission of letters of request.

Parties were obliged to execute letters of request relating to offences referred to in the Convention of 1949 in accordance with their domestic law and practice. Transmission between States was to be effected by direct communication between their judicial authorities, between their Ministers of Justice, or between another competent authority of the requesting State and the Minister of Justice of the State requested, or by way of request from the diplomatic or consular representative of a requesting State within the State to which the request was made, sent direct to the competent judicial authority or to the authority indicated by the government of the state to which the request was made, in which case papers constituting the execution of the letters of request were to be sent direct to the representative.

Dealings were to be at the highest level, and were, unless otherwise agreed, to be prepared in the language of the authority making the request, although the State requested letters could also require a translation in its own language, certified correct by the requesting authority.

Each Party was required to notify all the others of the transmission methods it was prepared to recognize, but until it had done so, its existing procedure for letters of request was to remain in force. Execution was not to give rise to any claim for reimbursement of charges or expenses other than expenses of experts. Further, no undertaking to adopt any provision contrary to the domestic criminal law within a jurisdiction in relation to form and methods of proof was to be construed from the wording of the Convention of 1949.[286]

## Article 14

States were required to establish or maintain services to co-ordinate and centralize data resulting from investigation of offences under the Convention of 1949. These agencies were to compile data to facilitate the preventive and punitive aspects of the Convention of 1949 and to liaise closely with their counterparts in other States.[287]

## Article 15

This article related to communication of information related to prior convictions and offences. Article 15 provided:

To the extent permitted by domestic law and to the extent to which the authorities responsible for the services referred to in Article 14 may judge desirable, they shall furnish to the authorities responsible for the corresponding services in other States the following information: (1) particulars of any offence referred to in the present Convention or any attempt to commit such offence; (2) particulars of any search for and any prosecution, arrest, conviction, refusal of admission or expulsion of persons guilty of any of the offences referred to in the present Convention, the movements of such persons and any other useful information with regard to them. The information so furnished shall include descriptions of the offenders, their fingerprints, photographs, methods of operation, police records and records of conviction.[288]

## Article 16

This provision obliged States, in relation to the offence set out in Article 1, to agree to take measures to prevent prostitution and encourage rehabilitation and social adjustment of victims of prostitution through public and private educational, health, social, economic and other related services.[289]

## Article 17

Article 17 related to the protection of emigrants. Under Article 17 parties undertook in connection with immigration and emigration to adopt or maintain whatever measures were required by the Convention of 1949 in order to check the traffic in persons of either sex for the purpose of prostitution.[290] The specific measures were:

(1) to make such regulations as are necessary for the protection of immigrants and emigrants, and in particular, women and children, both at the place of arrival and departure and while en route; (2) to arrange for appropriate publicity warning the public of the dangers of the aforesaid traffic; (3) to take appropriate measures to ensure supervision of railway stations, airports, seaports and en route, and of other public places, in order to prevent international traffic in persons for the purpose of prostitution; (4) to take appropriate measures in order that the appropriate authorities be informed of the arrival of persons who appear, prima facie, to be the principals and accomplices in or victim of such traffic.[291]

## Article 18

Under Article 18 parties undertook, subject to their local law, to take declarations from foreign prostitutes in order to establish their identity and civil status and establish the cause of their leaving their home State. The authorities in the state of origin were thereupon to be apprised of the situation with a view to their eventual repatriation.[292]

## Article 19

Under Article 19 parties undertook, subject to their local law, and without prejudice to other prosecutions:

(1) pending the completion of arrangements for the registration of destitute victims of international traffic in persons for the purpose of prostitution, to make suitable provisions for their temporary care and maintenance; (2) to repatriate persons referred to in Article 18 who desire to be repatriated or who may be claimed by persons exercising authority over them or whose expulsion is ordered in conformity with the law. Repatriation shall take place only after agreement is reached with the State of destination as to identity and nationality as well as to the place and date of arrival at frontiers. Each Party to the present Convention shall facilitate the passage of such persons through its territory.[293]

Where persons requiring repatriation were unable to meet the cost themselves, and had no spouse, relative, or guardian to pay for them, the State or residence was to bear the cost of repatriation as far as the nearest frontier or part of embarkation or airport, and the state of origin was to bear the cost of the remainder of the journey.[294]

## Article 20

Article 20 related to employment agencies. Article 20 obliged States to take necessary measures to supervise employment agencies in order to prevent persons seeking employment, in particular women and children, being exposed to the danger of prostitution.[295]

## Article 21

This provision required States to communicate to the Secretary-General of the United Nations any laws and regulations already promulgated within their own jurisdictions relating to the subjects of the Convention of 1949, and to similarly report, on an annual basis, any new laws, along with the measures taken by States concerning the application of the Convention of 1949.[296] The information 'was to be published by the Secretary-General of the United Nations and circulated among members of the United Nations and to non-member States to which the Convention of 1949 had been officially communicated pursuant to Article 23.[297]

## Article 22

Unresolved disputes between parties concerning the instrument's interpretation or application were to be referred to the International Court of Justice at the request of any disputing party.[298]

## Article 27

Each State that was a party to the Convention of 1949 undertook to adopt, in accordance with its constitution, all legislative or other measures necessary to ensure the application of the Convention of 1949 in its local jurisdiction.[299]

## Other Provisions

The remaining provisions concerned a range of matters: signature, ratification and accession,[300] entry into force,[301] denunciation,[302] obligation on the Secretary-General to inform States of certain information,[303] and termination of earlier instruments (the Agreement of 1904, Convention of 1910, Convention of 1921 and Convention of 1933).[304]

## Final Protocol

The Final Protocol stated that 'nothing in the present convention shall be deemed to prejudice any legislation which ensures, for the enforcement of the provisions for securing the suppression of the traffic in persons and the exploitation of others for the purposes of prostitution, stricter conditions than those provided by the present convention. The provisions of Articles 23 to 26 inclusive of the convention shall apply to the present Protocol'.[305]

## The Convention of 1949 and Trafficking of Children for the Sexual Exploitation of Prostitution

In this context, the provisions of the Convention of 1949 applied to female children of any race as well as to male children of any race.[306]

# Conclusion

## THE DEVELOPMENT OF INTERNATIONAL LAW, 1864–1950

The preceding chapters demonstrate that in the period 1864–1950, international law in relation to the trafficking of children for the sexual exploitation of prostitution developed progressively in five areas: (1) from being a gender-specific to a gender-neutral conceptualization; (2) from being a race-specific to a race-neutral conceptualization; (3) from no obligation upon States to a criminalize the offence to such an enjoined obligation; (4) from a minimal description of the act of trafficking to a broader description of the act of trafficking; and (5) from an implicit connection between the act of trafficking and the exploitative end purpose of prostitution to an express statement of this connection.[1]

### Gender

The Agreement of 1904 conceptualized trafficking in a gender-specific manner. Use of the phrase 'women and girls underage'[2] in the preamble, and thereafter the phrase 'women and girls'[3] in the provisions of the treaty excluded application of the Agreement of 1904 to male children.[4] The Convention of 1910 continued this exclusionary framework, based on such gender-specific conceptualization,[5] and also adopted the analogous phrase 'woman or girl underage' with linguistic variations.[6] It was not until 1921 that international law developed an inclusive character. That arose with the conclusion of the Convention of 1921, which replaced the earlier terminology with 'children of both sexes'[7] and 'children'[8] in its provisions so that the measures set out therein now also applied to male children.[9] The Convention of 1933, as Chapter 3 details, which historically in part emerged from a background of concern about the problem of the traffic in girls who were being trafficked by traffickers who presented them as being overage by the use of false birth certificates and passports, was gender-specific.[10] In 1949, as Chapter 4 details, the Agreement of 1904 and the Conventions of 1910, 1921, and 1933 were consolidated by the conclusion of the Convention of 1949. The term 'person' was used throughout the treaty along with the term 'children'[11] and the phrase 'traffic in persons of either sex',[12] which together ensured that any gender discrimination was eliminated.[13]

## Race

The Agreement of 1904 used the phrases 'White Slave Traffic',[14] 'criminal traffic known as the White Slave Traffic',[15] and 'criminal traffic',[16] thereby suggesting exclusion of its measures from application to children of races other than whites.[17] The Convention of 1910 continued this discriminatory framework with its use of the phrases 'White Slave Traffic'[18] and 'traffic known as the White Slave Traffic'.[19] International law in this area developed with the Convention of 1921, which in accordance with Recommendation 13 of the Conference of 1921 abolished the phrase 'White Slave Traffic' and replaced it with the phrase 'traffic in women and children'. Thus, by 1921 the race discriminatory character of the instruments had ended, and children of all races were afforded protection.[20] This remained the norm thereafter. The Convention of 1933 used the phrases 'traffic in women of full age'[21] and 'traffic in women and children'[22] and the Convention of 1949 used the phrases 'traffic in persons'[23] and 'traffic in women and children'.[24]

## Legislative Measures

The Agreement of 1904, as detailed in Chapter 1, obliged States to undertake certain measures, notably, the establishment of a central authority;[25] watching of ports and railway stations;[26] repatriation of prostitutes;[27] and supervision of employment agencies.[28] It was not until 1910 that international law in this area began to develop. The Convention of 1910 obliged States in Article 1 to punish traffickers.

Whoever, in order to gratify the passions of another person, has procured, enticed, or led away, even with her consent, a woman or girl underage, for immoral purposes, shall be punished, notwithstanding that the various acts constituting the offence may have been committed in different countries.[29]

The year 1921 saw further developments. The Convention of 1921 obliged States first, 'to take all measures to discover and prosecute persons engaged in the traffic of children of both sexes and who committed offences within the meaning of Article 1 of the Convention of 1910',[30] and second, 'to take the necessary steps to secure the punishment of attempts to commit the offence and, within legal limits, acts preparatory to the commission of the offence, as set out in Article 1 of the Convention of 1910'.[31]

In 1933 the offence of trafficking set out in Article 1 of the Convention of 1910 and extended by the Convention of 1921 was further modified by the Convention of 1933. First, there was substitution of the phrase 'woman or girl underage' by the phrase 'woman or girl of full age'. Second, there was inclusion of the phrase 'to be carried out in another country'. Third, the term 'country' was for the first time defined. Punishment for attempted offences and preparatory acts (as established by the Convention of 1921 to apply to the offence in Article 1 of the Convention of 1910) was retained by the Convention of 1933 in these terms:

Whoever in order to gratify the passions of another person, has procured, enticed or led away even with her consent, a woman or girl of full age for immoral purposes to be carried out in another country, shall be punished, notwithstanding that the various acts constituting the offence may have been committed in different countries. Attempted offences, and, within legal limits, acts preparatory to the offences in question, shall also be punishable. For the purposes of the present Article, the term 'country' includes the colonies and protectorates of the High Contracting Party concerned, as well as territories under his suzerainty and territories for which a mandate has been entrusted to him.[32]

The Convention of 1949 developed international law in this area even further. The offence depicted in the Convention of 1933 was modified and a number of new offences adopted. The modifications were:

The phrase 'woman or girl' was replaced with the phrase 'another person.

The phrase 'immoral purposes' was replaced with the phrase 'purposes of prostitution'.

The phrase 'to be carried out in another country' was removed.

The definition of the term 'country' was removed.

The phrase 'notwithstanding that the various acts constituting the offence may have been committed in different countries' was removed.

Thus, the offence first introduced in 1910 now in 1950 read:

The Parties to the present Convention agree to punish any person who, to gratify the passions of another, procures, entices or leads away, for the purposes of prostitution, another person, even with the consent of that person.[33]

In relation to the new offences, these were:

punishment of 'any person who, to gratify the passions of another, exploited the prostitution of another person even with the consent of that person';[34]

punishment of 'any person who kept or managed, or knowingly financed or took part in the financing of a brothel';[35] and

punishment of 'any person who knowingly let or rented a building or other place, or any part thereof, for the purpose of the prostitution of others'.[36]

To the extent permitted by domestic law, attempts to commit any of these new offences and acts preparatory to their commission also required punishment,[37] as did intentional participation.[38]

## Description of the Act of Trafficking

The Agreement of 1904 described the act of trafficking as 'procuring'.[39] The only change during the period 1864–1950 came in 1910, when the Convention of 1910 provided new elements—'procured, enticed or lead away even with her consent'.[40] This description remained unchanged in the Conventions of 1921, 1933, and 1949.

## CONNECTION BETWEEN THE ACT OF TRAFFICKING AND THE EXPLOITATIVE END PURPOSE OF PROSTITUTION

International law in this area developed slowly. The Agreement of 1904 provided only an implicit connection between the act of trafficking and the exploitative end purpose of prostitution when it used the phrases 'immoral purposes'[41] and 'immoral life'[42] and the term 'prostitutes'[43] in its provisions.[44] The Convention of 1910 continued this implicit connection, also employing the phrases 'immoral purposes'[45] and 'immoral life',[46] as did the Convention of 1921.[47] Even as late as 1933 this implicit connection between the act of trafficking and the exploitative end purpose of prostitution was discernible only in the way provisions were framed: the Convention of 1933, like its predecessors, used the phrase 'immoral purposes'.[48] It was not until some forty-five years later, upon the conclusion of the Convention of 1949, that international law in this area developed. Thus, it marked a conceptual departure when the Convention of 1949 adopted the phrases 'for the purpose of prostitution',[49] 'for purposes of prostitution'[50] and 'for the purpose of the prostitution of others',[51] thereby providing an explicit, express, and direct connection between the act of trafficking and the exploitative end purpose of prostitution.[52]

# Endnotes

## CHAPTER 1

1. Advisory Committee on the Traffic of Women and Protection of Children, . *Report on the Fourth Session, Reply of the British Government to Questionnaire on the Subject of Licensed Houses*, LON Assembly, 4th sess., Annex IV, [23], LON Doc. A.22.1925.IV (1925).

2. Ibid.

3. Ibid.

4. Ibid.

5. Advisory Committee on the Traffic of Women and Protection of Children, *Report on the Fourth Session, Reply of the British Government to Questionnaire on the Subject of Licensed Houses*, LON Assembly, 4th sess., Annex IV, [23], LON Doc. A.22.1925.IV (1925).

6. Ibid.

7. Ibid.

8. Ibid.

9. Advisory Committee on the Traffic of Women and Protection of Children, *Report on the Fourth Session, Reply of the British Government to Questionnaire on the Subject of Licensed Houses*, LON Assembly, 4th sess., Annex IV, [23], LON Doc. A.22.1925.IV (1925).

10. Ibid.

11. Advisory Committee on the Traffic of Women and Protection of Children, *Report on the Fourth Session, Reply of the British Government to Questionnaire on the Subject of Licensed Houses*, LON Assembly, 4th sess., Annex IV, [24], LON Doc. A.22.1925.IV (1925).

12. Ibid.

13. Ibid.

14. Ibid.

15. Advisory Committee on the Traffic of Women and Protection of Children, *Report on the Fourth Session, Reply of the British Government to Questionnaire on*

the *Subject of Licensed Houses*, LON Assembly, 4th sess., Annex IV, [24], LON Doc. A.22.1925.IV (1925).

16. Ibid.

17. Ibid.

18. Ibid.

19. Advisory Committee on the Traffic of Women and Protection of Children, *Report on the Fourth Session, Reply of the British Government to Questionnaire on the Subject of Licensed Houses*, LON Assembly, 4th sess., Annex IV, [24–25], LON Doc. A.22.1925.IV (1925).

20. Advisory Committee on the Traffic of Women and Protection of Children, *Report on the Fourth Session, Reply of the British Government to Questionnaire on the Subject of Licensed Houses*, LON Assembly, 4th sess., Annex IV, [25], LON Doc. A.22.1925.IV (1925).

21. Ibid.

22. Ibid.

23. Advisory Committee on the Traffic of Women and Protection of Children, *Report on the Fourth Session, Reply of the British Government to Questionnaire on the Subject of Licensed Houses*, LON Assembly, 4th sess., Annex IV, [25], LON Doc. A.22.1925.IV (1925).

24. Ibid.

25. Ibid.

26. Advisory Committee on Social Questions, *Prevention of Prostitution: A Study of Measures Adopted or Under Construction Particularly with Regard to Minors*, LON Council, [9], LON Doc. C.26.M.26.1943.IV (1943).

27. Advisory Committee on the Traffic of Women and Protection of Children, *Report on the Fourth Session, Reply of the British Government to Questionnaire on the Subject of Licensed Houses*, LON Assembly, 4th sess., Annex IV, [25], LON Doc. A.22.1925.IV (1925): the 1870 agitation had prompted the government of the day to appoint a Royal Commission to enquire into the administration and operation of the Contagious Diseases Acts. The Commission reported in 1871. Its findings were not unanimous. The majority recommended discontinuance of the periodical examination of prostitutes. It also advised reinstatement of the provisions of the principle of the Act of 1864 relating to detention of women infected with disease. A further recommendation was to the effect that as long as proper hospital accommodation was provided, the system should be extended upon request to any place in the United Kingdom (except London and Westminster). It should in any event be extended to the Metropolis, at least in part. The report languished unimplemented. Another select committee of the House of Commons, established in 1879, reported in 1882. It recommended against the repeal of the Contagious Diseases Acts, by an 8:5 majority. In 1883 a solid majority

of the House passed a motion of disapproval of the compulsory examination of women under the Contagious Diseases Acts, making administration of the Contagious Diseases Acts difficult to carry out. Ultimately, the Acts were repealed in 1886.

28. Ibid. The name of the association was the Ladies National Association. See, Kathleen Barry, *Female Sexual Slavery,* (New York University Press: New York, 1979), p. 16.

29. Ibid. Advisory Committee on Social Questions, *Prevention of Prostitution: A Study of Measures Adopted or Under Construction Particularly with Regard to Minors,* LON Council, [9], LON Doc. C.26.M.26.1943.IV (1943).

30. Advisory Committee on the Traffic of Women and Protection of Children, *Report on the Fourth Session, Reply of the British Government to Questionnaire on the Subject of Licensed Houses,* LON Assembly, 4th sess., Annex IV, [25], LON Doc. A.22.1925.IV (1925).

31. *Report of the Special Body of Experts on Traffic in Women and Children, Part One,* LON Council, [6], LON Doc. C.52.M.52.1927.IV (1927).

32. Advisory Committee on the Traffic of Women and Protection of Children, *Report on the Fourth Session, Reply of the British Government to Questionnaire on the Subject of Licensed Houses,* LON Assembly, 4th sess., Annex IV, [25], LON Doc. A.22.1925.IV (1925); *Report of the Special Body of Experts on Traffic in Women and Children, Part One,* LON Council, [6], LON Doc. C.52.M.52.1927. IV (1927).

33. *Report of the Special Body of Experts on Traffic in Women and Children, Part One,* LON Council, [7], LON Doc. C.52.M.52.1927.IV (1927).

34. Jonathan S. Ignarski, 'Traffic in Persons', in R. Bernhardt (ed.), *Encyclopaedia of Public International Law,* Volume 4, (North-Holland: Amsterdam/New York, 2000), p. 893.

35. *Report of the Special Body of Experts on Traffic in Women and Children, Part One,* LON Council, [7], LON Doc. C.52.M.52.1927.IV (1927).

36. Ibid. Advisory Committee on the Traffic of Women and Protection of Children, *Report on the Fourth Session, Reply of the British Government to Questionnaire on the Subject of Licensed Houses,* LON Assembly, [26], LON Doc. A.22.1925.IV (1925).

37. *Report of the Special Body of Experts on Traffic in Women and Children, Part One,* LON Council, [7], LON Doc. C.52.M.52.1927.IV (1927).

38. Kathleen Barry, *Female Sexual Slavery,* (New York University Press: New York, 1979), p. 24.

39. *Report of the Special Body of Experts on Traffic in Women and Children, Part One,* LON Council, [7], LON Doc. C.52.M.52.1927.IV (1927).

40. Ibid.

41. *Official Records of the International Conference on Women and Children*, LON Council, 4th plen. mtg, [68], LON Doc. C.484.M.339.1921.IV (1921).

42. Ibid.

43. Ibid.

44. Ibid.

45. *Official Records of the International Conference on Women and Children*, LON Council, 4th plen. mtg, [68], LON Doc. C.484.M.339.1921.IV (1921).

46. Ibid.

47. *Report of the Special Body of Experts on Traffic in Women and Children, Part One*, LON Council, [7], LON Doc. C.52.M.52.1927.IV (1927).

48. Ibid.

49. Advisory Committee on Social Questions, *Prevention of Prostitution, A Study of Measures Adopted or Under Construction Particularly with Regard to Minors*, LON Council, [10], LON Doc. C.26.M.26.1943.IV (1943).

50. Advisory Committee on Traffic in Women and Children, *Preparatory Documents, Federation of National Union for the Protection of Girls Report on Its Activities*, LON Council, 1st sess., [8], LON Doc. C.365.M.216.1922.IV (1922).

51. Ibid. The International Union of the Girls' Friendly Society became the Federation of the National Unions of Girls' Friendly Society in 1921.

52. Advisory Committee on Traffic in Women and Children, *Preparatory Documents, Jewish Association for the Protection of Girls Report to the League of Nations Advisory Committee on the Suppression of the Traffic in Women and Children*, LON Council, 1st sess., [9], LON Doc. C.365.M.216.1922.IV (1922).

53. Ibid.

54. Official Records of the International Conference on Women and Children, *Report of the International Bureau for the Suppression of the White Slave Traffic and the International Traffic in Women*, LON Council, 1st plen. mtg, [13], LON Doc. C.484.M.339.1921.IV (1921).

55. Advisory Committee on Traffic in Women and Children, *Preparatory Documents, International Catholic Association for the Protection of Girls Report to the Association*, LON Council, 1st sess., [14], LON Doc. C.365.M.216.1922.IV (1922).

56. Advisory Committee on Social Questions, *Prevention of Prostitution, A Study of Measures Adopted or Under Construction Particularly with Regard to Minors*, LON Council, [10], LON Doc. C.26.M.26.1943.IV (1943).

57. Official Records of the International Conference on Women and Children, *Opening Speech by the President*, LON Council, 1st plen. mtg, [7–8], LON Doc. C.484.M.339.1921.IV (1921).

58. Official Records of the International Conference on Women and Children, *Opening Speech by the President*, LON Council, 1st plen. mtg, [8], LON Doc. C.484.M.339.1921.IV (1921).

59. Advisory Committee on Traffic in Women and Children, *Preparatory Documents, International Bureau for the Suppression of the Traffic in Women and Children*, LON Council, 1st sess., [16], LON Doc. C.365.M.216.1922.IV (1922).

60. *Report of the Special Body of Experts on Traffic in Women and Children, Part One*, LON Council, [7], LON Doc. C.52.M.52.1927.IV (1927); Official Records of the International Conference on Women and Children, *Standing Advisory Committee Motion by Mr Harris (Great Britain)*, LON Council, 2nd plen. mtg, [26], LON Doc. C.484.M.339.1921.IV (1921).

61. Official Records of the International Conference on Women and Children, *Report of the International Bureau for the Suppression of the White Slave Traffic and the International Traffic in Women*, LON Council, 1st plen. mtg, [13], LON Doc. C.484.M.339.1921.IV (1921).

62. Ibid.

63. Ibid.

64. Ibid.

65. Official Records of the International Conference on Women and Children, *Report of the International Bureau for the Suppression of the White Slave Traffic and the International Traffic in Women*, LON Council, 1st plen. mtg, [13], LON Doc. C.484.M.339.1921.IV (1921).

66. The International Bureau was known as the International Bureau for the Suppression of the White Slave Traffic: Memorandum by the Secretary General, *The Suppression of the White Slave Traffic in Women and Children*, LON Assembly, LON Doc. [A].20/48/8.IV] (1920). The International Bureau was also referred to as the International Bureau for the Suppression of the Traffic in Women and Children: Memorandum by the Secretary General, *The Suppression of the White Slave Traffic in Women and Children*, LON Assembly, LON Doc. [A].20/48/8.IV] (1920); Advisory Committee on Traffic in Women and Children, *Preparatory Documents, International Bureau for the Suppression of the Traffic in Women and Children*, LON Council, 1st sess., [16], LON Doc. C.365.M.216.1922.IV (1922); Report by the Delegate of Roumania, *Note on International Measures to be Taken for the Suppression of Traffic in Women and Children*, LON Assembly, [2], LON Doc. [A.20/48/225(a).IV] (1920). The International Bureau was also referred to as the International Bureau for the Suppression of the White Slave Traffic and the International Traffic in Women, *Note by the Secretary-General*, LON Council, LON Doc. C.473.M.348.1921.IV (1921).

67. Official Records of the International Conference on Women and Children, *Report of the International Bureau for the Suppression of the White Slave Traffic and the International Traffic in Women*, LON Council, 1st plen. mtg, [13], LON Doc. C.484.M.339.1921.IV (1921); Advisory Committee on Traffic in Women and Children, *Preparatory Documents, International Bureau for the Suppression of the Traffic in Women and Children*, LON Council, 1st sess., [16],

LON Doc. C.365.M.216.1922.IV (1922); Report by the Delegate of Roumania, *Note on International Measures to be taken for the Suppression of Traffic in Women and Children*, LON Assembly, [2], LON Doc. [A.20/48/225(a).IV] (1920); Memorandum by the Secretary-General, *The Suppression of the White Slave Traffic in Women and Children*, LON Assembly, LON Doc. [A].20/48/8.[IV] (1920); International Conference on Traffic in Women and Children, *General Report on the Work of the Conference*, LON Council, [2], LON Doc. C.227.M.166.1921.IV (1921).

68. Official Records of the International Conference on Women and Children, *Opening Speech by the President*, LON Council, 1st plen. mtg, [8], LON Doc. C.484.M.339.1921.IV (1921).

69. Advisory Committee on Traffic in Women and Children, *Preparatory Documents, International Bureau for the Suppression of the Traffic in Women and Children*, LON Council, 1st sess., [16], LON Doc. C.365.M.216.1922.IV (1922); Official Records of the International Conference on Women and Children, *Opening Speech by the President*, LON Council, 1st plen. mtg, [8], LON Doc. C.484.M.339.1921.IV (1921); Official Records of the International Conference on Women and Children, *Report of the International Bureau for the Suppression of the White Slave Traffic and the International Traffic in Women*, LON Council, 1st plen. mtg, [13], LON Doc. C.484.M.339.1921.IV (1921).

70. Ibid. This document states the meeting occurred in May 1902; Official Records of the International Conference on Women and Children, *Standing Advisory Committee Motion by Mr Harris (Great Britain)*, LON Council, 2nd plen. mtg, [27], LON Doc. C.484.M.339.1921.IV (1921) states the meeting was in 1902; *International Convention for the Suppression of the White Slave Traffic*, opened for signature 4 May 1910, 8 LNTS 278, preamble (entered into force 5 July 1920) states the meeting occurred from 15 to 25 July 1902; Cf, Report by the Delegate of Roumania, *Note on International Measures to be taken for the Suppression of Traffic in Women and Children*, LON Assembly, [2], LON Doc. [A.20/48/225(a).IV] (1920) which states that the conference was in 1904 and the purpose was to draw up an agreement and a proposal for a convention; only the agreement was signed.

71. Advisory Committee on Traffic in Women and Children, *Preparatory Documents*, LON Council, 1st sess., [16], LON Doc. C.365.M.216.1922.IV (1922); Official Records of the International Conference on Women and Children, *Report of the International Bureau for the Suppression of the White Slave Traffic and the International Traffic in Women*, LON Council, 1st plen. mtg, [13], LON Doc. C.484.M.339.1921.IV (1921).

72. *International Agreement for the Suppression of the White Slave Traffic*, opened for signature 18 May 1904, 1 LNTS 83, preamble (entered into force 18 July 1905).

73. The other objective was to secure to women of full age who had suffered abuse or compulsion effective protection against the criminal traffic known as the White Slave Traffic, *International Agreement for the Suppression of the White Slave Traffic*, opened for signature 18 May 1904, 1 LNTS 83, preamble (entered into force 18 July 1905).

74. *Report of the Special Body of Experts on Traffic in Women and Children, Part One*, LON Council, [36], LON Doc. C.52.M.52.1927.IV (1927).

75. Ibid.

76. International Agreement for the Suppression of the White Slave Traffic, opened for signature 18 May 1904, 1 LNTS 83, Article 1 (entered into force 18 July 1905).

77. *Report of the Special Body of Experts on Traffic in Women and Children, Part One*, LON Council, [37], LON Doc. C.52.M.52.1927.IV (1927).

78. International Agreement for the Suppression of the White Slave Traffic, opened for signature 18 May 1904, 1 LNTS 83, Article 2 (entered into force 18 July 1905).

79. Ibid. Included were immigration officers and other such officials, along with, at least in some countries, agents of voluntary societies. Officials relied on these agents for information and assistance. In some jurisdictions railway officials were briefed and assigned the task of detection of trafficking-related activities at transport hubs: *Report of the Special Body of Experts on Traffic in Women and Children Part One*, LON Council, [37], LON Doc. C.52.M.52.1927. IV (1927).

80. Ibid.

81. Ibid.

82. *International Agreement for the Suppression of the White Slave Traffic*, opened for signature 18 May 1904, 1 LNTS 83, Article 3 (entered into force 18 July 1905).

83. Ibid.

84. Ibid.

85. *International Agreement for the Suppression of the White Slave Traffic*, opened for signature 18 May 1904, 1 LNTS 83, Article 4 (entered into force 18 July 1905).

86. *International Agreement for the Suppression of the White Slave Traffic*, opened for signature 18 May 1904, 1 LNTS 83, Article 5 (entered into force 18 July 1905).

87. *Report of the Special Body of Experts on Traffic in Women and Children, Part One*, LON Council, [37], LON Doc. C.52.M.52.1927.IV (1927).

88. *International Agreement for the Suppression of the White Slave Traffic*, opened for signature 18 May 1904, 1 LNTS 83, Article 6 (entered into force 18 July 1905).

89. *International Agreement for the Suppression of the White Slave Traffic*, opened for signature 18 May 1904, 1 LNTS 83, Article 7 (entered into force 18 July 1905).

90. *International Agreement for the Suppression of the White Slave Traffic*, opened for signature 18 May 1904, 1 LNTS 83, Article 8 (entered into force 18 July 1905).

91. Ibid.

92. *International Agreement for the Suppression of the White Slave Traffic*, opened for signature 18 May 1904, 1 LNTS 83, Article 9 (entered into force 18 July 1905).

93. *International Agreement for the Suppression of the White Slave Traffic*, opened for signature 18 May 1904, 1 LNTS 83, Proces–Verbal de Signature arts 1–3 (entered into force 18 July 1905).

94. Tom Obokata, *Trafficking of Human Beings from a Human Rights Perspective: Towards a Holistic Approach*, (Martinus Nijhoff: Netherlands, 2006), p. 13.

95. Advisory Committee on Traffic in Women and Children, *Preparatory Documents, International Bureau for the Suppression of the Traffic in Women and Children*, LON Council, 1st sess., [16], LON Doc. C.365.M.216.1922.IV (1922); Official Records of the International Conference on Women and Children, *Report of the International Bureau for the Suppression of the White Slave Traffic and the International Traffic in Women*, LON Council, 1st plen. mtg, [14], LON Doc. C.484.M.339.1921.IV (1921).

96. Advisory Committee on Traffic in Women and Children, *Preparatory Documents, International Bureau for the Suppression of the Traffic in Women and Children*, LON Council, 1st sess., [16], LON Doc. C.365.M.216.1922.IV (1922).

97. Ibid.

98. Advisory Committee on Traffic in Women and Children, *Preparatory Documents, International Bureau for the Suppression of the Traffic in Women and Children*, LON Council, 1st sess., [16–17], LON Doc. C.365.M.216.1922. IV (1922); Official Records of the International Conference on Women and Children, *Report of the International Bureau for the Suppression of the White Slave Traffic and the International Traffic in Women*, LON Council, 1st plen. mtg, [14], LON Doc. C.484.M.339.1921.IV (1921).

99. Report by the Delegate of Roumania, *Note on International Measures to be taken for the Suppression of Traffic in Women and Children*, LON Assembly, [2], LON Doc. [A.20/48/225(a).IV] (1920).

100. Radhika Coomaraswamy, Report of the Special Rapportuer on Violence against Women, Its Causes and Consequences on Trafficking in Women, Women's Migration and Violence against Women, UN ESCOR, [Para 18], UN Doc. E/CN.4. 2000/68 (2000).

101. Advisory Committee on Traffic in Women and Children, *Preparatory Documents, International Bureau for the Suppression of the Traffic in Women and Children*, LON Council, 1st sess., [17], LON Doc. C.365.M.216.1922.IV (1922). In September 1904 the International Bureau conducted a conference at Zurich in preparation for the Paris Congress: Official Records of the International Conference on Women and Children, *Report of the International Bureau for the Suppression of the White Slave Traffic and the International Traffic in Women*, LON Council, 1st plen. mtg, [15], LON Doc. C.484.M.339.1921.IV (1921).

102. *International Convention for the Suppression of the White Slave Traffic*, opened for signature 4 May 1910, 8 LNTS 278, (entered into force 5 July 1920).

103. *International Convention for the Suppression of the White Slave Traffic*, opened for signature 4 May 1910, 8 LNTS 278, preamble (entered into force 5 July 1920).

104. *International Convention for the Suppression of the White Slave Traffic*, opened for signature 4 May 1910, 8 LNTS 278, Final Protocol, para A (entered into force 5 July 1920). The Final Protocol interpreted Articles 1, 2, and 3 of this Convention. States exercising legislative sovereignty were to provide for the execution of the stipulations agreed upon, or for their extension, in the manner described: *International Convention for the Suppression of the White Slave Traffic*, opened for signature 4 May 1910, 8 LNTS 278, Final Protocol, preamble (entered into force 5 July 1920). The Final Protocol and the Convention were considered to be one piece; the Protocol had the same force, validity and duration as the Convention: *International Convention for the Suppression of the White Slave Traffic*, opened for signature 4 May 1910, 8 LNTS 278, Final Protocol, (entered into force 5 July 1920); *International Convention for the Suppression of the White Slave Traffic*, opened for signature 4 May 1910, 8 LNTS 278, Article 9 (entered into force 5 July 1920).

105. *Report of the Special Body of Experts on Traffic in Women and Children, Part One*, LON Council, [38], LON Doc. C.52.M.52.1927.IV (1927). Note that the Convention of 1910 pursuant to Article 2 also mandated legislative measures to prevent exploitation of 'women and girls over age' for prostitution in a foreign country.

106. Ignarski, *Traffic in Persons*, p. 894.

107. *International Convention for the Suppression of the White Slave Traffic*, opened for signature 4 May 1910, 8 LNTS 278, Article 3 (entered into force 5 July 1920). Note Article 3 also applied to the offence in Article 2 of the Convention of 1910 concerning a woman or girl over-age.

108. *International Convention for the Suppression of the White Slave Traffic*, opened for signature 4 May 1910, 8 LNTS 278, Article 1 (entered into force 5 July 1920).

109. *International Convention for the Suppression of the White Slave Traffic*, opened for signature 4 May 1910, 8 LNTS 278, Final Protocol, para B (entered

into force 5 July 1920). The Final Protocol interpreted Articles 1, 2, and 3 of this Convention. States exercising legislative sovereignty were to provide for the execution of the stipulations agreed upon, or for their extension, in the manner described: *International Convention for the Suppression of the White Slave Traffic*, opened for signature 4 May 1910, 8 LNTS 278, Final Protocol, preamble (entered into force 5 July 1920). The Final Protocol and the Convention were considered to be one piece; the Protocol had the same force, validity and duration as the Convention: *International Convention for the Suppression of the White Slave Traffic*, opened for signature 4 May 1910, 8 LNTS 278, Final Protocol, (entered into force 5 July 1920); *International Convention for the Suppression of the White Slave Traffic*, opened for signature 4 May 1910, 8 LNTS 278, Article 9 (entered into force 5 July 1920).

110. *International Convention for the Suppression of the White Slave Traffic*, opened for signature 4 May 1910, 8 LNTS 278, Final Protocol, para A (entered into force 5 July 1920). The Final Protocol interpreted Articles 1, 2, and 3 of this Convention. States exercising legislative sovereignty were to provide for the execution of the stipulations agreed upon, or for their extension, in the manner described: *International Convention for the Suppression of the White Slave Traffic*, opened for signature 4 May 1910, 8 LNTS 278, Final Protocol, preamble (entered into force 5 July 1920). The Final Protocol and the Convention were considered to be one piece; the Protocol had the same force, validity and duration as the Convention: *International Convention for the Suppression of the White Slave Traffic*, opened for signature 4 May 1910, 8 LNTS 278, Final Protocol, (entered into force 5 July 1920); *International Convention for the Suppression of the White Slave Traffic*, opened for signature 4 May 1910, 8 LNTS 278, Article 9 (entered into force 5 July 1920).

111. *International Convention for the Suppression of the White Slave Traffic*, opened for signature 4 May 1910, 8 LNTS 278, Final Protocol, para D (entered into force 5 July 1920) which stated that the case of detention, against her will, of a woman or girl in a brothel could not, in spite of its gravity, be dealt with in the present Convention, seeing that it is governed exclusively by internal legislation. The Final Protocol interpreted Articles 1, 2, and 3 of this Convention. States exercising legislative sovereignty were to provide for the execution of the stipulations agreed upon, or for their extension, in the manner described: *International Convention for the Suppression of the White Slave Traffic*, opened for signature 4 May 1910, 8 LNTS 278, Final Protocol, preamble (entered into force 5 July 1920). The Final Protocol and the Convention were considered to be one piece; the Protocol had the same force, validity and duration as the Convention: *International Convention for the Suppression of the White Slave Traffic*, opened for signature 4 May 1910, 8 LNTS 278, Final Protocol, (entered into force 5 July 1920);

*International Convention for the Suppression of the White Slave Traffic*, opened for signature 4 May 1910, 8 LNTS 278, Article 9 (entered into force 5 July 1920).

112. *International Convention for the Suppression of the White Slave Traffic*, opened for signature 4 May 1910, 8 LNTS 278, Final Protocol, para C (entered into force 5 July 1920). The Final Protocol interpreted Articles 1, 2, and 3 of this Convention. States exercising legislative sovereignty were to provide for the execution of the stipulations agreed upon, or for their extension, in the manner described: *International Convention for the Suppression of the White Slave Traffic*, opened for signature 4 May 1910, 8 LNTS 278, Final Protocol, preamble (entered into force 5 July 1920). The Final Protocol and the Convention were considered to be one piece; the Protocol had the same force, validity and duration as the Convention: *International Convention for the Suppression of the White Slave Traffic*, opened for signature 4 May 1910, 8 LNTS 278, Final Protocol, (entered into force 5 July 1920); *International Convention for the Suppression of the White Slave Traffic*, opened for signature 4 May 1910, 8 LNTS 278, Article 9 (entered into force 5 July 1920).

113. Article 2 of the Convention of 1910 states: 'Whoever, in order to gratify the passions of another person, has, by fraud, or by means of violence, threats, abuse of authority, or any other method of compulsion, procured, enticed, or led away a woman or girl over age, for immoral purposes, shall also be punished, notwithstanding that the various acts constituting the offence may have been committed in different countries.'

114. *International Convention for the Suppression of the White Slave Traffic*, opened for signature 4 May 1910, 8 LNTS 278, Final Protocol, para C (entered into force 5 July 1920). The Final Protocol interpreted Articles 1, 2, and 3 of this Convention. States exercising legislative sovereignty were to provide for the execution of the stipulations agreed upon, or for their extension, in the manner described: *International Convention for the Suppression of the White Slave Traffic*, opened for signature 4 May 1910, 8 LNTS 278, Final Protocol, preamble (entered into force 5 July 1920). The Final Protocol and the Convention were considered to be one piece; the Protocol had the same force, validity and duration as the Convention: *International Convention for the Suppression of the White Slave Traffic*, opened for signature 4 May 1910, 8 LNTS 278, Final Protocol, (entered into force 5 July 1920); *International Convention for the Suppression of the White Slave Traffic*, opened for signature 4 May 1910, 8 LNTS 278, Article 9 (entered into force 5 July 1920).

115. *International Convention for the Suppression of the White Slave Traffic*, opened for signature 4 May 1910, 8 LNTS 278, Article 5 (entered into force 5 July 1920). Note, Article 5 also applied to the offence stipulated in Article 2 of the Convention of 1910.

116. *International Convention for the Suppression of the White Slave Traffic*, opened for signature 4 May 1910, 8 LNTS 278, Article 6 (entered into force 5 July 1920). Note, Article 6 also applied to the offence stipulated in Article 2 of the Convention of 1910.

117. Ibid.

118. *International Convention for the Suppression of the White Slave Traffic*, opened for signature 4 May 1910, 8 LNTS 278, Article 7 (entered into force 5 July 1920). Note, Article 7 also applied to the offence stipulated in Article 2 of the Convention of 1910.

119. *International Convention for the Suppression of the White Slave Traffic*, opened for signature 4 May 1910, 8 LNTS 278, Article 2 (entered into force 5 July 1920).

120. *International Convention for the Suppression of the White Slave Traffic*, opened for signature 4 May 1910, 8 LNTS 278, Article 4 (entered into force 5 July 1920).

121. *International Convention for the Suppression of the White Slave Traffic*, opened for signature 4 May 1910, 8 LNTS 278, Article 8 (entered into force 5 July 1920).

122. *International Convention for the Suppression of the White Slave Traffic*, opened for signature 4 May 1910, 8 LNTS 278, Article 9 (entered into force 5 July 1920).

123. *International Convention for the Suppression of the White Slave Traffic*, opened for signature 4 May 1910, 8 LNTS 278, Article 10 (entered into force 5 July 1920).

124. *International Convention for the Suppression of the White Slave Traffic*, opened for signature 4 May 1910, 8 LNTS 278, Article 11 (entered into force 5 July 1920).

125. *International Convention for the Suppression of the White Slave Traffic*, opened for signature 4 May 1910, 8 LNTS 278, Article 12 (entered into force 5 July 1920).

126. Report by the Delegate of Roumania, *Note on International Measures to be Taken for the Suppression of Traffic in Women and Children*, LON Assembly, [3], LON Doc. [A.20/48/225(a).IV] (1920).

127. *Report of the Special Body of Experts on Traffic in Women and Children, Part One*, LON Council, [7], LON Doc. C.52.M.52.1927.IV (1927). The USA amended its immigration law after this investigation. The White Slave Traffic Act came into force in 1910. The Act included strong sanctions against interstate and international transport and commerce in women or girls for immoral purposes: *Report of the Special Body of Experts on Traffic in Women and Children Part One*, LON Council, [7], LON Doc. C.52.M.52.1927.IV (1927).

128. *International Convention for the Suppression of the White Slave Traffic*, opened for signature 4 May 1910, 8 LNTS 278, Final Protocol, para B (entered into force 5 July 1920).

129. Obokata, *Trafficking of Human Beings*, p. 14.

130. International Conference on Traffic in Women and Children, *General Report on the Work of the Conference*, LON Council, [2], LON Doc. C.227.M.166.1921.IV (1921); Memorandum by the Secretary-General, *The Suppression of the White Slave Traffic in Women and Children*, LON Assembly, LON Doc. [A].20/48/8.IV] (1920); Advisory Committee on Traffic in Women and Children, *Preparatory Documents, International Bureau for the Suppression of the Traffic in Women and Children*, LON Council, 1st sess., [17], LON Doc. C.365.M.216.1922.IV (1922).

131. International Conference on Traffic in Women and Children, *General Report on the Work of the Conference*, LON Council, [2], LON Doc. C.227.M.166.1921.IV (1921); Memorandum by the Secretary-General, *The Suppression of the White Slave Traffic in Women and Children*, LON Assembly, LON Doc. [A].20/48/8.IV] (1920).

132. Advisory Committee on Traffic in Women and Children, *Preparatory Documents, International Bureau for the Suppression of the Traffic in Women and Children*, LON Council, 1st sess., [17], LON Doc. C.365.M.216.1922.IV (1922); Official Records of the International Conference on Women and Children, *Report of the International Bureau for the Suppression of the White Slave Traffic and the International Traffic in Women*, LON Council, 1st plen. mtg, [15], LON Doc. C.484.M.339.1921.IV (1921).

133. Official Records of the International Conference on Women and Children, *Report of the International Bureau for the Suppression of the White Slave Traffic and the International Traffic in Women*, LON Council, 1st plen. mtg, [15], LON Doc. C.484.M.339.1921.IV (1921).

134. Advisory Committee on Traffic in Women and Children, *Preparatory Documents, International Bureau for the Suppression of the Traffic in Women and Children*, LON Council, 1st sess., [17], LON Doc. C.365.M.216.1922.IV (1922).

135. Official Records of the International Conference on Women and Children, *Report of the International Bureau for the Suppression of the White Slave Traffic and the International Traffic in Women*, LON Council, 1st plen. mtg, [15], LON Doc. C.484.M.339.1921.IV (1921).

136. Ibid.

137. Ibid.

138. Official Records of the International Conference on Women and Children, *Report of the International Bureau for the Suppression of the White Slave*

*Traffic and the International Traffic in Women*, LON Council, 1st plen. mtg, [16], LON Doc. C.484.M.339.1921.IV (1921).

139. Ibid.

140. Ibid.

141. Ibid.

142. Official Records of the International Conference on Women and Children, *Report of the International Bureau for the Suppression of the White Slave Traffic and the International Traffic in Women*, LON Council, 1st plen. mtg, [15], LON Doc. C.484.M.339.1921.IV (1921).

143. Official Records of the International Conference on Women and Children, *Report of the International Bureau for the Suppression of the White Slave Traffic and the International Traffic in Women*, LON Council, 1st plen. mtg, [16], LON Doc. C.484.M.339.1921.IV (1921); Advisory Committee on Traffic in Women and Children, *Preparatory Documents, International Bureau for the Suppression of the Traffic in Women and Children*, LON Council, 1st sess., [17], LON Doc. C.365.M.216.1922.IV (1922).

144. Advisory Committee on Traffic in Women and Children, *Preparatory Documents, International Bureau for the Suppression of the Traffic in Women and Children*, LON Council, 1st sess., [17], LON Doc. C.365.M.216.1922.IV (1922).

145. Official Records of the International Conference on Women and Children, *Report of the International Bureau for the Suppression of the White Slave Traffic and the International Traffic in Women*, LON Council, 1st plen. mtg, [15], LON Doc. C.484.M.339.1921.IV (1921); Advisory Committee on Traffic in Women and Children, *Preparatory Documents, International Bureau for the Suppression of the Traffic in Women and Children*, LON Council, 1st sess., [17], LON Doc. C.365.M.216.1922.IV (1922).

146. International Conference on Traffic in Women and Children, *General Report on the Work of the Conference*, LON Council, [2], LON Doc. C.227.M.166.1921.IV (1921).

147. *Report of the Special Body of Experts on Traffic in Women and Children, Part One*, LON Council, [8], LON Doc. C.52.M.52.1927.IV (1927).

## CHAPTER 2

1. League of Nations, *Monthly Summary of the League of Nations* (Vol. 1, 1921), p. 130.

2. Article 23(c) of the Covenant of the League of Nations. The Covenant of the League of Nations came into force on 10 January 1920.

3. Report by the Delegate of Roumania, *Note on International Measures to be Taken for the Suppression of Traffic in Women and Children*, LON Assembly, [3], LON Doc. [A.20/48/225(a).IV] (1920).

4. Report by the Delegate of Roumania, *Note on International Measures to be Taken for the Suppression of Traffic in Women and Children*, LON Assembly, [3], LON Doc. [A.20/48/225(a).IV] (1920); Memorandum by the Secretary-General, *The Suppression of the White Slave Traffic in Women and Children*, LON Assembly, LON Doc. [A].20/48/8.[IV] (1920); Traffic in Women and Children, *Resolution by the Council of the League of Nations, Meeting in Rome on 15th May 1920*, LON Council, LON Doc. 20/41/10.IV (1920). Dame Rachel Crowdy was the person appointed: Official Records of the International Conference on Traffic in Women and Children, *Opening Speech by the President*, LON Council [9], LON Doc. C.484.M.339.1921.IV (1921).

5. Report by the Delegate of Roumania, *Note on International Measures to be taken for the Suppression of Traffic in Women and Children*, LON Assembly, [3], LON Doc. [A.20/48/225(a).IV] (1920).

6. Traffic in Women and Children, *Resolution by the Council of the League of Nations, Meeting in Rome on 15th May 1920*, 20/41/10.IV (1920).

7. Report by the Delegate of Roumania, *Note on International Measures to be taken for the Suppression of Traffic in Women and Children*, LON Assembly, [2], LON Doc. [A.20/48/225(a).IV] (1920).

8. Report by the Delegate of Roumania, *Note on International Measures to be taken for the Suppression of Traffic in Women and Children*, LON Assembly, [3], LON Doc. [A.20/48/225(a).IV] (1920).

9. Ibid.

10. Ibid.

11. International Conference on Traffic in Women and Children, *General Report on the Work of the Conference*, LON Council, [2], LON Doc. C.227.M.166.1921.IV (1921).

12. *Resolution Adopted by the Assembly Concerning the Suppression of Traffic in Women and Children*, LON Assembly Res 17, LON Doc. [A].20/48/239.[IV] (1920); *Text of Motions Proposed by Committee II Regarding the Suppression of Traffic in Women and Children*, LON Assembly, LON Doc. [A].20/48/236. [IV] (1920); International Conference on Traffic in Women and Children, *General Report on the Work of the Conference*, LON Council, [2–3], LON Doc. C.227.M.166.1921.IV (1921); *Memorandum by the Secretary-General*, LON Council, LON Doc. [C].21/4/18.[IV] (1921); *Memorandum by the Secretary-General*, LON Council, LON Doc. [C].21/41/12.IV (1921).

13. Ibid.

14. Ibid.

15. Ibid. In addition, it was resolved by the Assembly that the Council constitute a commission of enquiry, funded by the League of Nations, to ascertain the current situation in relation to deported women and children in Armenia, Asia Minor, Turkey and adjacent territories. Membership of the three-person

Commission, chosen from residents of the districts concerned, was to reflect suitability to serve, and was to include at least one woman. The Secretariat was directed to accept all information supplied by the Commission along with whatever information from other countries was relevant to the inquiry. The Council would in turn report to the Assembly: *Resolution Adopted by the Assembly Concerning the Suppression of Traffic in Women and Children*, LON Assembly Res 17, LON Doc [A].20/48/239.[IV] (1920); *Text of Motions Proposed by Committee II Regarding the Suppression of Traffic in Women and Children*, LON Assembly, LON Doc [A].20/48/236.[IV] (1920).

16. International Conference on Traffic in Women and Children, *General Report on the Work of the Conference*, LON Council, [3], LON Doc. C.227.M.166.1921.IV (1921); *Memorandum by the Secretary-General*, LON Council, LON Doc. [C].21/41/12.IV (1921); *Memorandum by the Secretary-General*, LON Council, LON Doc. [C].21/4/18.[IV] (1921).

17. International Conference on Traffic in Women and Children, *General Report on the Work of the Conference*, LON Council, [4], LON Doc. C.227.M.166.1921.IV (1921).

18. Official Records of the International Conference on Women and Children, *Report of the International Bureau for the Suppression of the White Slave Traffic and the International Traffic in Women*, LON Council, 1st plen. mtg, [16], LON Doc. C.484.M.339.1921.IV (1921).

19. International Conference on Traffic in Women and Children, *General Report on the Work of the Conference*, LON Council, [3], LON Doc. C.227.M.166.1921.IV (1921); *Memorandum by the Secretary-General*, LON Council, LON Doc. [C].21/41/12.IV (1921); *Memorandum by the Secretary-General*, LON Council, LON Doc. [C].21/4/18.[IV] (1921).

20. International Conference on Traffic in Women and Children, *General Report on the Work of the Conference*, LON Council, [4–5], LON Doc. C.227.M.166.1921.IV (1921).

21. International Conference on Traffic in Women and Children, *General Report on the Work of the Conference*, LON Council, [3], LON Doc. C.227.M.166.1921.IV (1921); Traffic in Women and Children, *Resolution Adopted by the Council in Paris on February 22nd 1921*, LON Council, LON Doc. [C].21/41/13.[IV](1921).

22. Ibid. See generally, Gilbert A. Murray, *Report Submitted to the Second Assembly by the Fifth Committee*, LON Assembly, [2], LON Doc. A.132.1921.[IV] (1921).

23. International Conference on Traffic in Women and Children, *General Report on the Work of the Conference*, LON Council, [3], LON Doc. C.227.M.166.1921.IV (1921); International Conference on Women and Children, *Final Act*, LON Council, [2], LON Doc. C.223.M.162.1921.IV (1921); Gilbert A.

Murray, *Report Submitted to the Second Assembly by the Fifth Committee*, LON Assembly, [2], LON Doc. A.132.1921.[IV] (1921); *Report of the British Delegate*, LON Council, [1], LON Doc. [C.325.1921.IV] (1921). (Conference of 1921).

24. Gilbert A. Murray, *Report Submitted to the Second Assembly by the Fifth Committee*, LON Assembly, [2], LON Doc. A.132.1921.[IV] (1921). See, International Conference on Traffic in Women and Children, *General Report on the Work of the Conference*, LON Council, Annex I, [9], LON Doc. C.227.M.166.1921.IV (1921).

25. Gilbert A. Murray, *Report Submitted to the Second Assembly by the Fifth Committee*, LON Assembly, [2], LON Doc. A.132.1921.[IV] (1921).

26. Official Records of the International Conference on Women and Children, *Agenda of the International Conference on Traffic in Women and Children*, LON Council, [agenda], LON Doc. C.484.M.339.1921. IV (1921); International Conference on Traffic in Women and Children, *General Report on the Work of the Conference*, LON Council, [6], LON Doc. C.227.M.166.1921.IV (1921). The remaining agenda items were: 1. Verification of credentials; 2. Adoption of Rules of Procedure; 3. Appointment of Committees of Organization; 4. Statement by the President; 5. Report on the replies received to the Questionnaire; 6(a). Report on existing Traffic by the International Bureau for the Suppression of the Traffic in Women and Children; 6(b). Any other reports or evidence; 7. Appointment of Standing Committee to advise the Council on Traffic questions; 9(e). Any other suggestions; 11. Adoption of Report, including suggested amendments to the Convention, for submission to the Council and to the Assembly of the League of Nations.

27. Official Records of the International Conference on Women and Children, *Agenda of the International Conference on Traffic in Women and Children*, LON Council, [agenda], LON Doc. C.484.M.339.1921.IV (1921); International Conference on Traffic in Women and Children, *General Report on the Work of the Conference*, LON Council, [6], LON Doc. C.227.M.166.1921.IV (1921).

28. International Conference on Traffic in Women and Children, *General Report on the Work of the Conference*, LON Council, [10], LON Doc. C.227.M.166.1921.IV (1921).

29. Official Records of the International Conference on Women and Children, *Report Presented by M. Regnault (France) on the Replies Submitted by Various States to the Questionnaire of the Secretariat*, LON Council, 5th plen. mtg, [75], LON Doc. C.484.M.339.1921.IV (1921); International Conference on Traffic in Women and Children, *Report Presented by M. Regnault, Delegate of the French Republic, on the Replies from the Various States to the Questionnaire Sent Out by the Secretariat*, LON Council, [2], C.223(a). M.162(a).1921.IV (1921).

30. Official Records of the International Conference on Women and Children, *Report Presented by M. Regnault (France) on the Replies Submitted by Various*

*States to the Questionnaire of the Secretariat,* LON Council, 5th plen. mtg, [75], LON Doc. C.484.M.339.1921.IV (1921); International Conference on Traffic in Women and Children, *Report Presented by M. Regnault, Delegate of the French Republic, on the Replies from the Various States to the Questionnaire Sent Out by the Secretariat,* LON Council, [2], C.223(a). M.162(a).1921.IV (1921).

31. Official Records of the International Conference on Women and Children, *Report Presented by M. Regnault (France) on the Replies Submitted by Various States to the Questionnaire of the Secretariat,* LON Council, 5th plen. mtg, [75], LON Doc. C.484.M.339.1921.IV (1921); International Conference on Traffic in Women and Children, *Report presented by M. Regnault, Delegate of the French Republic, on the Replies from the Various States to the Questionnaire Sent Out by the Secretariat,* LON Council, [2-3], C.223(a). M.162(a).1921.IV (1921).

32. Official Records of the International Conference on Women and Children, *Report Presented by M. Regnault (France) on the Replies Submitted by Various States to the Questionnaire of the Secretariat,* LON Council, 5th plen. mtg, [75], LON Doc. C.484.M.339.1921.IV (1921); International Conference on Traffic in Women and Children, *Report Presented by M. Regnault, Delegate of the French Republic, on the Replies from the Various States to the Questionnaire Sent Out by the Secretariat,* LON Council, [3], C.223(a). M.162(a).1921.IV (1921).

33. Ibid.

34. Ibid.

35. Official Records of the International Conference on Women and Children, *Report Presented by M. Regnault (France) on the Replies Submitted by Various States to the Questionnaire of the Secretariat,* LON Council, 5th plen. mtg, [76], LON Doc. C.484.M.339.1921.IV (1921); International Conference on Traffic in Women and Children, *Report Presented by M. Regnault, Delegate of the French Republic, on the Replies from the Various States to the Questionnaire Sent Out by the Secretariat,* LON Council, [3], C.223(a). M.162(a).1921.IV (1921).

36. Ibid.

37. International Conference on Traffic in Women and Children, *Report Presented by M. Regnault, Delegate of the French Republic, on the Replies from the Various States to the Questionnaire Sent Out by the Secretariat,* LON Council, [3], C.223(a). M.162(a).1921.IV (1921).

38. Ibid.

39. Official Records of the International Conference on Women and Children, *Report Presented by M. Regnault (France) on the Replies Submitted by Various States to the Questionnaire of the Secretariat,* LON Council, 5th plen. mtg, [76], LON Doc. C.484.M.339.1921.IV (1921); International Conference on Traffic in Women and Children, *Report Presented by M. Regnault, Delegate of the French Republic, on the Replies from the Various States to the Questionnaire Sent Out by the Secretariat,* LON Council, [3], C.223(a). M.162(a).1921.IV (1921).

40. Ibid.

41. Ibid.

42. International Conference on Traffic in Women and Children, *Report Presented by M. Regnault, Delegate of the French Republic, on the Replies from the Various States to the Questionnaire Sent Out by the Secretariat*, LON Council, [3], C.223(a). M.162(a).1921.IV (1921).

43. Official Records of the International Conference on Women and Children, *Report Presented by M. Regnault (France) on the Replies Submitted by Various States to the Questionnaire of the Secretariat*, LON Council, 5th plen. mtg, [76], LON Doc. C.484.M.339.1921.IV (1921); International Conference on Traffic in Women and Children, *Report Presented by M. Regnault, Delegate of the French Republic, on the Replies from the Various States to the Questionnaire Sent Out by the Secretariat*, LON Council, [4], C.223(a). M.162(a).1921.IV (1921).

44. Ibid.

45. International Conference on Traffic in Women and Children, *Report Presented by M. Regnault, Delegate of the French Republic, on the Replies from the Various States to the Questionnaire Sent Out by the Secretariat*, LON Council, [4], C.223(a). M.162(a).1921.IV (1921).

46. Official Records of the International Conference on Women and Children, *Report Presented by M. Regnault (France) on the Replies Submitted by Various States to the Questionnaire of the Secretariat*, LON Council, 5th plen. mtg, [77], LON Doc. C.484.M.339.1921.IV (1921); International Conference on Traffic in Women and Children, *Report Presented by M. Regnault, Delegate of the French Republic, on the Replies from the Various States to the Questionnaire Sent Out by the Secretariat*, LON Council, [4], C.223(a). M.162(a).1921.IV (1921).

47. Ibid.

48. Official Records of the International Conference on Women and Children, *Report Presented by M. Regnault (France) on the Replies Submitted by Various States to the Questionnaire of the Secretariat*, LON Council, 5th plen. mtg, [77], LON Doc. C.484.M.339.1921.IV (1921); International Conference on Traffic in Women and Children, *Report Presented by M. Regnault, Delegate of the French Republic, on the Replies from the Various States to the Questionnaire Sent Out by the Secretariat*, LON Council, [5], C.223(a). M.162(a).1921.IV (1921).

49. Ibid.

50. International Conference on Traffic in Women and Children, *Report presented by M. Regnault, Delegate of the French Republic, on the Replies from the various States to the Questionnaire Sent Out by the Secretariat*, LON Council, [5], C.223(a). M.162(a).1921.IV (1921).

51. Official Records of the International Conference on Women and Children, *Report Presented by M. Regnault (France) on the Replies Submitted by Various States to the Questionnaire of the Secretariat*, LON Council, 5th plen. mtg,

[77–78], LON Doc. C.484.M.339.1921.IV (1921); International Conference on Traffic in Women and Children, *Report Presented by M. Regnault, Delegate of the French Republic, on the Replies from the Various States to the Questionnaire Sent Out by the Secretariat*, LON Council, [5], C.223(a). M.162(a).1921.IV (1921).

52. Official Records of the International Conference on Women and Children, *Report Presented by M. Regnault (France) on the Replies Submitted by Various States to the Questionnaire of the Secretariat*, LON Council, 5th plen. mtg, [78], LON Doc. C.484.M.339.1921.IV (1921); International Conference on Traffic in Women and Children, *Report Presented by M. Regnault, Delegate of the French Republic, on the Replies from the Various States to the Questionnaire Sent Out by the Secretariat*, LON Council, [5], C.223(a). M.162(a).1921.IV (1921).

53. International Conference on Traffic in Women and Children, *Report Presented by M. Regnault, Delegate of the French Republic, on the Replies from the Various States to the Questionnaire Sent Out by the Secretariat*, LON Council, [5], C.223(a). M.162(a).1921.IV (1921).

54. Official Records of the International Conference on Women and Children, *Report Presented by M. Regnault (France) on the Replies Submitted by Various States to the Questionnaire of the Secretariat*, LON Council, 5th plen. mtg, [78], LON Doc. C.484.M.339.1921.IV (1921); International Conference on Traffic in Women and Children, *Report Presented by M. Regnault, Delegate of the French Republic, on the Replies from the Various States to the Questionnaire Sent Out by the Secretariat*, LON Council, [5], C.223(a). M.162(a).1921.IV (1921).

55. Ibid.

56. Official Records of the International Conference on Women and Children, *Report Presented by M. Regnault (France) on the Replies Submitted by Various States to the Questionnaire of the Secretariat*, LON Council, 5th plen. mtg, [78], LON Doc. C.484.M.339.1921.IV (1921); International Conference on Traffic in Women and Children, *Report Presented by M. Regnault, Delegate of the French Republic, on the Replies from the Various States to the Questionnaire Sent Out by the Secretariat*, LON Council, [6], C.223(a). M.162(a).1921.IV.

57. Ibid.

58. Ibid.

59. Ibid.

60. Official Records of the International Conference on Women and Children, *Report Presented by M. Regnault (France) on the Replies Submitted by Various States to the Questionnaire of the Secretariat*, LON Council, 5th plen. mtg, [79], LON Doc. C.484.M.339.1921.IV (1921); International Conference on Traffic in Women and Children, *Report Presented by M. Regnault, Delegate of the French Republic, on the Replies from the Various States to the Questionnaire Sent Out by the Secretariat*, LON Council, [6], C.223(a). M.162(a).1921.IV (1921).

61. League of Nations, *Monthly Summary of the League of Nations*, (Vol. 1, 1921), p. 71.

62. Official Records of the International Conference on Women and Children, *Report of the International Bureau for the Suppression of the White Slave Traffic and the International Traffic in Women*, LON Council, 1st plen. mtg, [12–18], LON Doc. C.484.M.339.1921.IV (1921).

63. Official Records of the International Conference on Women and Children, *Report of the International Bureau for the Suppression of the White Slave Traffic and the International Traffic in Women*, LON Council, 1st plen. meeting, [17], LON Doc C.484.M.339.1921.IV (1921). In addition, the International Bureau recommended that the Conference consider preventive and remedial measures which incorporated philanthropic as well as official action. Such measures included uniform legislation loosely modeled on the British Children's Employment Act, 1913, and the Norwegian law, regulating employment of young girls in places of amusement (for example, theatres, circuses, concert halls, and music halls); uniform international legislation regulating employment agencies; attention to issues in emigration, including adequate international protection for women travelling alone; Advisory Committee support for an official commission in each country, with male and female members, charged with ascertaining the extent and causes of the trafficking problem in their own country and making recommendations to the Advisory Committee about the best ways to suppress that trafficking; repatriation; and a united and consistent international response to victims of trafficking. This last could best be achieved by co-operation between counsels, police authorities and philanthropic societies: Official Records of the International Conference on Women and Children, *Report of the International Bureau for the Suppression of the White Slave Traffic and the International Traffic in Women*, LON Council, 1st plen. mtg, [17], LON Doc C.484.M.339.1921.IV (1921).

64. International Conference on Women and Children, *Final Act*, LON Council, [3], LON Doc. C.223.M.162.1921.IV (1921).

65. International Conference on Women and Children, *Final Act*, LON Council, [3], LON Doc. C.223.M.162.1921.IV (1921); International Conference on Traffic in Women and Children, *General Report on the Work of the Conference*, LON Council, Annex I, [10], LON Doc. C.227.M.166.1921.IV (1921).

66. International Conference on Women and Children, *Final Act*, LON Council, [3–7], LON Doc. C.223.M.162.1921.IV (1921); International Conference on Traffic in Women and Children, *General Report on the Work of the Conference*, LON Council, Annex I, [9–13], LON Doc. C.227.M.166.1921.IV (1921).

67. *Report of the British Delegate*, LON Council, [1], LON Doc. C.325.1921. IV (1921); Gilbert A Murray, *Report Submitted to the Second Assembly by the Fifth Committee*, LON Assembly, [2], LON Doc. A.132.1921.[IV] (1921).

68. International Conference on Women and Children, *Final Act*, LON Council, [4], LON Doc. C.223.M.162.1921.IV (1921); International Conference on Traffic in Women and Children, *General Report on the Work of the Conference*, LON Council, Annex I, [10], LON Doc. C.227.M.166.1921.IV (1921); Official Records of the International Conference on Women and Children, *Final Act*, LON Council, 7th plen. mtg, Annex, [135], LON Doc. C.484.M.339.1921.IV (1921).

69. International Conference on Women and Children, *Final Act*, LON Council, [4], LON Doc. C.223.M.162.1921.IV (1921); International Conference on Traffic in Women and Children, *General Report on the Work of the Conference*, LON Council, Annex I, [10–11], LON Doc. C.227.M.166.1921.IV (1921); Official Records of the International Conference on Women and Children, *Final Act*, LON Council, 7th plen. mtg, Annex [135], LON Doc. C.484.M.339.1921. IV (1921).

70. Official Records of the International Conference on Women and Children, *Final Act*, LON Council, 7th plen. mtg, Annex, [135], LON Doc. C.484.M.339.1921. IV (1921); International Conference on Women and Children, *Final Act*, LON Council, [4], LON Doc. C.223.M.162.1921.IV (1921); International Conference on Traffic in Women and Children, *General Report on the Work of the Conference*, LON Council, Annex I, [11], LON Doc. C.227.M.166.1921.IV (1921).

71. Official Records of the International Conference on Women and Children, *Final Act*, LON Council, 7th plen. mtg, Annex, [135], LON Doc. C.484.M.339.1921. IV (1921); International Conference on Women and Children, *Final Act*, LON Council, [5], LON Doc. C.223.M.162.1921.IV (1921); International Conference on Traffic in Women and Children, *General Report on the Work of the Conference*, LON Council, Annex I, [11], LON Doc. C.227.M.166.1921.IV (1921).

72. Ibid.

73. International Conference on Women and Children, *Final Act*, LON Council, [6], LON Doc. C.223.M.162.1921.IV (1921); International Conference on Traffic in Women and Children, *General Report on the Work of the Conference*, LON Council, Annex I, [13], LON Doc. C.227.M.166.1921.IV (1921); Official Records of the International Conference on Women and Children, *Final Act*, LON Council, 7th plen. mtg, Annex, [136], LON Doc. C.484.M.339.1921.IV (1921).

74. Official Records of the International Conference on Women and Children, *Statement by the Vice President*, LON Council, 4th plen. mtg, [72], LON Doc. C.484.M.339.1921.IV (1921).

75. Official Records of the International Conference on Women and Children, *Statement by the President*, LON Council, 4th plen. mtg, [73], LON Doc. C.484.M.339.1921.IV (1921). This Committee was the Committee appointed to examine the Recommendations of Private Associations.

76. Official Records of the International Conference on Women and Children, *Report by the Committee Appointed to Examine the Recommendations of Private Associations and the Question of the Traffic in Children*, LON Council, 5th plen. mtg, [95], LON Doc. C.484.M.339.1921.IV (1921).

77. Ibid.

78. Official Records of the International Conference on Women and Children, *Final Act*, LON Council, 7th plen. mtg, Annex, [136], LON Doc. C.484.M.339.1921. IV (1921); International Conference on Women and Children, *Final Act*, LON Council, [6], LON Doc. C.223.M.162.1921.IV (1921); International Conference on Traffic in Women and Children, *General Report on the Work of the Conference*, LON Council, Annex I, [12–13], LON Doc. C.227.M.166.1921.IV (1921).

79. Official Records of the International Conference on Women and Children, *Final Act*, LON Council, 7th plen. mtg, Annex, [135], LON Doc. C.484.M.339.1921. IV (1921); International Conference on Women and Children, *Final Act*, LON Council, [4], LON Doc. C.223.M.162.1921.IV (1921); International Conference on Traffic in Women and Children, *General Report on the Work of the Conference*, LON Council, Annex I, [10], LON Doc. C.227.M.166.1921.IV (1921).

80. Official Records of the International Conference on Women and Children, *Final Act*, LON Council, 7th plen. mtg, Annex, [135], LON Doc. C.484.M.339.1921. IV (1921); International Conference on Women and Children, *Final Act*, LON Council, [4], LON Doc. C.223.M.162.1921.IV (1921); International Conference on Traffic in Women and Children, *General Report on the Work of the Conference*, LON Council, Annex I, [11], LON Doc. C.227.M.166.1921.IV (1921).

81. Ibid.

82. Official Records of the International Conference on Women and Children, *Final Act*, LON Council, 7th plen. mtg, Annex, [135], LON Doc. C.484.M.339.1921. IV (1921); International Conference on Women and Children, *Final Act*, LON Council, [5], LON Doc. C.223.M.162.1921.IV (1921); International Conference on Traffic in Women and Children, *General Report on the Work of the Conference*, LON Council, Annex I, [11], LON Doc. C.227.M.166.1921.IV (1921).

83. Official Records of the International Conference on Women and Children, *Final Act*, LON Council, 7th plen. mtg, Annex, [136], LON Doc. C.484.M.339.1921. IV (1921); International Conference on Women and Children, *Final Act*, LON Council, [5], LON Doc. C.223.M.162.1921.IV (1921); International Conference on Traffic in Women and Children, *General Report on the Work of the Conference*, LON Council, Annex I, [11–12], LON Doc. C.227.M.166.1921.IV (1921).

84. Official Records of the International Conference on Women and Children, *Final Act*, LON Council, 7th plen. mtg, Annex, [136], LON Doc. C.484.M.339.1921. IV (1921); International Conference on Women and Children, *Final Act*, LON

Council, [5], LON Doc. C.223.M.162.1921.IV (1921); International Conference on Traffic in Women and Children, *General Report on the Work of the Conference*, LON Council, Annex I, [12], LON Doc. C.227.M.166.1921.IV (1921).

85. Ibid.

86. Ibid.

87. Ibid.

88. Official Records of the International Conference on Women and Children, *Final Act*, LON Council, 7th plen. mtg, Annex, [136], LON Doc. C.484.M.339.1921. IV (1921); International Conference on Women and Children, *Final Act*, LON Council, [6], LON Doc. C.223.M.162.1921.IV (1921); International Conference on Traffic in Women and Children, *General Report on the Work of the Conference*, LON Council, Annex I, [12], LON Doc. C.227.M.166.1921.IV (1921).

89. Ibid.

90. Official Records of the International Conference on Women and Children, *Final Act*, LON Council, 7th plen. mtg, Annex, [136], LON Doc. C.484.M.339.1921. IV (1921); International Conference on Women and Children, *Final Act*, LON Council, [6], LON Doc. C.223.M.162.1921.IV (1921); International Conference on Traffic in Women and Children, *General Report on the Work of the Conference*, LON Council, Annex I, [12], LON Doc. C.227.M.166.1921.IV (1921).

91. Official Records of the International Conference on Women and Children, *Final Act*, LON Council, 7th plen. mtg, Annex, [137], LON Doc. C.484.M.339.1921. IV (1921); International Conference on Women and Children, *Final Act*, LON Council, [6], LON Doc. C.223.M.162.1921.IV (1921); International Conference on Traffic in Women and Children, *General Report on the Work of the Conference*, LON Council, Annex I, [13], LON Doc. C.227.M.166.1921.IV (1921).

92. Official Records of the International Conference on Women and Children, *Final Act*, LON Council, 7th plen. mtg, Annex, [137], LON Doc. C.484.M.339.1921. IV (1921); International Conference on Women and Children, *Final Act*, LON Council, [7], LON Doc. C.223.M.162.1921.IV (1921); International Conference on Traffic in Women and Children, *General Report on the Work of the Conference*, LON Council, Annex I, [13], LON Doc. C.227.M.166.1921.IV (1921).

93. *Memorandum by the Secretary-General*, LON Council, LON Doc. [C.223(1).M.162(1).1921.IV] (1921); *Memorandum by the Secretary-General*, LON Council, [1], LON Doc. C.494.1921.IV (1921).

94. *Memorandum by the Secretary-General*, LON Council, LON Doc. [C.223(1).M.162(1).1921.IV] (1921); *Memorandum by the Secretary-General*, LON Council, [1], LON Doc. C.494.1921.IV (1921); Advisory Committee on Traffic in Women and Children, *Preparatory Documents, Preliminary Statement*, LON Council, 1st sess., [2], C.365.M.216.1922.IV (1922).

95. *Report of the British Delegate*, LON Council, [1], LON Doc. C.325.1921. IV (1921). See generally, Advisory Committee on Traffic in Women and Children,

*Preparatory Documents, Preliminary Statement,* LON Council, 1st sess., [2], C.365.M.216.1922.IV (1922); Gilbert A. Murray, *Report Submitted to the Second Assembly by the Fifth Committee,* LON Assembly, [2], LON Doc. A.132.1921.[IV] (1921).

96. *Report of the British Delegate,* LON Council, [1–2], LON Doc. C.325.1921. IV (1921). See generally, Gilbert A. Murray, *Report Submitted to the Second Assembly by the Fifth Committee,* LON Assembly, [2], LON Doc. A.132.1921.[IV] (1921).

97. *Draft of International Convention for the Suppression of the Traffic proposed by the Representative of Great Britain on the Council,* LON Council, LON Doc. C.240.M.176.1921.IV (1921).

98. *Report of the British Delegate,* LON Council, [2], LON Doc. C.325.1921. IV (1921).

99. *Draft of International Convention for the Suppression of the Traffic proposed by the Representative of Great Britain on the Council,* LON Council, [2], LON Doc. C.240.M.176.1921.IV (1921).

100. Ibid.

101. *Draft of International Convention for the Suppression of the Traffic Proposed by the Representative of Great Britain on the Council,* LON Council, [2–3], LON Doc. C.240.M.176.1921.IV (1921).

102. *Draft of International Convention for the Suppression of the Traffic proposed by the Representative of Great Britain on the Council,* LON Council, [3], LON Doc. C.240.M.176.1921.IV (1921).

103. *Report of the British Delegate,* LON Council, [2], LON Doc. C.325.1921. IV (1921).

104. *Traffic in Women and Children,* LON Council, [1], LON Doc. C.331.1921. IV (1921).

105. *Traffic in Women and Children,* LON Council, [2], LON Doc. C.331.1921. IV (1921).

106. Ibid.

107. Ibid.

108. *Traffic in Women and Children,* LON Council, [2–3], LON Doc. C.331.1921.IV (1921).

109. *Traffic in Women and Children,* LON Council, [3], LON Doc. C.331.1921. IV (1921).

110. Ibid.

111. Ibid.

112. *Traffic in Women and Children, Amended Draft of International Convention for the Suppression of the Traffic,* LON Assembly, LON Doc. A.58.1921. IV (1921). See also, *Report of the British Delegate,* LON Council, [2], LON Doc. C.325.1921.IV (1921).

113. *Report of the British Delegate,* LON Council, [2], LON Doc. C.325.1921. IV (1921).

114. Advisory Committee on Traffic in Women and Children, *Preparatory Documents, Preliminary Statement,* LON Council, 1st sess., [2], LON DOC C.365.M.216.1922.IV (1922).

115. Gilbert A. Murray, *Report Submitted to the Second Assembly by the Fifth Committee,* LON Assembly, [2], LON Doc. A.132.1921.[IV] (1921).

116. Gilbert A. Murray, *Report Submitted to the Second Assembly by the Fifth Committee,* LON Assembly, [3], LON Doc. A.132.1921.[IV] (1921); Advisory Committee on Traffic in Women and Children, *Preparatory Documents, Preliminary Statement,* LON Council, 1st sess., [2], C.365.M.216.1922.IV (1922).

117. Gilbert A. Murray, *Report Submitted to the Second Assembly by the Fifth Committee,* LON Assembly, [3], LON Doc. A.132.1921.[IV] (1921).

118. *Draft Convention on Traffic in Women and Children* (as revised by the Drafting Committee appointed by the Fifth Committee of the Assembly), LON Assembly, Article 1, LON Doc. A.125.1921.IV (1921).

119. *Draft Convention on Traffic in Women and Children* (as revised by the Drafting Committee appointed by the Fifth Committee of the Assembly), LON Assembly, Article 2, LON Doc. A.125.1921.IV (1921).

120. *Draft Convention on Traffic in Women and Children* (as revised by the Drafting Committee appointed by the Fifth Committee of the Assembly), LON Assembly, Article 4, LON Doc. A.125.1921.IV (1921).

121. *Draft Convention on Traffic in Women and Children* (as revised by the Drafting Committee appointed by the Fifth Committee of the Assembly), LON Assembly, Article 6, LON Doc. A.125.1921.IV (1921).

122. Gilbert A. Murray, *Report Submitted to the Second Assembly by the Fifth Committee,* LON Assembly, [3], LON Doc. A.132.1921.[IV] (1921).

123. Advisory Committee on Traffic in Women and Children, *Preparatory Documents, Preliminary Statement,* LON Council, 1st sess., [2], C.365.M.216.1922. IV (1922); Gilbert A. Murray, *Report Submitted to the Second Assembly by the Fifth Committee,* LON Assembly, [3], LON Doc. A.132.1921.[IV] (1921).

124. Advisory Committee on Traffic in Women and Children, *Preparatory Documents, Preliminary Statement,* LON Council, 1st sess., [2], C.365.M.216.1922. IV (1922).

125. *International Convention for the Suppression of the Traffic in Women and Children,* opened for signature 30 September 1921, 9 LNTS 415 (entered into force 15 June 1922).

126. *International Convention for the Suppression of the Traffic in Women and Children,* opened for signature 30 September 1921, 9 LNTS 415, Preamble (entered into force 15 June 1922).

127. *International Convention for the Suppression of the Traffic in Women and Children*, opened for signature 30 September 1921, 9 LNTS 415, Article 2 (entered into force 15 June 1922).

128. *International Convention for the Suppression of the Traffic in Women and Children*, opened for signature 30 September 1921, 9 LNTS 415, Article 3 (entered into force 15 June 1922). Article 3 of the Convention of 1921 also applied to Article 2 of the Convention of 1910.

129. *International Convention for the Suppression of the Traffic in Women and Children*, opened for signature 30 September 1921, 9 LNTS 415, Article 4 (entered into force 15 June 1922). Article 4 of the Convention of 1921 also applied to Article 2 of the Convention of 1910.

130. *International Convention for the Suppression of the Traffic in Women and Children*, opened for signature 30 September 1921, 9 LNTS 415, Article 5 (entered into force 15 June 1922).

131. *International Convention for the Suppression of the Traffic in Women and Children*, opened for signature 30 September 1921, 9 LNTS 415, Article 6 (entered into force 15 June 1922). Article 6 applies to women as well.

132. *International Convention for the Suppression of the Traffic in Women and Children*, opened for signature 30 September 1921, 9 LNTS 415, Article 7 (entered into force 15 June 1922). Article 7 also applied to women.

133. *International Convention for the Suppression of the Traffic in Women and Children*, opened for signature 30 September 1921, 9 LNTS 415, Article 1 (entered into force 15 June 1922).

134. *International Convention for the Suppression of the Traffic in Women and Children*, opened for signature 30 September 1921, 9 LNTS 415, Article 8 (entered into force 15 June 1922).

135. *International Convention for the Suppression of the Traffic in Women and Children*, opened for signature 30 September 1921, 9 LNTS 415, Article 9 (entered into force 15 June 1922).

136. *International Convention for the Suppression of the Traffic in Women and Children*, opened for signature 30 September 1921, 9 LNTS 415, Article 10 (entered into force 15 June 1922).

137. *International Convention for the Suppression of the Traffic in Women and Children*, opened for signature 30 September 1921, 9 LNTS 415, Article 11 (entered into force 15 June 1922).

138. *International Convention for the Suppression of the Traffic in Women and Children*, opened for signature 30 September 1921, 9 LNTS 415, Article 12 (entered into force 15 June 1922).

139. *International Convention for the Suppression of the Traffic in Women and Children*, opened for signature 30 September 1921, 9 LNTS 415, Article 13 (entered into force 15 June 1922).

140. *International Convention for the Suppression of the Traffic in Women and Children*, opened for signature 30 September 1921, 9 LNTS 415, Article 14 (entered into force 15 June 1922).

141. *International Convention for the Suppression of the Traffic in Women and Children*, opened for signature 30 September 1921, 9 LNTS 415, Article 5 (entered into force 15 June 1922).

142. Tom Obokata, *Trafficking of Human Beings from a Human Rights Perspective: Towards a Holistic Approach* (Martinus Nijhoff:: Netherlands, 2006), p. 16.

143. See generally, *Report of the Special Body of Experts on Traffic in Women and Children, Part One*, LON Council, [38], LON Doc. C.52.M.52.1927.IV (1927).

## CHAPTER 3

1. International Conference on Traffic in Women and Children, *General Report on the Work of the Conference*, LON Council, Annex I [12], LON Doc. C.227.M.166.1921.IV (1921); *Memorandum by the Secretary-General*, LON Council, [1], LON Doc. C.494.1921.IV (1921). The Final Act was presented to and considered by the Council at its session in September 1921 and a resolution approving the recommendations contained in the Final Act was passed. This included Recommendation XI: *Memorandum by the Secretary-General*, LON Council, [1], LON Doc. C.494.1921.IV (1921); *Memorandum by the Secretary-General*, LON Council, LON Doc. [C.223(1).M.162(1).1921.IV] (1921); *Report*, LON Council, [1], LON Doc. C.70.1922.IV (1922). On 14 January 1922, the Council considered the constitution of the Advisory Committee on Traffic in Women and Children and passed a resolution appointing the representatives and assessors: Advisory Committee on Traffic in Women and Children, *Preparatory Documents, Preliminary Statement*, LON Council, 1st sess., [3], LON Doc. C.365.M.216.1922.IV (1922). The Advisory Committee on Traffic in Women and Children held its first session from 28 June to 1 July 1922 at Geneva: Advisory Committee on the Traffic in Women and Children, *Report to the Council on the Work of the Committee at Its First Session*, LON Council, LON Doc. C.438.1922. IV (1922). Note, the Advisory Committee on Traffic in Women and Children had a number of name changes. The Advisory Committee on Traffic in Women and Children was reconstituted under the name of Advisory Committee on Traffic of Women and Protection of Children after the transfer to the League of Nations of the work of the International Association for the Promotion of Child Welfare: League of Nations, *The Committees of the League of Nations, Classified List and Essential Facts*, LON Council, [65], LON Doc. C.99.M.99.1945.V (1945); Advisory Committee on the Traffic in Women and Protection of Children, *Report of the Fourth Session*, LON Assembly, [1], LON Doc. A.22.1925.IV (1925).

See also, *Report by the British Representative*, LON Council, [1], LON Doc. C.810.1924.IV (1924). This name was later changed to the name of Advisory Commission for the Protection and Welfare of Children and Young People. This Advisory Commission was divided into two committees (a) Traffic in Women and Children Committee and (b) Child Welfare Committee: *The Committees of the League of Nations, Classified List and Essential Facts*, LON Council, [65], LON Doc. C.99.M.99.1945.V (1945). Thereafter the Advisory Commission for the Protection and Welfare of Children and Young People was reconstituted under the name Advisory Committee on Social Questions. The Advisory Committee on Social Questions replaced the Traffic in Women and Children Committee and Child Welfare Committee: *The Committees of the League of Nations, Classified List and Essential Facts*, LON Council, [65], LON Doc. C.99.M.99.1945.V (1945).

2. The Advisory Committee sat from March 22nd to 27th 1923: *Advisory Committee on Traffic in Women and Children, Report on the Work of the Committee during Its Second Session*, LON Council, [1], LON Doc. C.226.(1).M.166.1923.IV (1923).

3. *Report of the Special Body of Experts on Traffic in Women and Children Part One*, LON Council, [5], LON Doc. C.52.M.52.1927.IV (1927); Advisory Committee on Traffic in Women and Children, *Report on the Work of the Committee during Its Second Session*, LON Council, [6], LON Doc. C.226.(1).M.166.1923.IV (1923).

4. *Report of the Special Body of Experts on Traffic in Women and Children Part One*, LON Council, annex II, [50], LON Doc. C.52.M.52.1927.IV (1927).

5. Advisory Committee on Traffic in Women and Children, *Report on the Work of the Committee during Its Second Session*, LON Council, [6–7], LON Doc. C.226.(1).M.166.1923.IV (1923); M. Hymans, *Reports on the Work of the Advisory Committee during Its Second Session held at Geneva March 22nd–27th , 1923*, LON Assembly, [4], LON Doc. A.36.1923.IV (1923).

6. *Report of the Special Body of Experts on Traffic in Women and Children Part One*, LON Council, Annex I [49], LON Doc. C.52.M.52.1927.IV (1927); *Memorandum by the Secretary-General*, LON Council, [2], C.694.1923.IV (1923).

7. Ibid.

8. *Memorandum by the Secretary-General*, LON Council, [2], C.694.1923.IV (1923).

9. *Report of the Special Body of Experts on Traffic in Women and Children Part One*, LON Council, [48], LON Doc. C.52.M.52.1927.IV (1927).

10. Traffic in Women and Children, *Report of the Fifth Committee to the Assembly*, LON Assembly, [2], LON Doc. A.75.1923.IV (1923).

11. Ibid.

12. Fourth Assembly of the League of Nations, *Resolutions Adopted by the Assembly at Its Meeting held on Saturday, September 15th, 1923 (morning)*

(adopted on the Report of the Fifth Committee), LON Assembly, LON Doc. A.78.1923.IV (1923); *Memorandum by the Secretary-General*, LON Council, [3], C.694.1923.IV (1923).

13. *Memorandum by the Secretary-General*, LON Council, [2], C.694.1923.IV (1923).

14. *Memorandum by the Secretary-General*, LON Council, [3], C.694.1923.IV (1923).

15. *Report of the Special Body of Experts on Traffic in Women and Children Part One*, LON Council, [3], LON Doc. C.52.M.52.1927.IV (1927).

16. *Report of the Special Body of Experts on Traffic in Women and Children Part One*, LON Council, [22], LON Doc. C.52.M.52.1927.IV (1927).

17. Ibid.

18. Ibid.

19. *Report of the Special Body of Experts on Traffic in Women and Children Part One*, LON Council, [38], LON Doc. C.52.M.52.1927.IV (1927).

20. *Report of the Special Body of Experts on Traffic in Women and Children Part One*, LON Council, [38–39], LON Doc. C.52.M.52.1927.IV (1927).

21. *Report of the Special Body of Experts on Traffic in Women and Children Part One*, LON Council, [39], LON Doc. C.52.M.52.1927.IV (1927).

22. *Report of the Special Body of Experts on Traffic in Women and Children Part One*, LON Council, [46], LON Doc. C.52.M.52.1927.IV (1927); Report of the Secretary, *Amendments to the Conventions of 1910 and 1921: Elimination of Age Limit*, LON Council, [1], LON Doc. C.503.M.244.1932.IV (1932).

23. The Advisory Committee sat from April 25th to April 30th, 1927: Traffic in Women and Children Committee, *Report on the Work of the Sixth Session*, LON Council, [1], LON Doc. C.221.M.60.1927.IV (1927); *Report of the British Representative*, LON Council, [1], LON Doc. C.318.1927.IV (1927); Sir Austen Chamberlain, *Reports on the Work of the Committee during Its Sixth Session*, LON Assembly, [1] LON Doc. A.25.1927.IV (1927).

24. Traffic in Women and Children Committee, *Report on the Work of the Sixth Session*, LON Council, [4], LON Doc. C.221.M.60.1927.IV (1927); Sir Austen Chamberlain, *Reports on the Work of the Committee during Its Sixth Session*, LON Assembly, [6] LON Doc. A.25.1927.IV (1927); *Report of the British Representative*, LON Council, [3], LON Doc. C.318.1927.IV (1927).

25. The Advisory Committee sat from March 12th to 17th, 1928: Advisory Commission for the Protection and Welfare of Children and Young People, Traffic in Women and Children Committee, *Report of the Seventh Session*, LON Council, [1], LON Doc. C.154.1928.IV (1928); *Report by the British Representative*, LON Assembly, [1], LON Doc. A.9.1928.IV (1928); *Report by the British Representative*, LON Council, [1], LON Doc. C.274.1928.IV (1928).

26. Advisory Commission for the Protection and Welfare of Children and Young People, Traffic in Women and Children Committee, *Report of the Seventh Session*, LON Council, [5], LON Doc. C.154.1928.IV (1928); *Report by the British Representative*, LON Assembly, [6], LON Doc. A.9.1928.IV (1928).

27. The Advisory Committee sat from April 19th to 26th, 1929: Advisory Commission for the Protection and Welfare of Children and Young People, Traffic in Women and Children Committee, *Report of the Eighth Session*, LON Council, [1], LON Doc. C.170.1929.IV (1929); *Report by the British Representative*, LON Assembly, [3], LON Doc. A.14.1929.IV (1929).

28. Report of the Secretary, *Amendments to the Conventions of 1910 and 1921: Elimination of Age Limit*, LON Council, [2], LON Doc. C.503.M.244.1932. IV (1932).

29. Ibid.

30. Advisory Commission for the Protection and Welfare of Children and Young People, Traffic in Women and Children Committee, *Report of the Eighth Session*, LON Council, [6], LON Doc. C.170.1929.IV (1929); *Report by the British Representative*, LON Assembly, [8], LON Doc. A.14.1929.IV (1929); *Report by the British Representative*, LON Council, [3], LON Doc. C.276.1929.IV (1929).

31. Advisory Commission for the Protection and Welfare of Children and Young People, Traffic in Women and Children Committee, *Report of the Eighth Session*, LON Council, [6–7], LON Doc. C.170.1929.IV (1929); *Report by the British Representative*, LON Assembly, [8], LON Doc. A.14.1929.IV (1929); *Report by the British Representative*, LON Council, [3], LON Doc. C.276.1929. IV (1929).

32. Advisory Commission for the Protection and Welfare of Children and Young People, Traffic in Women and Children Committee, *Report of the Eighth Session*, LON Council, [7], LON Doc. C.170.1929.IV (1929); *Report by the British Representative*, LON Assembly, [8], LON Doc. A.14.1929.IV (1929).

33. Advisory Commission for the Protection and Welfare of Children and Young People, Traffic in Women and Children Committee, *Report of the Eighth Session*, LON Council, [7], LON Doc. C.170.1929.IV (1929); *Report by the British Representative*, LON Assembly, [8], LON Doc. A.14.1929.IV (1929); Report of the Secretary, *Amendments to the Conventions of 1910 and 1921: Elimination of Age Limit*, LON Council, [2], LON Doc. C.503.M.244.1932.IV (1932).

34. Report of the Secretary, *Amendments to the Conventions of 1910 and 1921: Elimination of Age Limit*, LON Council, [2], LON Doc. C.503.M.244.1932. IV (1932). The Committee sat from April 2nd to April 9th, 1930: Advisory Commission for the Protection and Welfare of Children and Young People, Traffic in Women and Children Committee, *Report on the Ninth Session*, LON Council, [1], LON Doc. C.216.M.104.1930.IV (1930).

35. *Report of the Fifth Committee to the Assembly,* LON Assembly, [1], LON Doc. A.76.1930. IV(1930).

36. Advisory Commission for the Protection and Welfare of Children and Young People, Traffic in Women and Children Committee, *Report on the Ninth Session,* LON Council, [5], LON Doc. C.216.M.104.1930.IV (1930).

37. Report of the Secretary, *Amendments to the Conventions of 1910 and 1921: Elimination of Age Limit,* LON Council, [2], LON Doc. C.503.M.244.1932. IV (1932); *Report by the Persian Representative,* LON Council, [4], LON Doc. C.253.1930.IV (1930); Advisory Commission for the Protection and Welfare of Children and Young People, Traffic in Women and Children Committee, *Report on the Ninth Session,* LON Council, [5,10], LON Doc. C.216.M.104.1930.IV (1930).

38. Report of the Secretary, *Amendments to the Conventions of 1910 and 1921: Elimination of Age Limit,* LON Council, [2], LON Doc. C.503.M.244.1932. IV (1932).

39. Traffic in Women and Children Committee, *Report on the Work of the Tenth Session,* LON Council, [4], LON Doc. C.267.M.122.1931.IV (1931). The Committee sat from April 21st to 27th, 1931. Traffic in Women and Children Committee, *Report on the Work of the Tenth Session,* LON Council, [1], LON Doc. C.267.M.122.1931.IV (1931).

40. Traffic in Women and Children Committee, *Report on the Work of the Tenth Session,* LON Council, [4], LON Doc. C.267.M.122.1931.IV (1931).

41. Ibid. See also, R*eport of the Fifth Committee to the Assembly,* LON Assembly, [1], LON Doc. A.72.1931.IV (1931).

42. *Report of the Fifth Committee to the Assembly,* LON Assembly, [1], LON Doc. A.72.1931.IV (1931).

43. The Committee sat from April 4th to 9th 1932: Report of the Secretary, *Amendments to the Conventions of 1910 and 1921: Elimination of Age Limit,* LON Council, [1], LON Doc. C.503.M.244.1932.IV (1932); Traffic in Women and Children Committee, *Report on the Work of the Eleventh Session,* LON Council, [1], LON Doc. C.390.M.220.1932.IV (1932).

44. Report of the Secretary, *Amendments to the Conventions of 1910 and 1921: Elimination of Age Limit,* LON Council, [2], LON Doc. C.503.M.244.1932. IV (1932).

45. Ibid.

46. Ibid.

47. Ibid.

48. Report of the Secretary, *Amendments to the Conventions of 1910 and 1921: Elimination of Age Limit,* LON Council, [2], LON Doc. C.503.M.244.1932. IV (1932).

49. Traffic in Women and Children Committee, *Report on the work of the Eleventh Session,* LON Council, [5], LON Doc. C.390.M.220.1932.IV (1932).

50. Report of the Secretary, *Amendments to the Conventions of 1910 and 1921: Elimination of Age Limit*, LON Council, [2–3], LON Doc. C.503.M.244.1932.IV (1932).

51. Report of the Secretary, *Amendments to the Conventions of 1910 and 1921: Elimination of Age Limit*, LON Council, [3], LON Doc. C.503.M.244.1932. IV (1932).

52. Ibid.

53. Report of the Secretary, *Amendments to the Conventions of 1910 and 1921: Elimination of Age Limit*, LON Council, [3], LON Doc. C.503.M.244.1932. IV (1932); Report of the Secretary, *Amendments to the Conventions of 1910 and 1921: Elimination of Age Limit*, LON Council, LON Doc. C.503.M.244.1932.IV Erratum (1932).

54. Report of the Secretary, *Amendments to the Conventions of 1910 and 1921: Elimination of Age Limit*, LON Council, [3], LON Doc. C.503.M.244.1932. IV (1932).

55. Ibid.

56. Ibid.

57. Ibid. See paragraph (a) where the Finish Penal Code is used as the example.

58. Report of the Secretary, *Amendments to the Conventions of 1910 and 1921: Elimination of Age Limit*, LON Council, [3], LON Doc. C.503.M.244.1932. IV (1932). See paragraph (b) where the Penal Code of Denmark is used as the example.

59. Report of the Secretary, *Amendments to the Conventions of 1910 and 1921: Elimination of Age Limit*, LON Council, [3], LON Doc. C.503.M.244.1932. IV (1932). See paragraph (c) which uses the Traffic in Women and Girls Act, 1928 of Siam as the example.

60. Report of the Secretary, *Amendments to the Conventions of 1910 and 1921: Elimination of Age Limit*, LON Council, [3–4], LON Doc. C.503.M.244.1932.IV (1932). See paragraph (d) which uses Article 532 of the Penal Code of Italy as the example.

61. Report of the Secretary, *Amendments to the Conventions of 1910 and 1921: Elimination of Age Limit*, LON Council, [4], LON Doc. C.503.M.244.1932.IV (1932). See paragraph (e) where the Japanese Penal Code is used as the example.

62. Report of the Secretary, *Amendments to the Conventions of 1910 and 1921: Elimination of Age Limit*, LON Council, [4], LON Doc. C.503.M.244.1932.IV (1932). See paragraph (g) where the Swedish Penal Code is used as the example.

63. Report of the Secretary, *Amendments to the Conventions of 1910 and 1921: Elimination of Age Limit*, LON Council, [4], LON Doc. C.503.M.244.1932. IV (1932). See paragraph (f) where the Criminal Law Amendment Act, 1885 of United Kingdom is used as the example.

64. Traffic in Women and Children Committee, *Report on the Work of the Eleventh Session*, LON Council, [5], LON Doc. C.390.M.220.1932.IV (1932).

65. Report of the Secretary, *Amendments to the Conventions of 1910 and 1921: Elimination of Age Limit*, LON Council, [4], LON Doc. C.503.M.244.1932. IV (1932).

66. Report of the Secretary, *Amendments to the Conventions of 1910 and 1921: Elimination of Age Limit*, LON Council, [5], LON Doc. C.503.M.244.1932. IV (1932); Traffic in Women and Children Committee, *Report on the Work of the Eleventh Session*, LON Council, [5], LON Doc. C.390.M.220.1932.IV (1932).

67. Report of the Secretary, *Amendments to the Conventions of 1910 and 1921: Elimination of Age Limit*, LON Council, [5], LON Doc. C.503.M.244.1932. IV (1932); Traffic in Women and Children Committee, *Report on the Work of the Eleventh Session*, LON Council, [5], LON Doc. C.390.M.220.1932.IV (1932). See also, *Report of the Fifth Committee to the Assembly*, LON Assembly, [2], LON Doc. A.55.1932.IV (1932).

68. *Report of the Fifth Committee to the Assembly*, LON Assembly, [2], LON Doc. A.55.1932.IV (1932).

69. League of Nations Official Journal, Report of the Traffic in Women and Children Committee on work of Its twelfth session (July 1933) 882.

70. *Report of the Fifth Committee to the Assembly*, LON Assembly, [2], LON Doc. A.55.1932.IV (1932).

71. Joint Session of the Traffic in Women and Children Committee and the Child Welfare Committee, *Report by the Representative of Panama*, LON Council, [5], LON Doc. C.306.1933.IV (1933); League of Nations Official Journal, *Report of the Traffic in Women and Children Committee on Work of Its twelfth Session* (July 1933) 882.

72. League of Nations Official Journal, *Report of the Traffic in women and Children Committee on Work of Its Twelfth Session* (July 1933) 882.

73. Joint Session of the Traffic in Women and Children Committee and the Child Welfare Committee, *Report by the Representative of Panama*, LON Council, [5–6], LON Doc. C.306.1933.IV (1933); League of Nations Official Journal, *Report of the Traffic in Women and Children Committee on Work of Its Twelfth Session* (July 1933) 882.

74. Joint Session of the Traffic in Women and Children Committee and the Child Welfare Committee, *Report by the Representative of Panama*, LON Council, [6], LON Doc. C.306.1933.IV (1933); *Draft Protocol for the Suppression of Traffic in Women of Full Age*, LON Assembly, Annex I, [2–3], LON Doc. A.24.1933.IV (1933).

75. *Draft Protocol for the Suppression of Traffic in Women of Full Age*, LON Assembly, Annex I, [2], LON Doc. A.24.1933.IV (1933).

76. Ibid.

77. Note by the Secretary-General, *Draft Protocol for the Suppression of Traffic in Women of Full Age*, LON Assembly, [1], LON Doc. A.24.1933.IV (1933).

78. Joint Session of the Traffic in Women and Children Committee and the Child Welfare Committee, *Report by the Representative of Panama*, LON Council, [6], LON Doc. C.306.1933.IV (1933).

79. Note by the Secretary-General, *Draft Protocol for the Suppression of Traffic in Women of Full Age*, LON Assembly, [1], LON Doc. A.24.1933.IV (1933).

80. Ibid.

81. Ibid.

82. Note by the Secretary-General, *Draft Protocol for the Suppression of Traffic in Women of Full Age*, LON Assembly, Annex II, [3], LON Doc. A.24.1933.IV (1933).

83. Note by the Secretary-General, *Draft Protocol for the Suppression of Traffic in Women of Full Age*, LON Assembly, [1], LON Doc. A.24(a).1933.IV (1933).

84. Note by the Secretary-General, *Draft Protocol for the Suppression of Traffic in Women of Full Age*, LON Assembly, Annex II, [4], LON Doc. A.24.1933.IV (1933).

85. Ibid.

86. Note by the Secretary-General, *Draft Protocol for the Suppression of Traffic in Women of Full Age*, LON Assembly, [1], LON Doc. A.24(a).1933.IV (1933).

87. Note by the Secretary-General, *Draft Protocol for the Suppression of Traffic in Women of Full Age*, LON Assembly, Annex II, [4], LON Doc. A.24.1933.IV (1933).

88. Note by the Secretary-General, *Draft Protocol for the Suppression of Traffic in Women of Full Age*, LON Assembly, [1], LON Doc. A.24(a).1933.IV (1933).

89. Note by the Secretary-General, *Draft Protocol for the Suppression of Traffic in Women of Full Age*, LON Assembly, Annex II, [4], LON Doc. A.24.1933.IV (1933).

90. Note by the Secretary-General, *Draft Protocol for the Suppression of Traffic in Women of Full Age*, LON Assembly, [3], LON Doc. A.24(a).1933.IV (1933).

91. Note by the Secretary-General, *Draft Protocol for the Suppression of Traffic in Women of Full Age*, LON Assembly, Annex II, [4], LON Doc. A.24.1933.IV (1933).

92. Note by the Secretary-General, *Draft Protocol for the Suppression of Traffic in Women of Full Age*, LON Assembly, [3], LON Doc. A.24(a).1933.IV (1933).

93. Note by the Secretary-General, *Draft Protocol for the Suppression of Traffic in Women of Full Age*, LON Assembly, Annex II, [5], LON Doc. A.24.1933.IV (1933).

94. Ibid.

95. Ibid.

96. Ibid.

97. Note by the Secretary-General, *Draft Protocol for the Suppression of Traffic in Women of Full Age*, LON Assembly, Annex II, [5], LON Doc. A.24.1933.IV (1933).

98. Note by the Secretary-General, *Draft Protocol for the Suppression of Traffic in Women of Full Age*, LON Assembly, Annex II, [5], LON Doc. A.24.1933.IV (1933).

99. Note by the Secretary-General, *Draft Protocol for the Suppression of Traffic in Women of Full Age*, LON Assembly, [3], LON Doc. A.24(a).1933.IV (1933).

100. Note by the Secretary-General, *Draft Protocol for the Suppression of Traffic in Women of Full Age*, LON Assembly, [2], LON Doc. A.24.1933.IV (1933).

101. Note by the Secretary-General, *Draft Protocol for the Suppression of Traffic in Women of Full Age*, LON Assembly, Annex II, [4], LON Doc. A.24.1933. IV (1933).

102. Note by the Secretary-General, *Draft Protocol for the Suppression of Traffic in Women of Full Age*, LON Assembly, Annex II, [4–5], LON Doc. A.24.1933.IV (1933).

103. Note by the Secretary-General, *Draft Protocol for the Suppression of Traffic in Women of Full Age*, LON Assembly, Annex II, [5], LON Doc. A.24.1933. IV (1933).

104. Ibid.

105. Ibid.

106. Ibid.

107. Article 4 states that any disputes arising between the High Contracting Parties on matters of interpretation or application of the Protocol which could not be satisfactorily settled by diplomacy was to be settled pursuant to whatever agreements were then in force between those Parties in relation to settlement of international disputes: *Note by the Secretary-General, Draft Protocol for the Suppression of Traffic in Women of Full Age*, LON Assembly, Annex I, [2], LON Doc A.24.1933.IV (1933).

108. Note by the Secretary General, *Draft Protocol for the Suppression of Traffic in Women of Full Age*, LON Assembly, Annex II, [5], LON Doc. A.24.1933. IV (1933).

109. Ibid.

110. Ibid.

111. Article 8 states that Protocol is to come into force after the Secretary-General of the League of Nations has received two ratifications or accessions. The Article also provides that the Protocol is to be registered by the Secretary-General of the League of Nations as soon as it enters into force: *Note by the Secretary-General, Draft Protocol for the Suppression of Traffic in Women of Full Age*, LON Assembly, Annex I, [3], LON Doc A.24.1933.IV (1933).

112. Note by the Secretary-General, *Draft Protocol for the Suppression of Traffic in Women of Full Age*, LON Assembly, Annex II, [5], LON Doc. A.24.1933. IV (1933).

113. Note by the Secretary-General, *Draft Protocol for the Suppression of Traffic in Women of Full Age*, LON Assembly, [3], LON Doc. A.24(a).1933.IV (1933).

114. Article 5 states that the French and English texts of the Protocol are authoritative, and that the Protocol is to be opened for signature (here there is standard wording concerning dates). Any State represented at the Conference (whether a Member of the League of Nations or not, including States to which the Council of the League had communicated the Protocol) was able to sign: *Note by the Secretary-General, Draft Protocol for the Suppression of Traffic in Women of Full Age*, LON Assembly, Annex I, [3], LON Doc A.24.1933.IV (1933).

115. Note by the Secretary-General, *Draft Protocol for the Suppression of Traffic in Women of Full Age*, LON Assembly, [3], LON Doc. A.24(a).1933.IV (1933).

116. Ibid.

117. Ibid.

118. Ibid.

119. Note by the Secretary-General, *Draft Protocol for the Suppression of Traffic in Women of Full Age*, LON Assembly, [3], LON Doc. A.24(a).1933.IV (1933).

120. Note by the Secretary-General, *Draft Protocol for the Suppression of Traffic in Women of Full Age*, LON Assembly, [1], LON Doc. A.24(a).1933.IV (1933).

121. Note by the Secretary-General, *Draft Protocol for the Suppression of Traffic in Women of Full Age*, LON Assembly, [1-2], LON Doc. A.24(a).1933.IV (1933).

122. Note by the Secretary-General, *Draft Protocol for the Suppression of Traffic in Women of Full Age*, LON Assembly, [2], LON Doc. A.24(a).1933.IV (1933).

123. Ibid.

124. Ibid.

125. Ibid.

126. Note by the Secretary-General, *Draft Protocol for the Suppression of Traffic in Women of Full Age*, LON Assembly, [2], LON Doc. A.24(a).1933.IV (1933).

127. Note by the Secretary-General, *Draft Protocol for the Suppression of Traffic in Women of Full Age*, LON Assembly, [2], LON Doc. A.24(a).1933.IV (1933).

128. Article 9, dealing with denunciation, provides that the Protocol may be denounced (by States on their own behalf, or for the territories referred

to in Article 10) by notification to the Secretary-General of the League of Nations. If that occurs, the denunciation takes effect one year later. Having received a denunciation, the Secretary-General is to notify all Members of the League of Nations and non-member States referred to in Article 5: *Note by the Secretary-General, Draft Protocol for the Suppression of Traffic in Women of Full Age,* LON Assembly, Annex I, [3], LON Doc A.24.1933.IV (1933).

129. Note by the Secretary-General, *Draft Protocol for the Suppression of Traffic in Women of Full Age,* LON Assembly, [3], LON Doc. A.24(a).1933.IV (1933).

130. *Traffic in Women and Children,* LON Assembly, LON Doc. A.47.1933. IV (1933). The revised draft Protocol may be found at: *Records of the Diplomatic Conference Concerning the Suppression of Traffic in Women of Full Age,* LON Council, Annex I, [15], LON Doc. C.649.M.310.1933.IV (1933).

131. Report by the Representative of Portugal, *Communication of the International Convention of the Traffic in Women of Full Age to States Non-Members of the League,* LON Council, [1], LON Doc. C.593.1933.IV (1933).

132. *Records of the Diplomatic Conference Concerning the Suppression of Traffic in Women of Full Age,* LON Council, [1], LON Doc. C.649.M.310.1933. IV (1933); Report by the Representative of Portugal, *Communication of the International Convention of the Traffic in Women of Full Age to States Non-Members of the League,* LON Council, [1], LON Doc. C.593.1933.IV (1933); International Convention for the Suppression of the Traffic in Women of Full Age, opened for signature 11 October 1933, 150 LNTS 431, preamble (entered into force 24 October 1934). (Conference of 1933)

133. Report by the Representative of Portugal, *Communication of the International Convention of the Traffic in Women of Full Age to States Non-Members of the League,* LON Council, [1], LON Doc. C.593.1933.IV (1933); *Records of the Diplomatic Conference Concerning the Suppression of Traffic in Women of Full Age,* LON Council, [5], LON Doc. C.649.M.310.1933.IV (1933).

134. *Records of the Diplomatic Conference Concerning the Suppression of Traffic in Women of Full Age,* LON Council, [6], LON Doc. C.649.M.310.1933.IV (1933).

135. Held on Monday, October 9th, 1933 at 10am: *Records of the Diplomatic Conference Concerning the Suppression of Traffic in Women of Full Age,* LON Council, [6], LON Doc. C.649.M.310.1933.IV (1933).

136. Anyone who procures, entices, or leads away any female of any age, even with their consent, for the gratification of some other person's desires for immoral purposes to be carried out in another country, is to be punished. Punishment is to be imposed even if the acts constituting the offence have been committed in different countries: *Records of the Diplomatic Conference Concerning the Suppression of Traffic in Women of Full Age,* LON Council, [7], LON Doc C.649.M.310.1933.IV (1933).

137. *Records of the Diplomatic Conference Concerning the Suppression of Traffic in Women of Full Age*, LON Council, [7], LON Doc. C.649.M.310.1933. IV (1933).

138. Here the term 'another country' includes any colonies, protectorates, and territories of the High Contracting Party and concerned as well as territories under his suzerainty or mandate, even if that other country has been excluded from the application of the Convention by a declaration made in accordance with Article 11: *Records of the Diplomatic Conference Concerning the Suppression of Traffic in Women of Full Age*, LON Council, [7], LON Doc C.649.M.310.1933.IV (1933).

139. *Records of the Diplomatic Conference Concerning the Suppression of Traffic in Women of Full Age*, LON Council, [7], LON Doc C.649.M.310.1933. IV (1933).

140. Ibid.

141. *Records of the Diplomatic Conference Concerning the Suppression of Traffic in Women of Full Age*, LON Council, [8], LON Doc C.649.M.310.1933.IV (1933). Article 11 provides for declaration by a High Contracting Party that acceptance of the Convention is not to be taken as acknowledgment of obligations in relation to other countries (colonies, protectorates and overseas territories), although a subsequent declaration may be made to render the Convention applicable to those other countries. Such declarations take effect after sixty days. Similarly, any High Contracting Party may declare a withdrawal by such other countries from the operation of the Convention, which then ceases to apply to those territories after one year. The Secretary-General of the League of Nations is to communicate notice of any denunciations and declarations under Articles 10 and 11 to all States (Members of the League and non-members mentioned in Article 6): *Records of the Diplomatic Conference concerning the Suppression of Traffic in Women of Full Age*, LON Council, Annex I, [16], LON Doc C.649.M.310.1933.IV (1933).

142. *Records of the Diplomatic Conference Concerning the Suppression of Traffic in Women of Full Age*, LON Council, [5], LON Doc. C.649.M.310.1933. IV (1933).

143. *Records of the Diplomatic Conference Concerning the Suppression of Traffic in Women of Full Age*, LON Council, [8], LON Doc. C.649.M.310.1933. IV (1933).

144. *Records of the Diplomatic Conference Concerning the Suppression of Traffic in Women of Full Age*, LON Council, [7], LON Doc. C.649.M.310.1933. IV (1933).

145. *Records of the Diplomatic Conference Concerning the Suppression of Traffic in Women of Full Age*, LON Council, [8], LON Doc. C.649.M.310.1933. IV (1933).

146. Ibid.

147. Ibid.

148. *Records of the Diplomatic Conference Concerning the Suppression of Traffic in Women of Full Age*, LON Council, [7], LON Doc. C.649.M.310.1933. IV (1933).

149. *Records of the Diplomatic Conference Concerning the Suppression of Traffic in Women of Full Age*, LON Council, [8], LON Doc. C.649.M.310.1933. IV (1933).

150. *Records of the Diplomatic Conference Concerning the Suppression of Traffic in Women of Full Age*, LON Council, [7], LON Doc. C.649.M.310.1933. IV (1933).

151. *Records of the Diplomatic Conference Concerning the Suppression of Traffic in Women of Full Age*, LON Council, [8], LON Doc. C.649.M.310.1933. IV (1933).

152. In jurisdictions where the laws could presently deal effectively with these offences, the High Contracting Parties agreed to take action to introduce sanctions to deal with them appropriately, according to their gravity: *Records of the Diplomatic Conference Concerning the Suppression of Traffic in Women of Full Age*, LON Council, [8], LON Doc C.649.M.310.1933.IV (1933).

153. *Records of the Diplomatic Conference Concerning the Suppression of Traffic in Women of Full Age*, LON Council, [8], LON Doc. C.649.M.310.1933. IV (1933).

154. *Records of the Diplomatic Conference Concerning the Suppression of Traffic in Women of Full Age*, LON Council, [9], LON Doc. C.649.M.310.1933. IV (1933).

155. *Records of the Diplomatic Conference Concerning the Suppression of Traffic in Women of Full Age*, LON Council, Annex 2, [17], LON Doc. C.649.M.310.1933. IV (1933).

156. *Records of the Diplomatic Conference Concerning the Suppression of Traffic in Women of Full Age*, LON Council, [9], LON Doc. C.649.M.310.1933. IV (1933).

157. *Records of the Diplomatic Conference Concerning the Suppression of Traffic in Women of Full Age*, LON Council, [9], LON Doc. C.649.M.310.1933.IV (1933). The meeting was held on Tuesday, 10 October 1933 at 10:15 am.

158. *Records of the Diplomatic Conference Concerning the Suppression of Traffic in Women of Full Age*, LON Council, [10], LON Doc. C.649.M.310.1933. IV (1933).

159. Ibid. For adoption of the preamble, see page 12 of this document.

160. *Records of the Diplomatic Conference Concerning the Suppression of Traffic in Women of Full Age*, LON Council, [10], LON Doc. C.649.M.310.1933. IV (1933).

161. Ibid.

162. Ibid. The delegate of the Irish Free State pointed out that he had abstained merely owing to lack of instructions from his government.

163. *Records of the Diplomatic Conference Concerning the Suppression of Traffic in Women of Full Age*, LON Council, [10], LON Doc. C.649.M.310.1933. IV (1933).

164. *Records of the Diplomatic Conference Concerning the Suppression of Traffic in Women of Full Age*, LON Council, [11], LON Doc. C.649.M.310.1933. IV (1933). Held on Wednesday, 11 October 1933 at 12 noon

165. *Records of the Diplomatic Conference Concerning the Suppression of Traffic in Women of Full Age*, LON Council, [12], LON Doc. C.649.M.310.1933. IV (1933). Held on Wednesday, 11 October 1933 at 12 noon.

166. Ibid.

167. *Records of the Diplomatic Conference Concerning the Suppression of Traffic in Women of Full Age*, LON Council, [13], LON Doc. C.649.M.310.1933. IV (1933).

168. Ibid.

169. Held on Wednesday, 11 October 1933 at 12 noon: *Records of the Diplomatic Conference Concerning the Suppression of Traffic in Women of Full Age*, LON Council, [12], LON Doc. C.649.M.310.1933.IV (1933).

170. Ibid.

171. Ibid.

172. Ibid.

173. Held on Wednesday, 11 October 1933 at 12 noon: *Records of the Diplomatic Conference Concerning the Suppression of Traffic in Women of Full Age*, LON Council, [12], LON Doc. C.649.M.310.1933.IV (1933).

174. Ibid.

175. Ibid.

176. *International Convention for the Suppression of the Traffic in Women of Full Age*, opened for signature 11 October 1933, 150 LNTS 431, Preamble (entered into force 24 October 1934).

177. *International Convention for the Suppression of the Traffic in Women of Full Age*, opened for signature 11 October 1933, 150 LNTS 431, Article 2 (entered into force 24 October 1934).

178. *International Convention for the Suppression of the Traffic in Women of Full Age*, opened for signature 11 October 1933, 150 LNTS 431, Article 1 (entered into force 24 October 1934).

179. Ibid.

180. *International Convention for the Suppression of the Traffic in Women of Full Age*, opened for signature 11 October 1933, 150 LNTS 431, Article 3 (entered into force 24 October 1934).

181. *International Convention for the Suppression of the Traffic in Women of Full Age*, opened for signature 11 October 1933, 150 LNTS 431, Article 4 (entered into force 24 October 1934).

182. *International Convention for the Suppression of the Traffic in Women of Full Age*, opened for signature 11 October 1933, 150 LNTS 431, Article 5 (entered into force 24 October 1934).

183. *International Convention for the Suppression of the Traffic in Women of Full Age*, opened for signature 11 October 1933, 150 LNTS 431, Article 6 (entered into force 24 October 1934).

184. *International Convention for the Suppression of the Traffic in Women of Full Age*, opened for signature 11 October 1933, 150 LNTS 431, Article 7 (entered into force 24 October 1934).

185. *International Convention for the Suppression of the Traffic in Women of Full Age*, opened for signature 11 October 1933, 150 LNTS 431, Article 8 (entered into force 24 October 1934).

186. *International Convention for the Suppression of the Traffic in Women of Full Age*, opened for signature 11 October 1933, 150 LNTS 431, Article 9 (entered into force 24 October 1934).

187. *International Convention for the Suppression of the Traffic in Women of Full Age*, opened for signature 11 October 1933, 150 LNTS 431, Article 10 (entered into force 24 October 1934).

## CHAPTER 4

1. *Report of the Special Body of Experts on Traffic in Women and Children Part One*, LON Council, [44], LON Doc. C.52.M.52.1927.IV (1927).

2. *Report of the Special Body of Experts on Traffic in Women and Children Part One*, LON Council, [47], LON Doc. C.52.M.52.1927.IV (1927).

3. The Advisory Committee sat from 25 April to 30 April 1927: Traffic in Women and Children Committee, *Report on the Work of the Sixth Session*, LON Council, [1], LON Doc. C.221.M.60.1927.IV (1927); *Report of the British Representative*, LON Council, [1], LON Doc. C.318.1927.IV (1927); Sir Austen Chamberlain, *Reports on the Work of the Committee during Its Sixth Session*, LON Assembly, [1] LON Doc. A.25.1927.IV (1927).

4. Traffic in Women and Children Committee, *Report on the Work of the Sixth Session*, LON Council, [3], LON Doc. C.221.M.60.1927.IV (1927); Sir Austen Chamberlain, *Reports on the Work of the Committee during Its Sixth Session*, LON Assembly, [5] LON Doc. A.25.1927.IV (1927).

5. Ibid.

6. The Advisory Committee sat from 12 March to 17 March 1928: Advisory Commission for the Protection and Welfare of Children and Young People, Traffic

in Women and Children Committee, *Report of the Seventh Session*, LON Council, [1], LON Doc. C.154.1928.IV (1928); *Report by the British Representative*, LON Assembly, [1], LON Doc. A.9.1928.IV (1928); *Report by the British Representative*, LON Council, [1], LON Doc. C.274.1928.IV (1928).

7. Children and Young People, Traffic in Women and Children Committee, *Report of the Seventh Session*, LON Council, [4], LON Doc. C.154.1928.IV (1928); *Report by the British Representative*, LON Assembly, [5], LON Doc. A.9.1928.IV (1928).

8. Ibid.

9. Ibid.

10. T. Hainari (Finland), *Report of the Fifth Committee to the Assembly*, LON Assembly, LON Doc. A.55.1928.IV (1928).

11. The Committee on Traffic in Women and Children, *Concise Study of the Laws and Penalties Relating to Souteneurs*, Part I, LON Council, [3], LON Doc. C.441.M.188.1931.IV (1931).

12. The Advisory Committee sat from 19 April to 26 April 1929: Advisory Commission for the Protection and Welfare of Children and Young People, Traffic in Women and Children Committee, *Report of the Eighth Session*, LON Council, [1], LON Doc. C.170.1929.IV (1929).

13. The Advisory Commission for the Protection and Welfare of Children and Young People, Traffic in Women and Children Committee, *Report of the Eighth Session*, LON Council, [6], LON Doc. C.170.1929.IV (1929); *Report of the Eighth Session Adopted by the Committee*, LON Assembly, [8], LON Doc. A.14.1929.IV (1929).

14. Ibid.

15. Ibid.

16. *Report of the Fifth Committee to the Assembly*, LON Assembly, [2], LON Doc. A.60.1929.IV (1929).

17. Ibid.

18. The Advisory Committee sat from 2 April to 9 April 1930: Advisory Commission for the Protection and Welfare of Children and Young People, Traffic in Women and Children Committee, *Report on the Ninth Session*, LON Council, [1], LON Doc. C.216.M.104.1930.IV (1930); *Report by the Persian Representative*, LON Council, [1], LON Doc. C.253.1930.IV (1930).

19. The Advisory Commission for the Protection and Welfare of Children and Young People, Traffic in Women and Children Committee, *Report on the Ninth Session*, LON Council, [5], LON Doc. C.216.M.104.1930.IV (1930). See also, *Report by the Persian Representative*, LON Council, [4], LON Doc. C.253.1930.IV (1930).

20. Ibid.

21. The Advisory Commission for the Protection and Welfare of Children and Young People, Traffic in Women and Children Committee, *Report on the Ninth Session*, LON Council, [5], LON Doc. C.216.M.104.1930.IV (1930).

22. Ibid.

23. Ibid.

24. The Advisory Committee sat from 21 April to 27 April 1931: Traffic in Women and Children Committee, *Report on the Work of the Tenth Session*, LON Council, [1], LON Doc. C.267.M.122.1931.IV (1931); *Report by the Persian Representative*, LON Council, [1], LON Doc. C.336.1931.IV (1931).

25. Traffic in Women and Children Committee, *Report on the Work of the Tenth Session*, LON Council, [4], LON Doc. C.267.M.122.1931.IV (1931); *Report by the Persian Representative*, LON Council, [2], LON Doc. C.336.1931.IV (1931).

26. Traffic in Women and Children Committee, *Report on the Work of the Tenth Session*, LON Council, [4], LON Doc. C.267.M.122.1931.IV (1931).

27. Ibid.

28. Ibid.

29. Ibid.

30. Traffic in Women and Children Committee, *Report on the Work of the Tenth Session*, LON Council, [4], LON Doc. C.267.M.122.1931.IV (1931).

31. Ibid.

32. For the text of the revised preliminary draft Protocol see, Traffic in Women and Children Committee, *Report on the Work of the Tenth Session*, LON Council, Appendix, [9], LON Doc. C.267.M.122.1931.IV (1931).

33. Traffic in Women and Children Committee, *Report on the Work of the Tenth Session*, LON Council, [4], LON Doc. C.267.M.122.1931.IV (1931); *Report by the Persian Representative*, LON Council, [2], LON Doc. C.336.1931.IV (1931).

34. Traffic in Women and Children Committee, *Report on the Work of the Tenth Session*, LON Council, Appendix, [9], LON Doc. C.267.M.122.1931.IV (1931).

35. Ibid.

36. Ibid.

37. Traffic in Women and Children Committee, *Report on the Work of the Tenth Session*, LON Council, Appendix, [9], LON Doc. C.267.M.122.1931.IV (1931).

38. Ibid.

39. Ibid.

40. Ibid

41. Traffic in Women and Children Committee, *Report on the Work of the Eleventh Session*, LON Council, [6], LON Doc. C.390.M.220.1932.IV (1932).

42. The Committee sat from 4 April to 9 April 1932: Report of the Secretary, *Amendments to the Conventions of 1910 and 1921: Elimination of Age Limit*, LON Council, [1], LON Doc. C.503.M.244.1932.IV (1932); Traffic in Women and

Children Committee, *Report on the Work of the Eleventh Session*, LON Council, [1], LON Doc. C.390.M.220.1932.IV (1932).

43. Traffic in Women and Children Committee, *Report on the Work of the Eleventh Session*, LON Council, [6], LON Doc. C.390.M.220.1932.IV (1932).

44. Ibid.

45. Traffic in Women and Children Committee, *Report on the Work of the Eleventh Session*, LON Council, [6], LON Doc. C.390.M.220.1932.IV (1932).

46. Ibid.

47. Ibid.

48. *Joint Session of the Traffic in Women and Children Committee and Child Welfare Committee and Session of the Traffic in Women and Children Committee*, LON Council, [30], LON Doc. C.306.1933.IV (1933).

49. Ibid.

50. Ibid.

51. Ibid.

52. *Joint Session of the Traffic in Women and Children Committee and Child Welfare Committee and Session of the Traffic in Women and Children Committee*, LON Council, [30], LON Doc. C.306.1933.IV (1933).

53. Ibid.

54. Ibid.

55. Ibid.

56. *Joint Session of the Traffic in Women and Children Committee and Child Welfare Committee and Session of the Traffic in Women and Children Committee*, LON Council, [30], LON Doc. C.306.1933.IV (1933).

57. The Committee sat from 4 April to 7 April 1934: Advisory Commission for the Protection and Welfare of Children and Young People, *Report on the Work of the Commission in 1934, Report of the Work of the Thirteenth Session of the Traffic in Women and Children Committee*, LON Council, [2], LON Doc. C.149.M.62.1934.IV (1934).

58. The Advisory Commission for the Protection and Welfare of Children and Young People, *Report on the Work of the Commission in 1934, Report of the Work of the Thirteenth Session of the Traffic in Women and Children Committee*, LON Council, [6], LON Doc. C.149.M.62.1934.IV (1934).

59. Ibid.

60. Ibid.

61. Ibid.

62. The Advisory Commission for the Protection and Welfare of Children and Young People, *Report on the Work of the Commission in 1934, Report of the Work of the Thirteenth Session of the Traffic in Women and Children Committee*, LON Council, [6], LON Doc. C.149.M.62.1934.IV (1934).

63. *Report by the Fifth Committee to the Assembly*, LON Assembly, [2], LON Doc. A.38.1934.IV (1934).

64. The Advisory Commission for the Protection and Welfare of Children and Young People, *Report on the Work of the Commission in 1935, Report of the Work of the Fourteenth Session of the Traffic in Women and Children Committee*, LON Council, [39], LON Doc. C.187.M.104.1935.IV (1935).

65. Ibid.

66. The Advisory Committee sat from 2 May to 9 May 1935: Advisory Commission for the Protection and Welfare of Children and Young People, *Report on the Work of the Commission in 1935, Report of the Work of the Fourteenth Session of the Traffic in Women and Children Committee*, LON Council, [2], LON Doc. C.187.M.104.1935.IV (1935).

67. The Advisory Commission for the Protection and Welfare of Children and Young People, *Report on the Work of the Commission in 1935, Report of the Work of the Fourteenth Session of the Traffic in Women and Children Committee*, LON Council, [40], LON Doc. C.187.M.104.1935.IV (1935).

68. Ibid.

69. Ibid.

70. Ibid.

71. The Advisory Commission for the Protection and Welfare of Children and Young People, *Report on the Work of the Commission in 1935, Report of the Work of the Fourteenth Session of the Traffic in Women and Children Committee*, LON Council, [39], LON Doc. C.187.M.104.1935.IV (1935).

72. The Advisory Commission for the Protection and Welfare of Children and Young People, *Report on the Work of the Commission in 1935, Report of the Work of the Fourteenth Session of the Traffic in Women and Children Committee*, LON Council, [40], LON Doc. C.187.M.104.1935.IV (1935).

73. The Advisory Commission for the Protection and Welfare of Children and Young People, *Report on the Work of the Commission in 1936, Report of the Work of the Fifteenth Session of the Traffic in Women and Children Committee*, LON Council, [8], LON Doc. C.204.M.127. 1936.IV (1936).

74. The Advisory Committee sat from 20 April to 27 April 1936: Advisory Commission for the Protection and Welfare of Children and Young People, *Report on the Work of the Commission in 1936, Report of the Work of the Fifteenth Session of the Traffic in Women and Children Committee*, LON Council, [2], LON Doc. C.204.M.127. 1936.IV (1936); Report by the Representative of Chile, *Report on the Work of Its Fifteenth Session*, LON Council, [1], LON Doc. C.231.1936.IV (1936).

75. The Advisory Commission for the Protection and Welfare of Children and Young People, *Report on the Work of the Commission in 1936, Report of the*

*Work of the Fifteenth Session of the Traffic in Women and Children Committee,* LON Council, [8], LON Doc. C.204.M.127. 1936.IV (1936).

76. Ibid.

77. Ibid., *Report Submitted by the Fifth Committee to the Assembly,* LON Assembly, [2], LON Doc. A.62.1936.IV (1936).

78. The First Draft Convention can be found at Advisory Commission for the Protection and Welfare of Children and Young People, *Report on the Work of the Commission in 1936, Report of the Work of the Fifteenth Session of the Traffic in Women and Children Committee,* LON Council, Appendix, [12–13], LON Doc. C.204.M.127. 1936.IV (1936).

79. The Advisory Commission for the Protection and Welfare of Children and Young People, *Report on the Work of the Commission in 1936, Report of the Work of the Fifteenth Session of the Traffic in Women and Children Committee,* LON Council, [8], LON Doc. C.204.M.127. 1936.IV (1936).

80. The Advisory Commission for the Protection and Welfare of Children and Young People, *Report on the Work of the Commission in 1936, Report of the Work of the Fifteenth Session of the Traffic in Women and Children Committee,* LON Council, Appendix, [12], LON Doc. C.204.M.127. 1936.IV (1936).

81. Ibid.

82. The Advisory Commission for the Protection and Welfare of Children and Young People, *Report on the Work of the Commission in 1936, Report of the Work of the Fifteenth Session of the Traffic in Women and Children Committee,* LON Council, Appendix, [12], LON Doc. C.204.M.127. 1936.IV (1936).

83. Ibid.

84. Ibid.

85. Ibid.

86. The Advisory Commission for the Protection and Welfare of Children and Young People, *Report on the Work of the Commission in 1936, Report of the Work of the Fifteenth Session of the Traffic in Women and Children Committee,* LON Council, Appendix, [12], LON Doc. C.204.M.127. 1936.IV (1936).

87. Advisory Commission for the Protection and Welfare of Children and Young People, *Report on the Work of the Commission in 1936, Report of the Work of the Fifteenth Session of the Traffic in Women and Children Committee,* LON Council, Appendix, [14], LON Doc. C.204.M.127. 1936.IV (1936).

88. The Advisory Commission for the Protection and Welfare of Children and Young People, *Report on the Work of the Commission in 1936, Report of the Work of the Fifteenth Session of the Traffic in Women and Children Committee,* LON Council, [8], LON Doc. C.204.M.127. 1936.IV (1936).

89. Ibid. Report by the Representative of Chile, *Report on the Work of Its Fifteenth Session,* LON Council, [3], LON Doc. C.231.1936.IV (1936); The

Advisory Committee on Social Questions, *Report on the Work of the Committee in 1937 (First session)*, LON Council, [29], LON Doc. C.235.M.169.1937.IV (1937).

90. The Advisory Committee on Social Questions, *Report on the Work of the Committee in 1937 (First session)*, LON Council, [29], LON Doc. C.235.M.169.1937.IV (1937); *Report Submitted by the Fifth Committee to the Assembly*, LON Assembly, [2], LON Doc. A.62.1936.IV (1936).

91. *Report Submitted by the Fifth Committee to the Assembly*, LON Assembly, [2], LON Doc. A.62.1936.IV (1936).

92. Ibid.

93. The Advisory Committee on Social Questions, *Report on the Work of the Committee in 1937 (First session)*, LON Council, [1], LON Doc. C.235.M.169.1937. IV (1937).

94. The Advisory Committee on Social Questions, *Report on the Work of the Committee in 1937 (First session)*, LON Council, [29], LON Doc. C.235.M.169.1937.IV (1937).

95. Ibid. *Report Submitted by the Fifth Committee to the Assembly*, LON Assembly, [4], LON Doc. A.65.1937.IV (1937).

96. The Advisory Committee on Social Questions, *Report on the Work of the Committee in 1937 (First session)*, LON Council, [29], LON Doc. C.235.M.169.1937.IV (1937); Report by the Representative of Chile, *Convention for the Suppression of the Exploitation of Prostitution of Others*, LON Council, LON Doc. C.357.1937.IV (1937).

97. The Advisory Committee on Social Questions, *Report on the Work of the Committee in 1937 (First session)*, LON Council, [29], LON Doc. C.235.M.169.1937.IV (1937).

98. The Advisory Committee on Social Questions, *Report on the work of the Committee in 1937 (First session)*, LON Council, [30], LON Doc. C.235.M.169.1937.IV (1937).

99. The Advisory Committee on Social Questions, *Report on the Work of the Committee in 1937 (First session)*, LON Council, [29], LON Doc. C.235.M.169.1937.IV (1937).

100. The Advisory Committee on Social Questions, *Report on the Work of the Committee in 1937 (First session)*, LON Council, [29–30], LON Doc. C.235.M.169.1937.IV (1937).

101. The Advisory Committee on Social Questions, *Report on the Work of the Committee in 1937 (First session)*, LON Council, [30], LON Doc. C.235.M.169.1937.IV (1937).

102. Ibid.

103. The Advisory Committee on Social Questions, *Report on the Work of the Committee in 1937 (First session)*, LON Council, [30], LON Doc. C.235.M.169.1937.IV (1937).

104. Ibid.

105. Ibid.

106. Ibid. See, *Report Submitted by the Fifth Committee to the Assembly*, LON Assembly, [4], LON Doc. A.65.1937.IV (1937).

107. The Advisory Committee on Social Questions, *Report on the Work of the Committee in 1937 (First session)*, LON Council, [30], LON Doc. C.235.M.169.1937.IV (1937).

108. Ibid.

109. Ibid.

110. The Advisory Committee on Social Questions, *Report on the Work of the Committee in 1937 (First session)*, LON Council, [31], LON Doc. C.235.M.169.1937.IV (1937); Advisory Committee on Social Questions, *Report of the Sub-Committee Entrusted with Drawing up the Second Draft of a Convention for Suppressing the Exploitation of the Prostitution of Others (Paris session)*, LON Council, [1], LON Doc. C.331.M.233.1937.IV (1937).

111. Ibid.

112. The Advisory Committee on Social Questions, *Report of the Sub-Committee Entrusted with Drawing up the Second Draft of a Convention for Suppressing the Exploitation of the Prostitution of Others (Paris session)*, LON Council, [2], LON Doc. C.331.M.233.1937.IV (1937). The second draft convention may be found at Advisory Committee on Social Questions, *Report of the Sub-Committee Entrusted with Drawing up the Second Draft of a Convention for Suppressing the Exploitation of the Prostitution of Others (Paris session)*, LON Council, Annex [6–9], LON Doc. C.331.M.233.1937.IV (1937).

113. The Advisory Committee on Social Questions, *Report of the Sub-Committee Entrusted with Drawing up the Second Draft of a Convention for Suppressing the Exploitation of the Prostitution of Others (Paris session)*, LON Council, Annex [6], LON Doc. C.331.M.233.1937.IV (1937).

114. Ibid.

115. Ibid.

116. Ibid.

117. The Advisory Committee on Social Questions, *Report of the Sub-Committee Entrusted with Drawing up the Second Draft of a Convention for Suppressing the Exploitation of the Prostitution of Others (Paris session)*, LON Council, [2], LON Doc. C.331.M.233.1937.IV (1937).

118. Ibid.

119. The Advisory Committee on Social Questions, *Report of the Sub-Committee Entrusted with Drawing up the Second Draft of a Convention for Suppressing the Exploitation of the Prostitution of Others (Paris session)*, LON Council, [2–3], LON Doc. C.331.M.233.1937.IV (1937).

120. The Advisory Committee on Social Questions, *Report of the Sub-Committee Entrusted with Drawing up the Second Draft of a Convention for Suppressing the Exploitation of the Prostitution of Others (Paris session)*, LON Council, [3], LON Doc. C.331.M.233.1937.IV (1937).

121. Ibid.

122. Ibid.

123. Ibid.

124. The Advisory Committee on Social Questions, *Report of the Sub-Committee Entrusted with Drawing up the Second Draft of a Convention for Suppressing the Exploitation of the Prostitution of Others (Paris session)*, LON Council, [3], LON Doc. C.331.M.233.1937.IV (1937).

125. Ibid.

126. The Advisory Committee on Social Questions, *Report of the Sub-Committee Entrusted with Drawing up the Second Draft of a Convention for Suppressing the Exploitation of the Prostitution of Others (Paris session)*, LON Council, [3], LON Doc. C.331.M.233.1937.IV (1937).

127. Ibid.

128. The Advisory Committee on Social Questions, *Report of the Sub-Committee Entrusted with Drawing up the Second Draft of a Convention for Suppressing the Exploitation of the Prostitution of Others (Paris session)*, LON Council, [3], LON Doc. C.331.M.233.1937.IV (1937).

129. Ibid.

130. The Advisory Committee on Social Questions, *Report of the Sub-Committee Entrusted with Drawing up the Second Draft of a Convention for Suppressing the Exploitation of the Prostitution of Others (Paris session)*, LON Council, [3], LON Doc. C.331.M.233.1937.IV (1937).

131. Ibid.

132. Ibid.

133. The Advisory Committee on Social Questions, *Report of the Sub-Committee Entrusted with Drawing up the Second Draft of a Convention for Suppressing the Exploitation of the Prostitution of Others (Paris session)*, LON Council, [3–4], LON Doc. C.331.M.233.1937.IV (1937).

134. The Advisory Committee on Social Questions, *Report of the Sub-Committee Entrusted with Drawing up the Second Draft of a Convention for Suppressing the Exploitation of the Prostitution of Others (Paris session)*, LON Council, [4], LON Doc. C.331.M.233.1937.IV (1937).

135. Ibid.

136. The Advisory Committee on Social Questions, *Report of the Sub-Committee Entrusted with Drawing up the Second Draft of a Convention for Suppressing the Exploitation of the Prostitution of Others (Paris session)*, LON Council, [5], LON Doc. C.331.M.233.1937.IV (1937).

137. The Advisory Committee on Social Questions, *Report of the Sub-Committee Entrusted with Drawing up the Second Draft of a Convention for Suppressing the Exploitation of the Prostitution of Others (Paris session)*, LON Council, [6], LON Doc. C.331.M.233.1937.IV (1937).

138. Ibid.

139. Ibid.

140. The Advisory Committee on Social Questions, *Report on the Work of the Committee in 1938 (Second session)*, LON Council, [20], LON Doc. C.147.M.88.1938.IV (1938); Suppression of the Exploitation of the Prostitution of Others, *Note by the Secretary-General*, LON Assembly, [1], LON Doc. A.13.1938. IV (1938).

141. For the comments of the sub-committee, see Advisory Committee on Social Questions, *Report of the Sub-Committee Entrusted with Drawing up the Second Draft of a Convention for Suppressing the Exploitation of the Prostitution of Others*, LON Council, [2–6], LON Doc. C.331.M.233.1937.IV (1937).

142. The Advisory Committee on Social Questions, *Report on the Work of the Committee in 1938 (Second session)*, LON Council, [20], LON Doc. C.147.M.88.1938.IV (1938); Suppression of the Exploitation of the Prostitution of Others, *Note by the Secretary-General*, LON Assembly, [1], LON Doc. A.13.1938. IV (1938).

143. *Suppression of the Exploitation of the Prostitution of Others, General Remarks Concerning the Draft*, LON Assembly, [2], LON Doc. A.13.1938.IV (1938).

144. Ibid.

145. Ibid.

146. Ibid.

147. *Suppression of the Exploitation of the Prostitution of Others, General Remarks Concerning the Draft*, LON Assembly, [2], LON Doc. A.13.1938.IV (1938).

148. Ibid.

149. *Suppression of the Exploitation of the Prostitution of Others, General Remarks Concerning the Draft*, LON Assembly, [2], LON Doc. A.13.1938.IV (1938).

150. Ibid.

151. Ibid.

152. *Suppression of the Exploitation of the Prostitution of Others, General Remarks Concerning the Draft*, LON Assembly, [2–3], LON Doc. A.13.1938.IV (1938).

153. *Suppression of the Exploitation of the Prostitution of Others, General Remarks Concerning the Draft*, LON Assembly, [3], LON Doc. A.13.1938.IV (1938).

154. Ibid.

155. Ibid.

156. Ibid. While the Norway Government stated its agreement with the object and fundamental principles of the draft convention, it felt bound to add some further remarks on the draft. It also had some reservations about some of the detailed provisions, which were incompatible with then-current Norwegian legislation. The offences mentioned in Articles 1 and 2 were already subject to criminal sanction in Norway under the Norwegian Penal Code: Articles 202, 204, and 206. However, Article 3 listed several circumstances, agreed by the contracting States to be considered aggravating, which would require changes in the Norwegian Penal Code. Since different jurisdictions had different approaches to aggravating circumstances, the Norway Government preferred an approach that merely referred in the convention to the national legislations. Norway added that under its Penal Code, aggravating circumstances included: habitual action, coercion, threats or trickery, or taking advantage of feeble-mindedness; acting out of a desire for gain, or offending against a wife, child, or a person under the offender's authority or supervision; abuse of official position or position as a clergyman, doctor or teacher; and incitement to immoral conduct of a person under 18 years of age, or sending a person out of the country for immoral purposes (Penal Code Sections 204 and 206, second paragraph). Norway felt that the last paragraph of Article 7 should be omitted. Merely being a national of the State in question seemed to be insufficient justification for limiting the maximum penalty. The Norway Government also preferred wording that would enable proceedings to be waived for special reasons in cases determined by law. Under the Norwegian Criminal Procedure Code (Section 85, paragraph 2), such waiver of proceedings was possible in certain circumstances, including lack of public interest considerations, effluxion of time, and mitigating circumstances. Waiver could be made conditional upon victim compensation or good behaviour for a period not exceeding the period of sanction or a maximum of two years. Finally, Norway pointed out that the enumerations in Article 10 of certain acts to be treated as *ipso jure* grounds of extradition, were incompatible with the Norwegian extradition system. Under the Norwegian Extradition Law (Law of 13 June 1908), a minimum penalty was fixed in limitation of the right of extradition. However, acts subject to sanction, such as those mentioned in the convention, were dealt with by the general provisions of the Extradition Law, which meant that the Norway government was able to accept the present wording of Article 10 of the draft convention: *Suppression of the Exploitation of the Prostitution of Others, General Remarks Concerning the Draft*, LON Assembly, Appendix, [6], LON Doc A.13.1938.IV (1938).

157. *Suppression of the Exploitation of the Prostitution of Others, General Remarks Concerning the Draft*, LON Assembly, [3], LON Doc. A.13.1938.IV (1938).

158. The Committee examined the draft International Convention for Suppressing the Exploitation of Prostitution as the Council of Ministries had requested. It focused on Article 2, which provided: 'the High Contracting Parties agree to punish any person who exploits immorality either by aiding, abetting, or facilitating the prostitution of third parties, or by deriving any material profit there from'. The Committee agreed that the Penal Code of Siam precluded compliance with this article, and also agreed that enactment of penal legislation implementing the provisions set out in the Article would have the effect of a sudden and total abolition of licensed or tolerated houses. The Committee referred to a recent issue of a similar nature relating to the Conference of Central Authorities of Eastern Countries at Bandoeng, and the experience with resolutions recommending administrative, medical and social measures to accompany abolitionist legislation, and concluded that a gradual and progressive introduction of such laws in Siam to implement Article 2 of the draft convention was preferable. The Committee was therefore of the view that Article 2 could not be implemented as currently framed. Similar, though less severe, difficulties were noted in relation to Article 1. The Committee, having observed the abrupt departure from existing Siamese legal procedures that would result from an introduction of special measures relating to extradition, letters of request and prosecution of Siamese nationals for offences committed abroad, proposed: (1) a modification of Articles 1 and 2 to include the words, 'to punish to the fullest extent compatible with their existing national laws and with the subsequent development of state laws'; and (2) introduction of a new provision that would restrict incorporation of new legal procedures to those which would conform to the limits of existing domestic law, in the same manner as Article 13, Section 8, of the Convention of 1936 for the Suppression of the Illicit Traffic in Dangerous Drugs, to wit: 'nothing in the present article shall be construed as an undertaking on the part of the High Contracting Parties to adopt in criminal matters any form or methods of proof contrary to their laws or to execute letters of request otherwise than within the limits of their laws': *Suppression of the Exploitation of the Prostitution of Others, General Remarks Concerning the Draft*, LON Assembly, Appendix [6-7], LON Doc. A.13.1938.IV (1938).

159. *Suppression of the Exploitation of the Prostitution of Others, General Remarks Concerning the Draft*, LON Assembly, [3], LON Doc. A.13.1938.IV (1938).

160. *Suppression of the Exploitation of the Prostitution of Others, General Remarks Concerning the Draft*, LON Assembly, [3], LON Doc. A.13.1938.IV (1938).

161. Ibid.

162. Ibid.

163. Ibid.

164. *Suppression of the Exploitation of the Prostitution of Others, General Remarks Concerning the Draft*, LON Assembly, [3], LON Doc. A.13.1938.IV (1938).

165. *Suppression of the Exploitation of the Prostitution of Others, General Remarks Concerning the Draft*, LON Assembly, [4], LON Doc. A.13.1938.IV (1938).

166. *Suppression of the Exploitation of the Prostitution of Others, Further Government Answers Received*, LON Assembly, [1], LON Doc. A.13.1938.IV Addendum (1938).

167. Ibid.

168. *Suppression of the Exploitation of the Prostitution of Others, Further Government Answers Received*, LON Assembly, [2], LON Doc. A.13.1938.IV Addendum (1938).

169. Ibid.

170. Ibid.

171. *Report Submitted by the Fifth Committee to the Assembly*, LON Assembly, [1], LON Doc. A.63.1938.IV (1938).

172. *Report Submitted by the Fifth Committee to the Assembly*, LON Assembly, [2], LON Doc. A.63.1938.IV (1938).

173. Ibid.

174. *Suppression of the Traffic in Women and Children*, ESC Res 43(IV), UN ESCOR, 4th sess., 24, UN Doc. E/437 (1947); Department of Public Information United Nations, *Yearbook of the United Nations 1946–47* (1947) 521; Department of Public Information United Nations, *Yearbook of the United Nations 1947–48* (1949) 617.

175. Department of Public Information United Nations, *Yearbook of the United Nations 1947–48* (1949) 617.

176. Resolutions adopted by the Economic and Social Council during Its Fifth Session from 19 July to 16 August 1947, UN ESCOR, UN Doc. E/573 (1947).

177. Unification of the International Agreements and Conventions for the suppression of the traffic in women and children, ESC Res 83(V), UN ESCOR, 5th sess., 53–54, UN Doc. E/573 (1947).

178. Resolutions adopted by the Economic and Social Council during Its Seventh Session from 19 July to 29 August 1948, UN ESCOR, UN Doc. E/1065 (1948).

179. *Suppression of the Traffic in Women and Children*, ESC Res 155 (VII) E.I., UN ESCOR, 7th sess., 34–35, UN Doc. E/1065 (1948); Department of Public Information United Nations, *Yearbook of the United Nations 1947–48* (1949) 617.

180. *Suppression of the Traffic in Women and Children*, ESC Res 155 (VII) E.I., UN ESCOR, 7th sess., 35, UN Doc. E/1065 (1948); Department of Public Information United Nations, *Yearbook of the United Nations 1947–48* (1949) 617.

181. *Suppression of the Traffic in Women and Children*, ESC Res 155 (VII) E.II., UN ESCOR, 7th sess., 35–36, UN Doc. E/1065 (1948).

182. Columbia University Press in cooperation with the United Nations, *Yearbook of the United Nations 1948–49* (1950) 609.

183. Ibid.

184. Ibid.

185. Columbia University Press in cooperation with the United Nations, *Yearbook of the United Nations 1948–49* (1950) 609.

186. Ibid.

187. *Draft Convention for the Suppression of the Traffic in Persons and of the Exploitation of the Prostitution of Others*, ESC Res 243(IX) B, UN ESCOR, 9th sess., Annex, 43, UN Doc. E/1553 (1949).

188. *Draft Convention for the Suppression of the Traffic in Persons and of the Exploitation of the Prostitution of Others*, ESC Res 243(IX) B, UN ESCOR, 9th sess., Annex, 43–44, UN Doc. E/1553 (1949).

189. *Draft Convention for the Suppression of the Traffic in Persons and of the Exploitation of the Prostitution of Others*, ESC Res 243(IX) B, UN ESCOR, 9th sess., Annex, 44, UN Doc. E/1553 (1949).

190. Ibid.

191. Ibid.

192. Ibid.

193. *Draft Convention for the Suppression of the Traffic in Persons and of the Exploitation of the Prostitution of Others*, ESC Res 243(IX) B, UN ESCOR, 9th sess., Annex, 44, UN Doc. E/1553 (1949).

194. Ibid.

195. Ibid.

196. *Draft Convention for the Suppression of the Traffic in Persons and of the Exploitation of the Prostitution of Others*, ESC Res 243(IX) B, UN ESCOR, 9th sess., Annex, 44–45, UN Doc. E/1553 (1949).

197. *Draft Convention for the Suppression of the Traffic in Persons and of the Exploitation of the Prostitution of Others*, ESC Res 243(IX) B, UN ESCOR, 9th sess., Annex, 45, UN Doc. E/1553 (1949).

198. Ibid.

199. Ibid.

200. Ibid.

201. *Draft Convention for the Suppression of the Traffic in Persons and of the Exploitation of the Prostitution of Others*, ESC Res 243(IX) B, UN ESCOR, 9th sess., Annex, 45–46, UN Doc. E/1553 (1949).

202. Ibid.

203. *Draft Convention for the Suppression of the Traffic in Persons and of the Exploitation of the Prostitution of Others*, ESC Res 243(IX) B, UN ESCOR, 9th sess., Annex, 46, UN Doc. E/1553 (1949).

204. Ibid.

205. Ibid.

206. *Draft Convention for the Suppression of the Traffic in Persons and of the Exploitation of the Prostitution of Others*, ESC Res 243(IX) B, UN ESCOR, 9th sess., Annex, 47, UN Doc. E/1553 (1949).

207. Ibid.

208. *Draft Convention for the Suppression of the Traffic in Persons and of the Exploitation of the Prostitution of Others*, ESC Res 243(IX) B, UN ESCOR, 9th sess., Annex, 47, UN Doc. E/1553 (1949).

209. Ibid.

210. Ibid.

211. *Draft Convention for the Suppression of the Traffic in Persons and of the Exploitation of the Prostitution of Others*, ESC Res 243(IX) B, UN ESCOR, 9th sess., Annex, 48, UN Doc. E/1553 (1949).

212. Ibid.

213. Ibid.

214. Ibid.

215. *Draft Convention for the Suppression of the Traffic in Persons and of the Exploitation of the Prostitution of Others*, ESC Res 243(IX) B, UN ESCOR, 9th sess., Annex, 48, UN Doc. E/1553 (1949).

216. Ibid.

217. *Draft Convention for the Suppression of the Traffic in Persons and of the Exploitation of the Prostitution of Others*, ESC Res 243(IX) B, UN ESCOR, 9th sess., Annex, 48–49, UN Doc. E/1553 (1949).

218. Ibid.

219. *Draft Convention for the Suppression of the Traffic in Persons and of the Exploitation of the Prostitution of Others*, ESC Res 243(IX) B, UN ESCOR, 9th sess., Annex, 49, UN Doc. E/1553 (1949).

220. Ibid.

221. Ibid.

222. Ibid.

223. *Draft Convention for the Suppression of the Traffic in Persons and of the Exploitation of the Prostitution of Others*, ESC Res 243(IX) B, UN ESCOR, 9th sess., Annex, 49, UN Doc. E/1553 (1949).

224. *Draft Convention for the Suppression of the Traffic in Persons and of the Exploitation of the Prostitution of Others*, ESC Res 243(IX) B, UN ESCOR, 9th sess., Annex, 50, UN Doc. E/1553 (1949).

225. *Draft Convention for the Suppression of the Traffic in Persons and of the Exploitation of the Prostitution of Others*, ESC Res 243(IX) B, UN ESCOR, 9th sess., 42, UN Doc. E/1553 (1949).

226. The Social Committee held Its meetings on 7 and 8 July 1949 (81st to 83rd meetings): Columbia University Press in cooperation with the United Nations, *Yearbook of the United Nations 1948–49* (1950) 609.

227. Columbia University Press in cooperation with the United Nations, *Yearbook of the United Nations 1948–49* (1950) 609.

228. Ibid.

229. Ibid.

230. Ibid.

231. Columbia University Press in cooperation with the United Nations, *Yearbook of the United Nations 1948–49* (1950) 609.

232. Ibid.

233. Ibid.

234. Ibid.

235. Columbia University Press in cooperation with the United Nations, *Yearbook of the United Nations 1948–49* (1950) 610.

236. Resolutions adopted by the Economic and Social Council during Its Ninth Session from 5 July to 15 August 1949, UN ESCOR, UN Doc. E/1553 (1949).

237. Draft *Convention for the Suppression of the Traffic in Persons and of the Exploitation of the Prostitution of Others*, ESC Res 243(IX) B, UN ESCOR, 9th sess., 42, UN Doc. E/1553 (1949).

238. Ibid.

239. Columbia University Press in cooperation with the United Nations, *Yearbook of the United Nations 1948–49* (1950) 610.

240. Ibid., 610–11.

241. Columbia University Press in cooperation with the United Nations, *Yearbook of the United Nations 1948–49* (1950) 611.

242. Ibid.

243. Ibid., 610.

244. Ibid.

245. 169th, 190th, and 199th to 208th meeting on 19 October, 11 and 21 to 28 November 1949: Columbia University Press in cooperation with the United Nations, *Yearbook of the United Nations 1948–49* (1950) 610.

246. Columbia University Press in cooperation with the United Nations, *Yearbook of the United Nations 1948–49* (1950) 610.

247. Ibid.

248. Ibid.

249. Columbia University Press in cooperation with the United Nations, *Yearbook of the United Nations 1948–49 (1950)* 610.

250. Ibid. 'In addition to article 10 the sixth committee suggested the deletion also of article 26 (specifying as to when a State shall become a party to the Convention) to be replaced by the second paragraph of article 25, as redrafted, and article 32 (regarding the registration of the convention by the Secretary-General), which it recommended, should be deleted in view of the recent amendment recommended for the rules on registration of treaties. It recommended a redraft of Article 24 which had been desired by the Third Committee, concerning signature and ratification of the convention, in line with changes recommended for other articles.'

251. Columbia University Press in cooperation with the United Nations, *Yearbook of the United Nations 1948–49* (1950) 610.

252. The Third Committee endorsed the Sixth Committee's proposal to delete Articles 10, 26, and 32. Along with the Third Committee's deletion of Article 27, this changed the numbering of provisions. The resultant numbering scheme was as follows (numbers in parentheses are those of the original Article): Articles 1–9 remained unchanged. Article 10 was deleted. Articles 11–24 were renumbered, as a result, by one number. Deletion of Articles 26, 27, and 32 resulted in the remaining articles being numbered thus: 25(28), 26(39), 27(30), and 28(31). The recommendation for a new version of Article 24 was also approved, along with approval for Articles 4, 7, 11, 13, 16, 19, and 20 in the form suggested by the Sixth Committee. Several changes were drafted into articles previously adopted by the Third Committee in a different form: Columbia University Press in cooperation with the United Nations, *Yearbook of the United Nations 1948–49* (1950) 611.

253. Held on 28 November 1949: Columbia University Press in cooperation with the United Nations, *Yearbook of the United Nations 1948–49* (1950) 611.

254. Columbia University Press in cooperation with the United Nations, *Yearbook of the United Nations 1948–49* (1950) 611.

255. Ibid.

256. Columbia University Press in cooperation with the United Nations, *Yearbook of the United Nations 1948–49* (1950) 611.

257. Ibid., 611–612.

258. Ibid., 612.

259. Formerly Article 24: Columbia University Press in cooperation with the United Nations, *Yearbook of the United Nations 1948–49* (1950) 612.

260. Columbia University Press in cooperation with the United Nations, *Yearbook of the United Nations 1948–49* (1950) 612.

261. Ibid.

262. Ibid.

263. Ibid. The remaining amendments involved first, an addition of words at the end of Article 25: 'such denunciation shall be operative only in respect of the State on whose behalf it was made, or if it was on behalf of a territory to which this convention has been extended under Article 24A, then only in respect of that territory', and second, insertion of a new sub-paragraph between existing Article 26(a) and 26(b), relating to notifications received in pursuant to Article 24A: Columbia University Press in cooperation with the United Nations, *Yearbook of the United Nations 1948–49* (1950) 612.

264. Columbia University Press in cooperation with the United Nations, *Yearbook of the United Nations 1948–49* (1950) 612.

265. Ibid.

266. Ibid., 613.

267. Ibid.

268. *Convention for the Suppression of the Traffic in Persons and of the Exploitation of the Prostitution of Others*, opened for signature 21 March 1950, 96 UNTS 1951 (entered into force 25 July 1951); Columbia University Press in cooperation with the United Nations, *Yearbook of the United Nations 1948–49* (1950) 613.

269. *Convention for the Suppression of the Traffic in Persons and of the Exploitation of the Prostitution of Others*, opened for signature 21 March 1950, 96 UNTS 1951, Preamble (entered into force 25 July 1951).

270. Ibid.

271. *Convention for the Suppression of the Traffic in Persons and of the Exploitation of the Prostitution of Others*, opened for signature 21 March 1950, 96 UNTS 1951, Final Protocol (entered into force 25 July 1951).

272. *Convention for the Suppression of the Traffic in Persons and of the Exploitation of the Prostitution of Others*, opened for signature 21 March 1950, 96 UNTS 1951, Article 1 (entered into force 25 July 1951).

273. Ibid.

274. *Convention for the Suppression of the Traffic in Persons and of the Exploitation of the Prostitution of Others*, opened for signature 21 March 1950, 96 UNTS 1951, Article 2 (entered into force 25 July 1951).

275. *Convention for the Suppression of the Traffic in Persons and of the Exploitation of the Prostitution of Others*, opened for signature 21 March 1950, 96 UNTS 1951, Article 3 (entered into force 25 July 1951).

276. *Convention for the Suppression of the Traffic in Persons and of the Exploitation of the Prostitution of Others*, opened for signature 21 March 1950, 96 UNTS 1951, Article 4 (entered into force 25 July 1951). 'To the extent permitted

by domestic law and acts of participation shall be treated as separate offences whenever this is necessary to prevent impunity.'

277. *Convention for the Suppression of the Traffic in Persons and of the Exploitation of the Prostitution of Others*, opened for signature 21 March 1950, 96 UNTS 1951, Article 5 (entered into force 25 July 1951).

278. *Convention for the Suppression of the Traffic in Persons and of the Exploitation of the Prostitution of Others*, opened for signature 21 March 1950, 96 UNTS 1951, Article 6 (entered into force 25 July 1951).

279. *Convention for the Suppression of the Traffic in Persons and of the Exploitation of the Prostitution of Others*, opened for signature 21 March 1950, 96 UNTS 1951, Article 7 (entered into force 25 July 1951).

280. Ibid.

281. *Convention for the Suppression of the Traffic in Persons and of the Exploitation of the Prostitution of Others*, opened for signature 21 March 1950, 96 UNTS 1951, Article 8 (entered into force 25 July 1951).

282. *Convention for the Suppression of the Traffic in Persons and of the Exploitation of the Prostitution of Others*, opened for signature 21 March 1950, 96 UNTS 1951, Article 9 (entered into force 25 July 1951).

283. *Convention for the Suppression of the Traffic in Persons and of the Exploitation of the Prostitution of Others*, opened for signature 21 March 1950, 96 UNTS 1951, Article 10 (entered into force 25 July 1951).

284. *Convention for the Suppression of the Traffic in Persons and of the Exploitation of the Prostitution of Others*, opened for signature 21 March 1950, 96 UNTS 1951, Article 11 (entered into force 25 July 1951).

285. *Convention for the Suppression of the Traffic in Persons and of the Exploitation of the Prostitution of Others*, opened for signature 21 March 1950, 96 UNTS 1951, Article 12 (entered into force 25 July 1951).

286. *Convention for the Suppression of the Traffic in Persons and of the Exploitation of the Prostitution of Others*, opened for signature 21 March 1950, 96 UNTS 1951, Article 13 (entered into force 25 July 1951).

287. *Convention for the Suppression of the Traffic in Persons and of the Exploitation of the Prostitution of Others*, opened for signature 21 March 1950, 96 UNTS 1951, Article 14 (entered into force 25 July 1951).

288. *Convention for the Suppression of the Traffic in Persons and of the Exploitation of the Prostitution of Others*, opened for signature 21 March 1950, 96 UNTS 1951, Article 15 (entered into force 25 July 1951).

289. *Convention for the Suppression of the Traffic in Persons and of the Exploitation of the Prostitution of Others*, opened for signature 21 March 1950, 96 UNTS 1951, Article 16 (entered into force 25 July 1951).

290. *Convention for the Suppression of the Traffic in Persons and of the Exploitation of the Prostitution of Others*, opened for signature 21 March 1950, 96 UNTS 1951, Article 17 (entered into force 25 July 1951).

291. Ibid.

292. *Convention for the Suppression of the Traffic in Persons and of the Exploitation of the Prostitution of Others*, opened for signature 21 March 1950, 96 UNTS 1951, Article 18 (entered into force 25 July 1951).

293. *Convention for the Suppression of the Traffic in Persons and of the Exploitation of the Prostitution of Others*, opened for signature 21 March 1950, 96 UNTS 1951, Article 19 (entered into force 25 July 1951).

294. Ibid.

295. *Convention for the Suppression of the Traffic in Persons and of the Exploitation of the Prostitution of Others*, opened for signature 21 March 1950, 96 UNTS 1951, Article 20 (entered into force 25 July 1951).

296. *Convention for the Suppression of the Traffic in Persons and of the Exploitation of the Prostitution of Others*, opened for signature 21 March 1950, 96 UNTS 1951, Article 21 (entered into force 25 July 1951).

297. Ibid.

298. *Convention for the Suppression of the Traffic in Persons and of the Exploitation of the Prostitution of Others*, opened for signature 21 March 1950, 96 UNTS 1951, Article 22 (entered into force 25 July 1951).

299. *Convention for the Suppression of the Traffic in Persons and of the Exploitation of the Prostitution of Others*, opened for signature 21 March 1950, 96 UNTS 1951, Article 27 (entered into force 25 July 1951).

300. *Convention for the Suppression of the Traffic in Persons and of the Exploitation of the Prostitution of Others*, opened for signature 21 March 1950, 96 UNTS 1951, Article 23 (entered into force 25 July 1951).

301. *Convention for the Suppression of the Traffic in Persons and of the Exploitation of the Prostitution of Others*, opened for signature 21 March 1950, 96 UNTS 1951, Article 24 (entered into force 25 July 1951).

302. *Convention for the Suppression of the Traffic in Persons and of the Exploitation of the Prostitution of Others*, opened for signature 21 March 1950, 96 UNTS 1951, Article 25 (entered into force 25 July 1951).

303. *Convention for the Suppression of the Traffic in Persons and of the Exploitation of the Prostitution of Others*, opened for signature 21 March 1950, 96 UNTS 1951, Article 26 (entered into force 25 July 1951).

304. *Convention for the Suppression of the Traffic in Persons and of the Exploitation of the Prostitution of Others*, opened for signature 21 March 1950, 96 UNTS 1951, Article 28 (entered into force 25 July 1951).

305. *Convention for the Suppression of the Traffic in Persons and of the Exploitation of the Prostitution of Others*, opened for signature 21 March 1950, 96 UNTS 1951, Final Protocol (entered into force 25 July 1951).

306. Tom Obokata, *Trafficking of Human Beings from a Human Rights Perspective: Towards a Holistic Approach* (Martinus Nijhoff: Netherlands, 2006), p. 17.

## CONCLUSION

1. Tom Obokata, *Trafficking of Human Beings from a Human Rights Perspective: Towards a Holistic Approach* (Martinus Nijhoff: Netherlands, 2006), pp. 13–17; Silvia Scarpa, *Trafficking in Human Beings: Modern Slavery* [2008]:50–55.

2. *International Agreement for the Suppression of the White Slave Traffic*, opened for signature 18 May 1904, 1 LNTS 83, Preamble (entered into force 18 July 1905).

3. Ibid. Articles 2 and 3 use the phrase 'women and girls', Articles 1, 3, and 6 use the phrase 'women or girls' and Article 4 uses the phrase 'woman or girl'.

4. Obokata, *Trafficking of Human Beings*, p. 13.

5. Ibid. p. 14.

6. *International Convention for the Suppression of the White Slave Traffic*, opened for signature 4 May 1910, 8 LNTS 278, Article 1, (entered into force 5 July 1920). Final Protocol (B) uses the phrase 'women or girls' and Final Protocol (D) uses the phrase 'woman or girl'.

7. *International Convention for the Suppression of the Traffic in Women and Children*, opened for signature 30 September 1921, 9 LNTS 415, Article 2 (entered into force 15 June 1922).

8. *International Convention for the Suppression of the Traffic in Women and Children*, opened for signature 30 September 1921, 9 LNTS 415, Articles 6 and 7 (entered into force 15 June 1922).

9. Obokata, *Trafficking of Human Beings*, p. 16.

10. *International Convention for the Suppression of the Traffic in Women of Full Age*, opened for signature 11 October 1933, 150 LNTS 431, Article 1 (entered into force 24 October 1934).

11. *Convention for the Suppression of the Traffic in Persons and of the Exploitation of the Prostitution of Others*, opened for signature 21 March 1950, 96 UNTS 1951, Article 17(1) and Article 20 (entered into force 25 July 1951).

12. *Convention for the Suppression of the Traffic in Persons and of the Exploitation of the Prostitution of Others*, opened for signature 21 March 1950, 96 UNTS 1951, Article 17 (entered into force 25 July 1951).

13. Obokata, *Trafficking of Human Beings*, p. 17; Scarpa, *Modern Slavery*, p. 52.

14. *International Agreement for the Suppression of the White Slave Traffic*, opened for signature 18 May 1904, 1 LNTS 83, Title (entered into force 18 July 1905).

15. *International Agreement for the Suppression of the White Slave Traffic*, opened for signature 18 May 1904, 1 LNTS 83, Preamble (entered into force 18 July 1905).

16. *International Agreement for the Suppression of the White Slave Traffic*, opened for signature 18 May 1904, 1 LNTS 83, Articles 2 and 3 (entered into force 18 July 1905).

17. Obokata, *Trafficking of Human Beings*, p. 13.

18. *International Convention for the Suppression of the White Slave Traffic*, opened for signature 4 May 1910, 8 LNTS 278, Title (entered into force 5 July 1920).

19. *International Convention for the Suppression of the White Slave Traffic*, opened for signature 4 May 1910, 8 LNTS 278, Preamble (entered into force 5 July 1920).

20. Obokata, *Trafficking of Human Beings*, p. 16.

21. *International Convention for the Suppression of the Traffic in Women of Full Age*, opened for signature 11 October 1933, 150 LNTS 431, Title (entered into force 24 October 1934).

22. *International Convention for the Suppression of the Traffic in Women of Full Age*, opened for signature 11 October 1933, 150 LNTS 431, Preamble (entered into force 24 October 1934).

23. *Convention for the Suppression of the Traffic in Persons and of the Exploitation of the Prostitution of Others*, opened for signature 21 March 1950, 96 UNTS 1951, Title and Preamble (entered into force 25 July 1951).

24. *Convention for the Suppression of the Traffic in Persons and of the Exploitation of the Prostitution of Others*, opened for signature 21 March 1950, 96 UNTS 1951, Preamble (entered into force 25 July 1951).

25. *International Agreement for the Suppression of the White Slave Traffic*, opened for signature 18 May 1904, 1 LNTS 83, Article 1(entered into force 18 July 1905).

26. *International Agreement for the Suppression of the White Slave Traffic*, opened for signature 18 May 1904, 1 LNTS 83, Article 2 (entered into force 18 July 1905).

27. *International Agreement for the Suppression of the White Slave Traffic*, opened for signature 18 May 1904, 1 LNTS 83, Articles 3, 4–5 (entered into force 18 July 1905).

28. *International Agreement for the Suppression of the White Slave Traffic*, opened for signature 18 May 1904, 1 LNTS 83, Article 6 (entered into force 18 July 1905).

29. *International Convention for the Suppression of the White Slave Traffic*, opened for signature 4 May 1910, 8 LNTS 278, Article 1 (entered into force 5 July 1920).

30. *International Convention for the Suppression of the Traffic in Women and Children*, opened for signature 30 September 1921, 9 LNTS 415, Article 2 (entered into force 15 June 1922).

31. *International Convention for the Suppression of the Traffic in Women and Children*, opened for signature 30 September 1921, 9 LNTS 415, Article 3 (entered into force 15 June 1922).

32. *International Convention for the Suppression of the Traffic in Women of Full Age*, opened for signature 11 October 1933, 150 LNTS 431, Article 1(entered into force 24 October 1934).

33. *Convention for the Suppression of the Traffic in Persons and of the Exploitation of the Prostitution of Others*, opened for signature 21 March 1950, 96 UNTS 1951, Article 1(1) (entered into force 25 July 1951).

34. *Convention for the Suppression of the Traffic in Persons and of the Exploitation of the Prostitution of Others*, opened for signature 21 March 1950, 96 UNTS 1951, Article 1(2) (entered into force 25 July 1951).

35. *Convention for the Suppression of the Traffic in Persons and of the Exploitation of the Prostitution of Others*, opened for signature 21 March 1950, 96 UNTS 1951, Article 2(1) (entered into force 25 July 1951).

36. *Convention for the Suppression of the Traffic in Persons and of the Exploitation of the Prostitution of Others*, opened for signature 21 March 1950, 96 UNTS 1951, Article 2(2) (entered into force 25 July 1951).

37. *Convention for the Suppression of the Traffic in Persons and of the Exploitation of the Prostitution of Others*, opened for signature 21 March 1950, 96 UNTS 1951, Article 3 (entered into force 25 July 1951).

38. *Convention for the Suppression of the Traffic in Persons and of the Exploitation of the Prostitution of Others*, opened for signature 21 March 1950, 96 UNTS 1951, Article 4 (entered into force 25 July 1951).

39. *International Agreement for the Suppression of the White Slave Traffic*, opened for signature 18 May 1904, 1 LNTS 83, Article 1 (entered into force 18 July 1905). See generally, Obokata, *Trafficking of Human Beings*, p. 15.

40. *International Convention for the Suppression of the White Slave Traffic*, opened for signature 4 May 1910, 8 LNTS 278, Article 1(entered into force 5 July 1920). See generally, Obokata, *Trafficking of Human Beings*, p. 15.

41. *International Agreement for the Suppression of the White Slave Traffic*, opened for signature 18 May 1904, 1 LNTS 83, Article 1 (entered into force 18 July 1905).

42. *International Agreement for the Suppression of the White Slave Traffic*, opened for signature 18 May 1904, 1 LNTS 83, Article 2 (entered into force 18 July 1905).

43. *International Agreement for the Suppression of the White Slave Traffic*, opened for signature 18 May 1904, 1 LNTS 83, Article 3 (entered into force 18 July 1905).

44. Obokata, *Trafficking of Human Beings*, p. 14.

45. *International Convention for the Suppression of the White Slave Traffic*, opened for signature 4 May 1910, 8 LNTS 278, Articles 1 and 2 (entered into force 5 July 1920).

46. *International Convention for the Suppression of the White Slave Traffic*, opened for signature 4 May 1910, 8 LNTS 278, Final Protocol (C) (entered into force 5 July 1920).

47. *International Convention for the Suppression of the Traffic in Women and Children*, opened for signature 30 September 1921, 9 LNTS 415, Article 2 (entered into force 15 June 1922). Article 2 of the Convention of 1921 refers to Article 1 of the Convention of 1910 which uses the phrase 'immoral purposes'.

48. *International Convention for the Suppression of the Traffic in Women of Full Age*, opened for signature 11 October 1933, 150 LNTS 431, Article 1 (entered into force 24 October 1934).

49. *Convention for the Suppression of the Traffic in Persons and of the Exploitation of the Prostitution of Others*, opened for signature 21 March 1950, 96 UNTS 1951, Preamble, Article 17, Article 17(3) and Article 19(1) (entered into force 25 July 1951).

50. *Convention for the Suppression of the Traffic in Persons and of the Exploitation of the Prostitution of Others*, opened for signature 21 March 1950, 96 UNTS 1951, Article 1(1) (entered into force 25 July 1951).

51. *Convention for the Suppression of the Traffic in Persons and of the Exploitation of the Prostitution of Others*, opened for signature 21 March 1950, 96 UNTS 1951, Article 2(2) (entered into force 25 July 1951).

52. Obokata, *Trafficking of Human Beings*, pp. 15–16. The Advisory Commission for the Protection and Welfare of Children and Young People, *Report on the Work of the Commission in 1934, Report of the Work of the Fourteenth Session of the Traffic in Women and Children Committee*, LON Council, [39], LON Doc. C.187.M.104.1935.IV (1935).

# Index

—❧ ❧—

administrative measures, 20, 86–87
Agreement of 1904 and Trafficking of
    Children for the Sexual Exploitation
    of Prostitution, The, 17–18
Amended Draft convention, 47–49
final wording of resolution, 49
anti-Semitism, 11

Becker, Lydia, 8
British Draft Convention, 43–45
    French amendments, 45–47
Butler, Josephine, 8

Cohen, Mr, 57–58
Contagious Diseases Act, 1864
    detention, 2
    examination orders, 2
    hospital certification, 1
    knowing acquiescence, 2–3
    method of uncovering the identity
        of women, 3
    offences, 2
    sunset clause, 3
Contagious Diseases Act, 1866
    appointment of visiting surgeons, 3
    focus on moral and religious
        instruction, 3
    JP-based system of information,
        4–5

medical examinations, periodical,
    4–5
regulatory power in treatment of
    detained women, 4
release from examination regime, 5
role of the metropolitan police, 5–6
sanctions applied to different
    offences, 5
voluntary examinations, 4
Contagious Diseases Act, 1869
    detention, 6
    detention period, 7
    effects of, 7–8
    examination procedure of
        voluntary and involuntary
        subjects, 6
    places under the legislation, 7
    release from examination regime, 7
    residential radius, 6
Convention for the Suppression of
    the Traffic in Persons and of the
    Exploitation of the Prostitution of
    Others, 1949, 133–41
    discussed responses to the First
        Draft Convention, 101–03
    Eighth Session of the Advisory
        Committee, 1929, 90–91
    Eleventh Session of the Advisory
        Committee, 1932, 94–95

Fifteenth Session of the Advisory
   Committee, 1936, 98–101
Fourteenth Session of the Advisory
   Committee, 1935, 97–98
IBUPL Draft Convention, 97
Ninth Session of the Advisory
   Committee, 1930, 91–92
Second Draft Convention, 103–116
Seventh Session of the Advisory
   Committee, 1928, 90
Sixth Session of the Advisory
   Committee, 1927, 89–90
Special Body of Experts, 88–89
Tenth Session of the Advisory
   Committee, 1931, 92–94
Thirteenth Session of the Advisory
   Committee, 1934, 96–97
Twelfth Session of the Advisory
   Committee, 1933, 95–96
Coote, Alexander, 13–14, 18
Council of the League of Nations
   (Council), 24
Covenant of the League of Nations,
   1919, 24–26
   Article 23(c) of, 24
   Brazilian Representative's
     submissions, 25
   Member of the Permanent
     Committee of Emigration, 26
   participating states, 25–26
   questionnaire, 1921, 27–29
   recommendations, 25
   responses to questionnaire, 1921,
     30–36
   Romania Representative's
     submissions, 25–26
Criminal Law Amendment Act, 1885
   leave a place of abode, 10
   leaving the jurisdiction, 9
   offences of procurement, 9–10

procurement for carnal connection
   (or its attempt), 9
prohibited procurement, 9
Cunha, M. Castao Da, 24

detention for treatment, 7
Drafting Committee, 47–48

Fifth Committee, 47, 49, 54, 64, 76–77
Fifth International Penitentiary
   Congress, 1895, 12–14
French amendments to British Draft
   Convention, 45–47

Guyot, Yves, 8

Hugo, Victor, 8

International Abolitionist Federation
   (IAF), 8
International Agreement for the
   Suppression of the White Slave
   Traffic, 1904, 15–16, 26, 30, 33,
   35, 146
administrative machinery of, 15–16
International Bureau for the
   Unification of Penal Law, Paris,
   1935, 97
International Catholic Association for
   the Protection of Girls (ICAPG), 12
International Conference on Traffic in
   Women and Children, 1921, 29–30
   Agenda item 9, 30
   'ages of consent' question,
     responses to, 32
   approval of the Final Act, 42
   distinction between seduction and
     procurement, 33
   Final Act of the Conference of
     1921, 37, 39, 42–43

New Convention, 43–45
new legislative provisions, 33
official supervisory services, 34–35
overseas employment agencies, 34
penal provisions on trafficking,
    31–32
penalties for 'reclusion', 33
problem of trafficking in native
    women and children, 35
provisions for punishing of
    offences, 31
recommendations, 39–42
repatriation of women and girls,
    relation of, 35
resolutions, 36–39
responses to questionnaire, 1921,
    30–36
women travellers, provisions for,
    34
International Convention for the
    Suppression of the Traffic in
    Women and Children 1921, 49–51
    effect of, 51
International Convention for the
    Suppression of the Traffic in
    Women of Full Age, 1933, 85–87
AC Draft Protocol to States,
    66–67
administrative measures, 86–87
Advisory Committee, 52–55
Advisory Committee Resolution,
    1932, 63–64
Advisory Committee Sessions,
    1927–30, 57–59
Amendments of the Conventions
    of 1910 and 1921, 64–85
appointment of a drafting
    committee, 81
assembly resolution, 1933, for
    diplomatic conference, 77

Completion of Consultation and
    Secretariat Report, 59
Conference of 1933 discussions on
    FC Draft Protocol, 78–81
DC Draft Convention, 82–83
eleventh session of the Advisory
    Committee, 1932, 59–64
Fifth Committee, 54, 76–77
final form of DC Draft
    Convention, 84–85
legislative measures, 86
new article relating to extradition,
    83
preamble, 81–82
proposed abolition of age limit,
    59–62
responses of participating
    countries, 67–76
Special Body of Experts, 55–56
International Convention for the
    Suppression of the White Slave
    Traffic, 1910, 18–21, 26, 30
    administration measures (Article 6
        and 7), 20
    legislative measures (Article 1 and
        5), 19–20
international law in relation to the
    trafficking of children for the
    sexual exploitation
    act of trafficking as 'procuring',
        145–146
    gender-specific conceptualization,
        142–143
    'immoral purposes' and 'immoral
        life', 146
    legislative measures, 143–145
    racial-specific conceptualization, 143
International Union of the Girls'
    Friendly Society (IUGFS), 10
Irish Free State, 85

Japanese Penal Code, 84–85
Jewish Association for the Protection
    of Women and Girls, 17
Justice of the Peace (JP), 2
    JP-based system of information, 4

legislative measures, 19–20, 86,
    143–45
London Congress, 1899, 14–18

maintenance of a register of women, 7
Martineau, Harriet, 8
medical examinations
    periodic, 4–5, 7

National Vigilance Association
    (NVA), 11, 17

Paris Congress, 1906, 18
periodic medical examinations, 4–5, 7
Permanent Committee for the
    Protection of Aborigines, 35
post-war revival of unification efforts,
    116
prostitution in England, 1
    State regulation of, 8–9
protection organizations for women,
    10–12

recommendations for preventing
    trafficking
    employment agencies, control of, 23
    employment of minors, 22
    entertainment venues, 22
    offences of procurement, 9–10, 22
    official commissions, 22
Regnault, M., 30–34, 36
Russian National Committee, 23

Second Draft Convention, 103–16
SG Draft Convention, 118
Snagge, T.W., 8–9
Snagge Inquiry, 8–9
Social Commission Fourth Session,
    1949, 118–128
Stansfield, Sir James, 8
State regulation of prostitution in
    England, 8–9

trafficking of girls, 11–12

UN Economic and Social Council
    (UN ESCOR), 116
    Fifth Session, 1947, 116–117
    Ninth Session, 1949, 128–129
    Seventh Session, 1947,
        117–118
    Social Commission Fourth
        Session, 1949, 118–128
    Third Committee Meetings, 1949,
        129–133

Versailles Treaty, 81
Vienna Congress, 1909, 18
vulnerability of women, 10–11

White Slave Traffic, 13–14. See also
    Covenant of the League of
    Nations, 1919; International
    Agreement for the Suppression of
    the White Slave Traffic,
    1904; International Convention
    for the Suppression of the
    Traffic in Women and Children
    1921
    conferences, 15–16, 18–23

# About the Author

Sunil Salankey Rao holds bachelor degrees in arts and law, and a Master of Laws with specialization in Public International Law from Monash University. He is presently Associate Lecturer at Monash University. He has a particular research interest in children's rights, and is also a consultant to UNICEF.

Rao held the position of lawyer in the Office of International Law, Attorney-General's Department, Australian Government, and was also Visiting Fellow at the British Institute of International and Comparative Law, and Visiting Scholar at the Lauterpacht Centre for International Law at Cambridge University.